AFTER THE FORESTS

Thailand's Captive Elephants and Their People

NIKKI SAVVIDES

Copyright © 2022 Nikki Savvides

ISBN: 978-1-922788-21-4
Published by Vivid Publishing
A division of Fontaine Publishing Group
P.O. Box 948, Fremantle
Western Australia 6959
www.vividpublishing.com.au

NATIONAL
LIBRARY
OF AUSTRALIA
A catalogue record for this
book is available from the
National Library of Australia

CONTENTS

PREFACE

This book is the culmination of numerous years of research both on the ground in Thailand and as an animal studies academic in my hometown of Sydney, Australia. Animal studies is a multidisciplinary field that aims to undo the entrenched human/animal binary that stems from human exceptionalism – the belief that our species is superior to others.[1] Animal studies has made great headway in undoing this binary by awakening us to the suffering we inflict on non-human species and asking us to find more ethical ways of treating them.[2] It allows us to examine the lived experiences of animals by acknowledging that they have agency – the ability to make their own decisions and to influence the world they live in, which we share with them.[3] In the case of elephants – who are known to have episodic and long-term memory, mirror self-recognition, social and vocal learning, behavioural innovation, anticipatory planning, and reactions to trauma and death (all facets of autonoetic awareness) – agency is surely part of their lived experiences, influencing their relationships with other elephants and people.[4] In my research I focused on recognising and interpreting elephant agency, and I describe these moments in this book as a means to explore how we might better understand their experiences and advocate for their welfare.

While much of my research formed part of my PhD – conducted in the Department of Gender and Cultural Studies at the University of Sydney between 2010 and 2013 – I have since continued to study Thailand's elephants as an independent researcher. But my involvement in the field of animal studies began much earlier. In 2005 I enrolled in a Master of Arts at the University of Sydney, where I completed my thesis about the ethics of human-horse relationships. At that time, animal studies was a relatively new discipline, and it had felt rather indulgent to write about something that was part of my everyday existence – the training and riding of horses. But studying the day-to-day lives of humans and animals in various contexts is common in animal studies and cultural studies, which value topics that are often overlooked as too ordinary or difficult to analyse because of their 'everyday-ness'. My immersion in these fields allowed me to investigate my relationship with horses, not simply as a hobby or daily practice but as a multispecies world with its own culture. I had been obsessed with horses since I was a child, passionate about equine welfare and finding more ethical ways to train them. I had always wanted to capture the complexity of my human–equine world, and academia allowed me to express my thoughts about the ethics of our relationships with a highly domesticated species.

In addition to my experiences with horses in Australia, some of the inspiration for my research into equine ethics arose while backpacking around Europe in 2003. Much of my holiday involved working with horses wherever I went – from the renowned Haflinger stud Fohlenhof Ebbs in Austria to a riding school in Inverness in the north of Scotland. During this trip I also worked with the famous *fiaker* (carriage) horses of Vienna after befriending several fiaker drivers who took tourists on trips around the city. The drivers let me help them out in exchange for as many carriage rides as I wanted. I mainly groomed and tacked up horses, took fares, and translated German to English for tourists, but by the end of my stay I had learned how to drive a fiaker – a far different experience than simply riding, especially on busy cobblestoned streets among pedestrians, bikes and traffic. The job was fulfilling – I spent every day immersed in the culture of the city – but I was always bothered by the conditions the horses experienced on a daily basis.

It was mid-summer and tourist season was in full swing, the horses run off their hooves with city tours of sites like the Vienna State Opera, Stephensplatz and the Spanish Riding School, loop after loop on an eternal circuit. Despite the popularity of the fiakers, there seemed to be less enthusiasm for the horses themselves; while some tourists wanted to pat the horses, more often than not the fiakers were laden with international visitors more interested in the novelty of their mode of transport than the animals shackled to them. The fiaker horses were undoubtedly part of the social fabric of a multispecies community, but their interests were curtailed in favour of those of the humans who used them as a source of employment or form of entertainment.

Memories of these experiences inspired me to study the use of animals in tourism for my PhD. I had been an avid traveller for years, yet had never travelled to Asia, and felt a trip to Thailand would be a great way to take a holiday while also finding a potential topic for my thesis. I searched for opportunities to investigate more ethical ways to interact with animals while travelling, and soon became interested in the phenomenon of volunteer tourism. Also known as 'responsible' or 'alternative' tourism, volunteer tourism provides a different way for people to interact with locals and animals while on holiday to more typical forms of mass tourism. Volunteering seemed to align with my wish to be a more ethical tourist, especially when it came to interacting with animals. So I decided to find a volunteer project I could participate in while travelling around Thailand, looking first to the bustling capital of Bangkok for ideas.

I soon found a fascinating volunteer culture in an area to the east of Bangkok known as Khlong Tan, where tourists largely from Western countries worked alongside expats and Bangkok locals to care for *soi* (street) dogs. There are some half a million of these dogs in Bangkok and most are in a dire state of health. The organisation I volunteered with implemented healthcare, neutering and vaccination programs, and my daily activities mainly involved exercising and socialising dogs (the latter to find them permanent homes) and assisting the vets and vet nurses with vaccinations and operations.[5]

During the two weeks I spent working with soi dogs, I had the first inklings of what a methodology would look like for studying animal-centred volunteer tourism. After discussion with my thesis supervisor, I learned that what I was proposing to do was a form of ethnography – what organisational theorist John van Maanen describes as 'the peculiar practice of representing the social reality of others through the analysis of one's own experience in the world of these others'. As van Maanen explains, ethnography is shaped by 'accident and happenstance ... as much as planning or foresight; numbing routine as much as living theatre; impulse as much as rational choice; mistaken judgments as much as accurate ones'.[6] Over the years to come, van Maanen's words would guide me well as my fieldwork took on its own life, with happy accidents, random meetings, failed plans and unexpected encounters all leading me deeper into the world of elephant captivity.

In its early stages, my ethnographic approach involved simply writing about my daily experiences and observations of human-dog relationships in Bangkok, both with the street dog welfare organisation and on the streets, where locals interacted with the dogs. I wrote pages of notes and voiced hours of thoughts on my digital recorder. These were the product of watching an array of multispecies encounters in the city which were influenced by various factors such as a fear of rabies or a desire to care for animals in need. I interviewed locals and learned about the practice of community dog-keeping in the process – a unique Bangkok tradition guided by the merit-making tenets of Theravada Buddhism. And through this process I developed a method for studying a range of human-animal relationships both in and outside tourism contexts. As well as volunteering with street dogs, I have worked in sea turtle conservation in Bali, Indonesia; with stray cows, dogs and donkeys at an animal hospital in Udaipur, India; and at a rehabilitation centre for macaque monkeys in Goa, India, most of whom had been rescued from a life of dancing for tourists. Most significantly, these ethnographic practices would shape the fieldwork I undertook with elephants, elephant caretakers known as 'mahouts', tourists, conservationists and welfare advocates in Thailand.

Ethnography is increasingly being used within animal studies, where it is often referred to as 'multispecies ethnography' – a term that theorists Eben Kirksey and Stefan Helmreich say encapsulates an intention to study 'the host of organisms whose lives and deaths are linked to human social worlds'.[7] While ordinary ethnography typically aims to reveal the worlds of the human subjects around the author, multispecies ethnography explores the worlds of both humans and non-humans. In Thailand, my own ethnographic process required immersion within communities of people living with captive elephants in different areas, where I rendered my observations of the elephant-related activities around me – many of which I participated in – through my own written self-reflections.[8] To complement this approach I used interviews and collaborative storytelling to share the experiences of tourists, sanctuary/welfare project operators and mahouts in their own words. This allowed me to develop reflexive relationships with the human subjects of my research; I provided the questions and framework for the stories to be told, but engaged with these subjects as research collaborators, co-constructing narratives with them about their lived experiences. This meant those subjects were active rather than passive participants in the fieldwork.[9] They drove its direction, with their dedication to elephants offering me the chance to gain unique insights into the frontline of elephant welfare and conservation.[10]

At the same time, ethnography allowed me to investigate the lives and experiences of elephants in intersubjective relationships with humans. In the field, I observed elephant interactions with mahouts and tourists and took notes on elephant behaviour for several hours each day at sanctuaries, community-based projects and other tourist sites. I took reflexive research notes on my own elephant encounters and over three thousand photos of my human and elephant subjects that were visual records I referred to when writing about my observations. While gaining unique insights into how human cultures have shaped and been shaped by elephants, I also learned much about elephant interests and how these could be upheld by the people who interacted with them – whether these were tourists; the operators of elephant camps, sanctuaries and elephant conservation/welfare projects; or mahouts from Indigenous tribes.

When beginning my research, I had no formal training in behaviourism and needed to find ways to recognise and understand elephant interests, guided by the work of elephant conservationists such as Raman Sukumar, Joy Poole, Peter Granli, Josh Plotnik and Franz de Waal. In their work with Asian elephants, Plotnik and De Waal stress the importance of understanding how elephants 'navigate their physical and social worlds'.[11] I was also guided by philosopher Helen Steward's suggestion that 'everyday thinking' can be used to understand animals' experiences, and aimed to identify easily recognisable, 'everyday' emotions like happiness, sadness, fear and anger among elephants.[12] I also drew on behavioural research from the veterinary and biological sciences and ethological studies of animal emotions and consciousness. Further, my methodology was based on the idea that our emotional responses to the more-than-human world can be considered just as valid as more 'scientific' analyses of animal behaviour. In the words of biologist and ethologist Marc Bekoff, '[s]tudies of animal thought, emotions, and self-awareness, as well as behavioral ecology and conservation biology, can all be compassionate as well as scientifically rigorous'.[13]

My fieldwork showed me that elephants actively seek happiness through social interactions, which provide them with great comfort. They show joy wallowing in mud; swimming and playing with their friends in dams and rivers; foraging for natural foods; eating sugarcane, watermelons and bananas in large quantities; scratching themselves on trees, rocks and one another; and covering themselves in dust and mud to protect themselves from mosquitoes and other insects. They certainly appear to enjoy and derive comfort from their freedom, and will take all opportunities to explore, forage, socialise and play when given time off their chains or outside their shelters.

I also observed what was not in the elephants' interests: punitive training methods and short chaining; a lack of shelter, access to water and natural food sources; and separation from other elephants – which, as closely knit herd animals, appeared to be one of the primary sources of their sadness.

One of the main ways I learned to understand elephant behaviour was by talking to their mahouts. I developed friendships with mahouts from the Guay tribe, who invited me to learn about their lives and cultural traditions. What mahout/elephant researcher Piers Locke terms 'ethnoelephantology' was the ultimate outcome of this process: an approach to studying elephants and mahouts as subjective actors and research informants.[14] I followed a similar methodology, which allowed me to explore the myriad facets of mahout-elephant relationships in the contemporary and historical landscape of Thai elephant tourism. By talking to people who lived so closely with elephants, I was able to understand more of the animals' lived experiences while also learning about the devastating impact of deforestation on elephant welfare. Fascinating yet heart-wrenching stories about life before and after deforestation revealed the complex interdependence of Indigenous people and their elephants as well as why they are reliant on tourism to survive. Along with the narratives of conservationists, welfarists and other advocates, these stories helped me to explore how we might provide a better future for Thailand's captive elephants.

MY JOURNEY

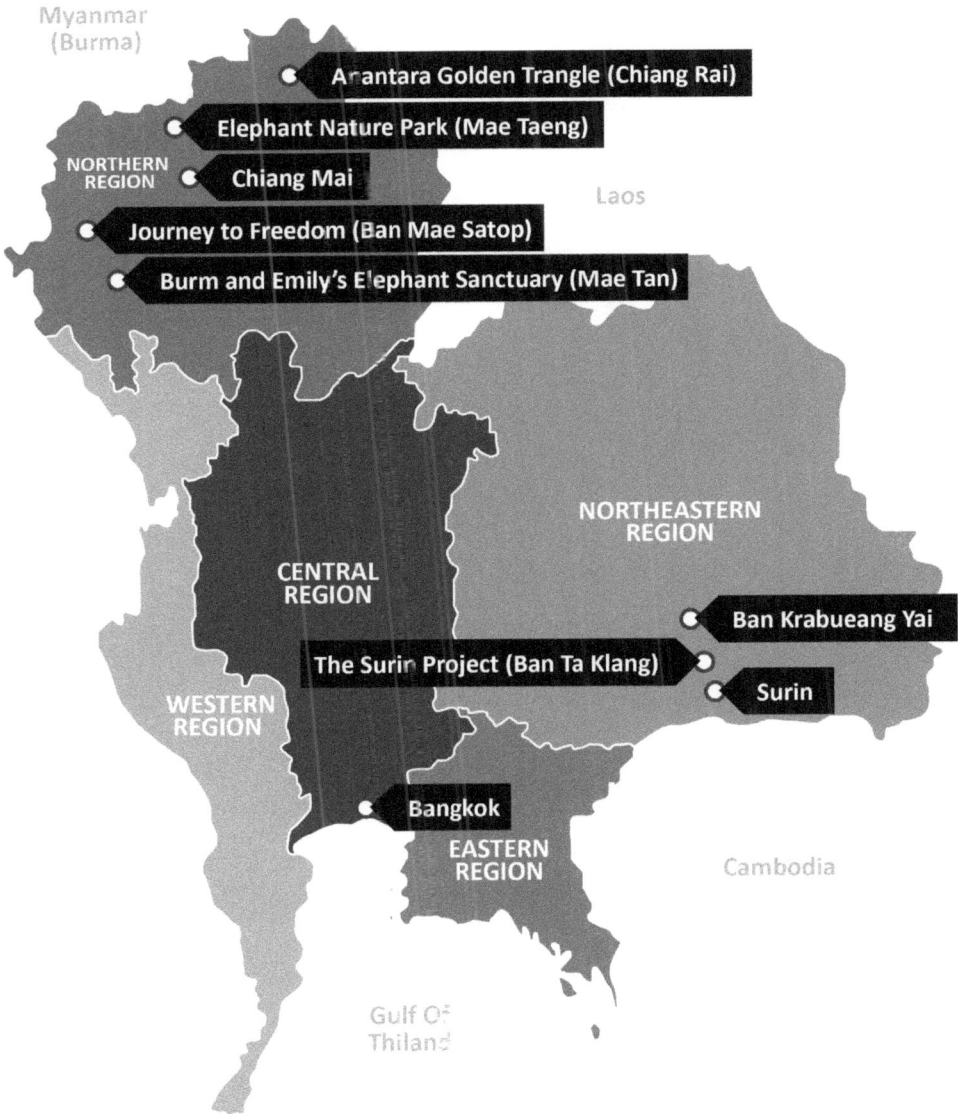

Myanmar
(Burma)

Anantara Golden Trangle (Chiang Rai)

Elephant Nature Park (Mae Taeng)

NORTHERN
REGION

Chiang Mai

Journey to Freedom (Ban Mae Satop)

Burm and Emily's Elephant Sanctuary (Mae Tan)

Laos

NORTHEASTERN
REGION

CENTRAL
REGION

Ban Krabueang Yai

The Surin Project (Ban Ta Klang)

Surin

WESTERN
REGION

Bangkok

EASTERN
REGION

Cambodia

Gulf Of
Thiland

For photos of the elephants and people I met on my
journey, visit my Instagram page @aftertheforests

Chapter 1

ENTER THE ELEPHANT

It was mid-morning, the sun illuminating the lushness of the fields and hills around me. Among the canopy, birds trilled as they flitted from tree to tree, their calls accompanied by the distant sound of gushing rapids. The smell of fresh grass and mud met my nostrils as Doc Ngern grabbed the bunch of ripening bananas from my hand and eagerly threw them back into the vast pink cavern of her mouth. Her strange set of yellow molars made quick work of the fruit, pulverising them to mash in an instant. I met her gaze, noticing how her eyes reflected the greenness around us. I took another bunch from the woven basket behind me and proffered it again; this time the wet tip of her trunk touched my hand, dripping warm slime down my fingers. Doc Ngern devoured the second bunch, then a third and fourth, then three whole pineapples, two small watermelons, a few pieces of lumpy pumpkin and several long, tubular yams. Each was crushed to oblivion in seconds. The basket now empty, her rough trunk snaked towards me, checking if I had indeed run out of food. I reached forwards and caressed the weaving coil of rumpled grey skin as she sniffed the air and my muddy boots. She made a grab for the basket, which I kicked further behind me and out of reach. Her trunk brushed my bare leg, its skin rough like tree bark, the black hairs covering it as coarse as brush bristles. I stood back before that powerful coil had any chance of pulling me off my feet. Doc Ngern regarded me with one gentle eye, her ears flapping lazily to dissuade the flies that buzzed around her head. Now that the food had run out, I was no longer of interest to her. With a brisk shake of her giant head, Doc Ngern turned away and strode back into the fields.

My momentary encounter with Doc Ngern – an eight-year-old Asian elephant whose name means 'silver flower' – occurred in 2008 at Elephant Nature Park, a 250-acre elephant sanctuary on the banks of the turgid Mae Taeng River in northern Thailand. Covered in a variety of native trees and thick grasses and surrounded by emerald hills, the sanctuary – also known as ENP – is one of a handful of places in Thailand where captive elephants roam. Back then I had no idea elephants like Doc Ngern would determine the course of my life and research for more than the next decade. What captivated me so completely were the stories of elephants like her, many whose lives are marked with neglect and abuse, despite the great love tourists and Thais alike have for these charismatic creatures.

Before arriving at ENP, Doc Ngern had lived for many years in an elephant camp (also known as a 'tourist camp' or 'trekking camp') where she took tourists on rides. She was mistreated in the camp and, in response, struck out at her trainer, seriously injuring him. Deemed too dangerous to be ridden by tourists, she had no value to the camp, which sold her to ENP, where she would spend the rest of her life wandering the fields and socialising with others of her species. Doc Ngern's acquisition from the camp constituted her 'rescue' – one of ENP's core operations, which involves the removal of elephants from situations in which their welfare is compromised and their rehoming in surroundings that aim to replicate their natural habitat.

Several thousand captive elephants like Doc Ngern work in

tourism in Thailand. They are classified under the 1939 Draught Animal Act as working livestock, similar to cattle, buffalo and oxen.[15] They are not afforded protection as an endangered or vulnerable species like their wild counterparts, who are categorised as such by the International Union for Conservation of Nature and listed under Appendix I of the Convention on International Trade in Endangered Species of Wild Fauna and Flora (CITES).[16] In terms of total numbers, statistics from a 2017 study show that there are 3783 captive elephants in Thailand and around 3100 to 3600 wild elephants.[17] Along with their protection under different legislation, as conservationists Alex Godfrey and Charatdao Kongmuang explain:

> The captive and wild populations of Asian elephants in Thailand are almost entirely geographically isolated from each other. The captive population, comprising approximately 60% of the total population, is found mainly in the North and Northeast of the country whereas the isolated wild populations ... are distributed primarily in the Central and Western regions, most of which are in protected areas.[18]

This geographical isolation means that the lives of captive and wild elephants are remarkably different. Most of today's captive elephants are the descendants of wild animals captured from the forests in Burma, Thailand and Cambodia over the past decades and centuries. The term 'captive' provides a fitting description for an animal that is neither wild nor domesticated, having 'never undergone systematic, multi-generational artificial selection by humans for specific physical or behavioral traits'.[19] To use the words of elephant specialist Richard

Lair, the captive Thai elephant is 'simply a wild animal in chains – but a wild animal frequently gentle and intelligent enough to be totally trustworthy'.[20]

At the time of my encounter with Doc Ngern in 2008, there were approximately forty to fifty elephant camps across Thailand; in 2017 there were 223 – the increase in number being indicative of their growing popularity.[21] At these camps, elephants work during the day and are chained in corrals or shelters overnight, usually by one front leg to a cement or steel post sunk into the ground on a chain that is anywhere between two to six metres in length. A raft of welfare issues is associated with camps, not least from chaining, which can cause joint damage, skin abrasions and poor foot health.[22] Further issues include a lack of socialisation and herd bonding, reproduction issues, and high levels of stress and injury.[23] These welfare issues are common not only to Thailand, but are generally associated with keeping elephants in captivity, including in zoos in the Global North.[24] Ultimately, by depriving elephants of opportunities for roaming, foraging and the expression of other natural behaviours, captivity compromises elephant welfare.[25] But in Thailand – like other countries with captive elephants in the Global South – socio-economic factors can exacerbate welfare issues associated with elephant tourism. Further, the destruction of elephant habitats through deforestation has meant that tourist camps are some of the few places around Thailand that are able to provide captive elephants with adequate food and care. These complex intersections between economic and environmental hardships mean that finding solutions to what is sometimes termed Thailand's 'elephant problem' is an equally complex undertaking.

Over the past two decades, criticisms of the treatment of captive elephants used in tourism in Thailand have spearheaded a movement that has changed the face of the industry. This has meant that many camps have improved their conditions, with positive welfare implications.[26] Further, attitudes towards elephant tourism have shifted in countries of the Global North, whose tourists drive much of the demand for elephant tourism.[27] Over the past two decades, a number of elephant sanctuaries have opened across the country, supported by tourists who not that long ago may have visited a camp instead. At these sanctuaries, tourists can observe and sometimes interact with elephants in more natural environments. The rise in sanctuary tourism has also led to an increase in tourist camps and other sites offering more 'elephant friendly' activities. At these sites, tourists might ride the elephants 'bareback', without sitting in a *howdah* – the heavy wooden (~25 kg) or steel (~15 kg) bench seat that is put on the elephant's back atop a thick saddle pad.[28] They might also feed elephants fruit and vegetables by hand and wash them in rivers and dams using buckets and scrubbing brushes.

At tourist sites around the country, elephants are cared for and controlled by their caretakers, known as 'mahouts'. Many mahouts are from Indigenous tribes, such as the Karen, Guay, Khmer and Lao Isan.[29] These mahouts can be considered Thailand's traditional 'elephant people', for whom, in anthropologist Peter Cuasay's words, 'the capture and keeping of elephants is a central tradition, an indigenous knowledge system, and a sacred collective undertaking'.[30] Also known as *kwan chang* in Thai – often translated as 'one who walks with elephants' – Indigenous mahouts have engaged in elephant-keeping practices along generational lines for centuries. This culture of mahoutship is accurately described by Nicolas Lainé of the Asian Elephant Specialist Group as 'the art of living and sharing life with elephants'.[31] Mahouts can be found across Asia, including in

India, Nepal and Indonesia; indeed, almost every captive elephant population across South and Southeast Asia is managed by mahouts.[32] And just as elephants rely on tourism for food and care, contemporary mahouts – many for whom elephant keeping is an entrenched cultural practice and occupation – rely on tourism for their livelihood.

Mahouts can be found at different tourist sites across Thailand, including traditional camps, sanctuaries, 'saddle off' projects and volunteer projects focused on elephant welfare and conservation activities, such as reforestation. Mahouts who work in traditional camps often live on-site and are provided with accommodation and meals; some are also able to access training courses.[33] Their primary source of income is provided by tourists who pay to spend the day riding an elephant; watching shows of elephants playing soccer, painting, and throwing darts; or viewing demonstrations of their traditional uses by Thai people, such as in logging. Mahouts at these sites engage in these activities with their elephants, either by taking tourists on elephant rides or directing and controlling the elephants in shows and demonstrations. Alternatively, mahouts may be employed by sanctuaries, where tourists pay to observe and sometimes interact with elephants for a day, or volunteer for a week or more at a time, staying on-site and participating in a variety of activities related to elephant care and maintaining or building sanctuary infrastructure.

In sanctuaries, mahouts ensure the safety of tourists while also monitoring and managing individual or herds of elephants, sometimes at close quarters, other times at more of a distance. Similarly, at saddle-off projects tourists can visit for a day and participate in activities such as walking with, observing, feeding and bathing elephants, with mahouts managing both tourist-elephant and herd interactions. These projects play a similar role to sanctuaries in that they provide a more natural home for elephants. Mahouts are also employed on community-based elephant welfare projects, where tourists pay to volunteer for several weeks or months. At these sites, tourists often live within the traditional villages of Indigenous elephant people, including the families of the mahouts who care for the projects' elephants. Daily tasks for tourists and mahouts alike include gathering elephant food, building fences and elephant shelters, and observing, interacting and walking with elephants for several hours a day.

While Indigenous mahouts in Thailand may have longstanding traditions involving elephants, environmental, socio-cultural and economic issues caused by deforestation have led to the ongoing marginalisation of their cultures while also harming their elephants. Further, a culture of mahoutship has evolved over recent decades that involves mahouts who do not have strong connections to ancient elephant cultures and participate in tourism for purely financial reasons. These less experienced mahouts may not have the appropriate knowledge or training, exacerbating elephant welfare issues such as those prevalent in camps. Contemporary mahoutship has thus been viewed as problematic and can be a controversial topic for animal welfare advocates. But the necessity of involving mahouts in a range of activities embedded in the tourism industry means that it is essential to create a dialogue with them and help them engage in more welfare-positive training and care practices. These include those derived from ancient Indigenous traditions and knowledge, and more contemporary behavioural research. This effort has been core to the work of elephant advocates and conservationists who have developed education and community outreach programs to facilitate more positive mahout-elephant relationships. These individuals recognise the complexity of mahout-elephant relationships in Thailand and understand how factors such as human poverty equally affect the lives of mahouts and those of their elephants. This provides a realistic approach to tackling Thailand's 'elephant problem' that addresses the use of harmful training methods while also recognising that tourism provides less than ideal but necessary employment for mahouts and elephants alike.

Thailand's Indigenous people first began capturing and training elephants from the forests that once covered much of the country possibly as long ago as 1000 BC.[34] Their resulting use for a variety of purposes – from warfare to logging to tourism – gives the elephants the unusual status of being 'captive' while still maintaining many of their wild characteristics. Perhaps this is why elephant tourism is so popular, driving tourists to seek encounters with creatures whose size, intelligence, power and mystique connect them to an imagined wilderness – imagined, in that the majority of elephant habitats have been shrinking worldwide, not least in Thailand, where the country's forests have been decimated due to logging and agricultural production. Today a mere 32 percent of Thailand's forest is suitable for elephant habitation, a reduction from 53 percent in 1961 and 70–80 percent in the early 1900s.[35]

The popularity of elephant tourism might be explained in terms of the species' famed high intelligence and social and emotional complexity.[36] Elephants are also common flagship species successfully used for conservation efforts,[37] especially in the Global North.[38] As aesthetically pleasing, charismatic megafauna with forward-facing eyes, they elicit emotional responses,[39] and their images have been used in successful conservation campaigns for biodiversity[40] and against the illegal ivory trade.[41] Elephants can be potent figures in encouraging tourists to engage in conservation projects,[42] and tourists who encounter elephants may consider them mystical, magical or sublime, their interactions providing visitors with a sense of spiritual awakening or connection.[43] Such perceptions may be a product of the contemporary conservation discourse that sets humanity in opposition to animality, and in doing so has avowed 'wildness' as reverent and sacred.[44] It is also possible that for many tourists, elephant encounters are 'back to nature' experiences – albeit with nature 'produced, reproduced and redesigned as a tourist attraction'.[45]

As I have experienced firsthand, elephant encounters can be fraught with danger. While many of my observations were conducted at a distance – often of elephants in fields, forests, rivers and dams some ten to fifty metres away – at other times I physically touched, washed and fed elephants, or observed relationships with their mahouts or tourists in close quarters. While most of my encounters were peaceful, in some of the closer interactions, elephants clearly showed their dissent through body language, and there were several instances where I was batted away by a trunk, tail or rear end, and in one particularly terrifying moment, charged. These were excellent reminders to keep my space from them, and many of my most interesting and informative encounters were conducted more remotely.

Such dangers appear unlikely to deter many tourists, perhaps due to their lack of understanding of the potential for injury, or simply because the desire to be close to elephants overrides any sense of fear. Tourists are drawn to camps despite various unfortunate incidents in recent years, including one case of a ridden elephant charging off into the jungle with terrified tourists onboard.[46] (Luckily, another group of tourists managed to subdue the elephant and rescue the group.)

This proximity to danger is usually mediated by methods of control, which include the restraining of elephants using chains and the use of an ankus or *takaw* (in Thai) – also known as a bull hook or simply 'the hook' – a sickle-shaped piece of metal atop a wooden rod that looks somewhat like a cane, but with a sharp metal point that inflicts pain if driven into the skin of the elephant.[47] The use of bull hooks by mahouts is another controversial topic, but it is through these means of control that camps and other tourist sites are able to provide tourists with the unique experience of encountering a 'wild' animal in relative security, using tools of captivity that essentially curtail the animal's 'wildness'.

While human fascination with and reverence for elephants may have positive implications for conservation, it has also contributed to the issues associated with tourism by providing financial support for activities that may be detrimental to elephant welfare. However, because mahouts and elephants rely on tourism for survival, completely boycotting activities like elephant riding is not a viable solution. Instead, shifting the industry towards a more sustainable and ethical focus is key. Tourists have been rapidly embracing changes to elephant tourism – increasingly choosing to participate in less intrusive elephant encounters in awareness of welfare issues. Much of this has been driven by a concerted effort by elephant advocates both within and outside Thailand to educate tourists and encourage them to visit sanctuaries and/or observe elephants in other more 'natural' environments. This effort has also improved the conditions at more traditional tourist camps.

It is important to note that much of the original criticism of Thai elephant tourism stemmed from the response to a video of a practice known as 'crushing', which has been used by welfare advocates to epitomise the cruelty often associated with the industry.[48] In 2002, People for the Ethical Treatment of Animals (PETA) disseminated this footage, which led to international condemnation of the treatment of elephants in Thailand. Essentially, the method shown in the video involved restraining a young elephant inside a wooden 'crush' and tormenting it for days to 'break' its spirit. The international response to the footage led to increased scrutiny of elephant camps, and the Thai government outlawed the practice of crushing. When I started my research, I believed that this method was used universally across Thailand. However, as my study continued, I learned that this was not the case, and that training methods differ around Thailand and generally come down to the particular beliefs and behaviours of certain people or groups. For example, I found that the restraining and training of a young elephant could be performed without the use of cruelty, but instead as a form of weaning or early schooling. As such it is important not to generalise and assume that all people who work with elephants use extreme measures, while also acknowledging that punitive training methods are highly problematic if and when they are purposely used to torment elephants. My own enlightenment to these issues was crucial to my attempts to fully understand the complex terrain of captive elephant management. Since the footage was released, there has been a general shift towards more gentle methods of training across the country,[49] another positive outcome of the work of conservation and welfare organisations as well as mahouts who actively eschew cruel training methods and seek more harmonious relationships with their elephants.

* * *

I encountered my first captive elephant in Chiang Mai, one of Thailand's northernmost cities, before I had heard of ENP or met Doc Ngern. This was the second city I visited in Thailand, having caught the comfortable overnight train there from Bangkok. After stepping out of the train and into the humidity, I lugged my backpack towards the tuktuk stand and hired a three-wheeler to take me to my lodgings for the next week, a backpacker hostel in the north of the city. The tuktuk navigated a glorious maze of intersecting roads that wove between the picturesque temples and bustling markets of the walled city, which was surrounded by a wide moat spanned by stone bridges. We putted over silted canals, racing alongside bikes and scooters on the narrow roads, until we reached a gated community of white-washed brick houses, their front gardens overgrown with vines and banana trees. One was my hostel, with four dormitory rooms and a large communal dining area.

After checking in and dumping my backpack on a lower bunk in the women's dorm, I headed to the communal space, where I made myself a tea and perched at a wobbly wooden table laden with the detritus of travellers since gone – a worn-out copy of *Lonely Planet Thailand* from 2001, three half-empty bottles of sunscreen, a tube of tropical strength DEET and a stack of crumpled leaflets advertising the city's attractions. 'Visit Tiger Temple!' one announced in bright yellow type above a photo of a white man patting a chained tiger. 'Ride Majestic Elephant in Jungle!' declared another atop an image of two white women on an elephant, surrounded by forest.

As I rifled through the other pamphlets, a trio of British women entered the room, two talking loudly to the other about their day spent at an elephant camp. Flushed with excitement, one of the women said: 'It was such an amazing experience. You have to try it!'

She turned to me, glancing at the pamphlet in my hand. 'Have you been?'

I shook my head.

'Oh, you really have to!' she enthused. 'It was incredible.'

I soon found myself being shown dozens of photos of elephants painting, playing soccer and basketball, and using their trunks to 'kiss' the woman and her friend on their cheeks. There were a few photos of the woman and her friend riding the elephant, too – almost carbon copies of the image on the Majestic Elephant pamphlet. I did not have any particular desire to ride an elephant, but the interaction piqued my interest. This would be further aroused the next day when I travelled to the highest point of the city to visit one of its most sacred sites.

Chiang Mai sits in a verdant valley in the shadow of the mountain Doi Suthep. On its summit is a holy temple nestled among shady oaks, magnolias and chestnut trees known as Wat Phra That Doi Suthep. Entry is via a 300-step stairway flanked by bejewelled stone serpents whose undulating bodies form stunning gold, green and crimson banisters. The temple grounds house numerous pavilions with red roofs and tiled floors of intersecting red, white and yellow patterns. A golden pagoda sits at the centre of the grounds surrounded by gold Buddhas in various poses who smile beatifically at the hundreds of tourists who visit the temple every day. And in one corner, on a marble plinth, stands a statue of a white elephant in crimson and gold finery, looking out over the temple grounds.

Founded in 1383, the temple was built on an auspicious site. As the legend goes, after a spiritual vision a monk named Sumanathera travelled to the village of Pang Cha, just north of Chiang Mai, where he found a piece of Buddha's collarbone. The bone had magical powers: it could move, it could duplicate itself and it could disappear. But King Nu Naone, of the northern Lanna Kingdom, heard of the magic bone and wanted it for himself. He commanded Sumanathera to bring it to him, but the bone broke into two pieces on arrival. King Nu Naone enshrined half the relic in a temple in Chiang Mai named Wat Suandok. He placed the other piece on the back of a sacred white elephant who carried it through wild jungle to the top of Doi Suthep. Once the elephant reached the mountain's peak, he trumpeted three times then lay down and died. The King took this as an omen and ordered the construction of the temple on the site. Since then, Wat Phra That Doi Suthep has become one of the most sacred sites in Thailand. Many Thais also call it Wat Changpheux – the Temple of the White Elephant.

Visitors will find statues of Ganesh, the Hindu god known as the Remover of Obstacles, nestled around Wat Phra That Doi Suthep. Ganesh, the Deva of arts, sciences, wisdom and intellect, has equal significance within the Thai Theravada Buddhist tradition, where he is known as Phra Phikanet. As an elephant-headed man, Phra Phikanet lives partway between the human and animal worlds, and his presence at numerous locations around the temple is a reminder of the significance of elephants in Thai culture. Thai people revere them as auspicious symbols of fortune who play a central role in Theravada Buddhism. They are also central to the animistic traditions of Thailand's Indigenous peoples – the holiest animal in ancient religions where nature and spirituality enmesh.

My trip up the mountain to Wat Phra That Doi Suthep began with a minibus crammed with eager tourists that dropped me off at the carpark at the foot of the gleaming serpentine stairway. Thirsty, I bought a bottle of lemonade from a street vendor to keep me going on the ascent. I was surprised to see a bull elephant with long pointed tusks in a pen behind the vendor. His front left foot was chained to a cement block sunk into the ground. The bull could just reach the bananas and chunks of pineapple proffered by tourists who were paying his mahout to feed him. The elephant's ribs protruded through his hide and he stood in a puddle of fly-blown manure and urine with no discernible source of water. The bull shifted from foot to foot as he listlessly chewed on the small pieces of fruit. I would see the same behaviour many times over the following years, the functionless movements known as 'stereotypies' that signify boredom, distress or anxiety and are commonly the outcome of poor welfare conditions.[50] Even without the knowledge I have now, I understood on Doi Suthep that the bull's behaviour was clearly a product of his misery. As I started the long climb to the temple, I looked back at the elephant and the crowd of tourists around him with the sense that something was terribly wrong.

That same night, I joined my new British friends from the hostel at a local bar where we drank cheap, potent spirits and shared travel stories. Barhopping, we headed out onto Ratchadamnoen Road, the busy thoroughfare that transects Chiang Mai's old city. As I walked tipsily past noisy bars and restaurants, I saw a young elephant, her mahout beside her, begging in front of a bar pumping techno out onto the street. A number of tourists had paid her mahout so that they could feed the elephant chunks of pineapple and small bunches of bananas, and have their photo taken with her. The elephant was skinny with a sunken back. Her eyes were fearful. Surrounded by cars and motorbikes she endured bright flashes from the tourists' cameras as she swayed from side to side, lifting one foot after another in a repetitive motion. I asked the mahout if I could buy some fruit, and he handed me a bundle of sugarcane in exchange for 40 baht (about $1.30), which the elephant grabbed from my hand and devoured. A motorbike careened down the road, honking and just missing a drunken tourist who had tumbled into the gutter. I had little time to pause before one of my British friends grabbed me by the elbow and pulled me off towards the next bar, leaving me to contemplate what I had just witnessed twice in one day – the abject status of the Thai elephant in two different tourism contexts. So began my introduction into the world of captive Thai elephants and the research that would define my life for the next decade.

Chapter 2

THE CAPTIVE
ELEPHANT IN THAILAND

The captive elephant's place in Thai culture and tourism – and indeed across many South and Southeast Asian countries, including India, Nepal, Cambodia and Burma – is marked by an inherent contradiction between reverence and mistreatment. For Thai people, elephants are core to spiritual beliefs in the magical-animism aspects of Theravada Buddhism, drawing on the special symbolism elephants hold within Buddhism across Asia, with Buddha himself being considered 'the reincarnation of a sacred white elephant'.[51] Just like at Wat Phra That Doi Suthep, temples around the country boast statues of elephants and the elephant-headed god Phra Pikanet, and it is commonly said that Thailand itself is shaped like an elephant's head, the northernmost provinces forming the face and ears, the southernmost the trunk.

Elephants are also emblematic of Thai royalty, and rare white elephants – those who meet certain specific criteria, including having light skin and white toenails and hair – represent the power and divinity of the king. King Bhumibol Aduljadev owned ten white elephants, kept in stables at two conservation sites where they remain today, now the property of his son and heir. Queen Sirikit designated reserved areas for elephant reintroduction in the late 1990s; these have been successful in rehabilitating a number of former working elephants. Images of white elephants adorn temples and flags and are the ultimate symbol of Thailand's sovereignty. Official Thai flags between the years 1817 and 1917 portrayed white elephants on red backgrounds, after which the official flag was changed to the modern version of blue, white and red horizontal stripes.

Thai people interested in elephant mythology may also consider white elephants to be somewhat supernatural, with strong connections to the spiritual world. One elephant I met during my fieldwork – a three-metre-tall bull known as Thong Bai – was viewed as especially supernatural due to his half-white status. Not white enough to be royal, he is also viewed by Indigenous elephant people as neither part of this world or the next. He is one of Thailand's most famous elephants, being the face of Chang Beer and featured in many of the company's advertisements as well as in several movies. While Thong Bai brought in money for his unusual looks and size, his mahouts seemed in endless peril. According to Guay people I spoke to who knew Thong Bai well, one mahout had broken his leg and another had died of a mysterious illness – all allegedly associated with the bull's supernaturalism. Thong Bai himself has experienced great suffering, spending most of his life chained up in the small village of Ban Ta Klang in the northeast of the country. Despite the fact that a large enclosure reinforced with cement and steel fences was built for Thong Bai in 2015, his owner has been reticent to use it because he is afraid to enter the enclosure to feed the elephant when he is not chained up. This is due to his size – and that of his tusks – but may also be connected to the mysticism surrounding the elephant. Whatever the case, attempts to liberate Thong Bai from his chains have been confounded by the beliefs of the humans who live in proximity to him. Indeed, Thong Bai's situation illustrates the tension that exists between reverence for and the abjection of elephants, and also represents the complexity of keeping bulls in captivity.

A fascinating treatise on Thai elephants published in 1929 by anthropologist Phya Indra Montri Srichandrakumara provides a detailed summary of the traditional use of captive elephants in Thailand:

> The elephant has been used in war, for which it has to be specially trained. Kings would fight in single combat on their elephants, and these animals were also used for dragging heavy ordnance from point to point and in many other ways assisting the soldier in his hazardous operations. In the everyday life of the people, elephants not many years back were very generally used for the transportation of heavy articles of commerce and to-day are still used for dragging timber from the forests and for freeing timber jammed by floods in the streams. They are also used for riding purposes but in a lessening degree every year.[52]

Such use contributed to deforestation – the most significant environmental crisis Thailand has faced in its history, and certainly what has had the biggest impact on the welfare and conservation of its elephants. As Thai economist Gadsaraporn Wannitikul notes, a range of factors led to this occurring:

> Population pressure, the demand for wood and forest products, logging and the weak implementation of

forest law and policy, various illegal encroachments, the development of forest lands for agriculture, shifting cultivation practices, road and highway development, and the construction of dams, among others.[53]

Logging, rice farming, slash-and-burn agriculture and road building led to the rampant deforestation that has caused irreversible damage to Thailand's once extensive wildlife habitats.[54] Today, many native species in Thailand are listed as threatened or endangered, primarily as a result of deforestation. Wild elephants are among those endangered, while the unprotected captive population declined dramatically from approximately 100,000 in the early 1900s to just 3,400 in 1985 – the direct result of habitat destruction and the expansion and gradual decline of the logging industry.[55] The clearing of the forest also made it harder for impoverished local people to find certain forest foods, with many valuable plants having been destroyed. It became easier for them to hunt animals that had become vulnerable as the trees disappeared and they were left exposed. Logging also pushed wild elephants out into villages, where human-animal conflict became an issue. Elephants would enter human territories, destroying crops and houses, often leading to their death at the hands of farmers armed with shotguns – an issue that is common across countries in Asia with large populations of elephants.[56]

The practice of logging in particular, both legal and illegal, was a key factor in deforestation and had profound implications for elephants and mahouts. The industry essentially used elephants to destroy their own habitats, particularly in the country's north, where loggers used the animals to access dense, otherwise impenetrable forests of valuable teak in remote regions.[57] The loggers would weaken old-growth trees by cutting partway through their trunks with saws and chainsaws, and the elephants would then push the trees over, lift them with their trunks and tusks and drag them away, pulling the logs behind them on long chains. As tools in the unsustainable logging industry, their usefulness only provided them with the basic foundations of care. Loggers were poorly paid mahouts who worked arduous days to support themselves and their families with the added challenge of feeding their elephants in areas where natural forest food was slowly disappearing. The relationship between mahout and elephant was uneasy: mahouts were reliant on their elephants financially yet were shackled to the task of feeding them, with each elephant requiring on average 250 kilograms of food a day. Elephants were enslaved in an industry in which they were neglected or abused, slowly forced to destroy their natural homes. This was a relationship marked at its core by dependence and poverty. It was also based around what could only ever be an industry in decline – yet one that would continue long after until the forests of Thailand were pushed beyond their limits.

In 1989 the livelihoods of mahouts and elephants were threatened when the government instated a national ban on logging – a reaction to serious flooding as a result of extensive erosion. This occurred not only due to teak logging in the north, but also because of increased agricultural production in southern provinces. As summarised by resource sociologist Sureeratna Lakanavician:

> Between 19 and 24 November 1988, heavy rains
> triggered massive landslides that affected 16 villages
> in southern Thailand. Three villages were buried

under 1 to 3 m of sand and debris. All of Thailand's eastern coastal provinces from Chumporn to Narathiwat were affected. The 1988 floods were particularly unusual because disastrous floods were previously rare in southern Thailand. Total damages from the flood were estimated to be 7 357 million baht … The severe floods also caused the death of 373 people, injured hundreds and rendered thousands homeless in Nakorn Srithammarat Province.[58]

The ban was enforced by the demarcation of protected forest areas; however, by this time more than 70 percent of Thailand's forests had already been destroyed.[59] As Lakanavician explains, 'the ban on commercial logging has not prevented further deterioration of the natural forests'.[60] Deforestation has continued due to 'shifting cultivation by tribal villagers, dam and road constructions, even gas pipelines, eucalyptus and pineapple plantations, as well as resort developments in forest reserve areas'.[61]

The ban had life-altering consequences for local communities reliant on logging for survival, including some 2000 mahouts and their elephants.[62] Needing to find an alternative form of income, some mahouts engaged in illegal logging, including near or over the Burmese border, a risky occupation for elephants, who were sometimes injured or killed by falling from cliffs, slipping down hills or stepping on landmines, the deadly relics of conflict between the Burmese government and Rohingya rebels.[63] Other mahouts took their elephants to cities like Bangkok to beg for money and food on the street, or to work in tourism. Street begging was a dangerous occupation, with traffic and pedestrian accidents as well as poor conditions causing harm to both elephants and humans. In 2010 – after many attempts to legislate against the practice – street begging was banned, and the majority moved to tourism camps to join thousands of other mahouts and elephants.[64] Support was also provided by the Thai Elephant Conservation Center (TECC) in Lampang, which took in a number of unemployed mahouts and elephants.[65] The Forest Industry Organization (FIO), which had employed some 200 working elephants since its establishment in 1947, developed a number of welfare efforts, first by establishing the Young Elephant Training Center in 1969, which eventually evolved into the TECC after the logging ban of 1989. After establishing the TECC's full-time mobile veterinary clinic and hospital, 'in 2002, FIO established the National Elephant Institute of Thailand (NEI) to promote the overall welfare of elephants and keepers' communities, for example, by helping to revise laws and develop self-sustaining, eco-friendly business models for the tourism industry'.[66] Today, tourists can visit the TECC to watch elephants and mahouts perform activities traditionally related to logging, and the centre also offers rides using howdahs. Many elephants at this site are kept on fairly long chains in green areas when not working, where they have access to natural foraging sites. In general, my impression during two visits in 2014 and 2015 was of a place that provides good welfare conditions and veterinary support and is therefore important in guiding more traditional tourism camps to improve their practices.

By the late 1990s the development of a raft of new elephant camps was supported by an influx of international tourists.[67] Likely inspired by Eastern mysticism, and following the hippie trail through South and Southeast Asia, these tourists wanted to find places off the beaten track to explore and immerse themselves in the exotic, foreign culture.[68] Elephant camps sprung up in places like Phuket and Pattaya – beachside idylls that held great attraction for this new wave of travellers. Entrepreneurs had discovered these Westerners wanted to interact with the majestic, intelligent creatures, and mobilised unemployed mahouts and elephants from the logging industry to work for them. It seemed to benefit all sides: mahouts and elephants were provided with an income, shelter and food; entrepreneurs made money from their investments; and tourists' desires to interact with elephants were fulfilled by the hugely popular practices of elephant riding and shows.

Elephant camps vary in size, set-up, location and conditions. I have visited several with decent welfare standards and others with crowded, poor conditions. Commonly, elephants are chained up in shelters or kept in corrals and work long hours during the day with their mahouts. As previously described, in these camps, elephants take tourists for rides, usually around the camp's property, out into areas of forest or along roads. They are also used in circuses and shows, where they exhibit learned behaviours like painting, playing soccer, throwing darts, spinning hoops on their trunks and other tricks. Tourists can also get up close to the animals, feed them food, stroke their trunks and have a photo taken. The chains used to tether elephants are a necessary evil in these spaces to protect the safety of humans and other elephants. But the welfare issues associated with these chains is one of the primary reasons that camps have come under fire, as with the forceful use of bull hooks and other punitive methods of training, as well as living conditions for elephants that are detrimental to their welfare.[69] Yet such conditions range across a spectrum, depending on the camp itself and on the people who care for elephants at these camps, including their mahouts, whose individual attitudes, behaviours, cultural practices, beliefs and life circumstances affect the care they give.[70]

I wanted to understand how these factors influenced mahout-elephant relationships without criticising a foreign culture and people, or by engaging in cultural relativism and excusing animal suffering in the face of tradition. This meant I needed to balance what critical race theorist Claire Jean Kim notes is 'a normative dilemma between respecting … cultural practices, on the one hand, and giving due consideration to the interests of the animals who are seriously harmed by these practices, on the other'.[71] As well as conducting numerous interviews with mahouts and observing mahout-elephant interactions for hundreds of hours, I explored these relationships by analysing historical information from elephant archives and museums, such as those at the TECC and the Surin Elephant Study Center in Ban Ta Klang, as well as related anthropological literature. While I certainly uncovered instances of cruelty towards and neglect of elephants, I also found many of kindness and care. I was intrigued by Srichandrakumara's suggestion that, in some places in Thailand, 'elephants take a place somewhat akin to the horse or ox, living with their owners on easy terms of intimacy and liking'.[72] This statement provides further evidence of a dichotomy within human-elephant relationships in Thailand – one of care and control, where the 'easy terms' of those relationships may have been tempered by the daily tasks the creatures were forced to perform in their service as nation-builders.

Environmental ethicist Napat Chaipraditkul suggests that Thai people's relationship with elephants can be understood as 'serving an anthropocentric attitude', with the animals' real relationship with humans being one of utility, rather than reverence.[73] However, such utility is common to many human-animal relationships in different cultural contexts and thus should be viewed as a universally human problem, rather than unique to Thai or Indigenous relationships with elephants. By comparing the Thai elephant to the horse or ox, Srichandrakumara's description reveals parallels between the treatment of these species, with each playing an important role in developing human civilisations. Srichandrakumara's ideas resonated with me as a researcher of equine ethics, for horses were also historically subjected to practices that caused them harm. Horses were and may still be 'broken in' using cruel methods, restrained using devices such as the Victorian-era bearing rein or the modern double bridle, and many suffer at our hands for the sake of entertainment, such as in racing, steeple-chasing and some less-than-ethical forms of equestrianism.[74] Indeed, such treatment can be associated with the keeping of many domestic animals, especially those used in industrialised farming. Without excusing mahouts who are intentionally cruel or neglectful, this was something I kept in mind as I began to explore the welfare issues associated with the use of captive elephants in tourism.

Different attitudes to elephant training exist throughout Thailand, and controversy has arisen over whether cruel practices are truly authentic of the traditions of elephant peoples around the country.[75] In my own research, I discovered that such differences arise from socio-cultural, environmental and economic factors that have shaped elephant-mahout relationships. Mahouts might choose cruelty over kindness in training for a number of reasons, many of which come down to the personality and attitude of the individual mahout as well as his background and socio-economic status. There are mahouts who care for their elephants despite their inability to adequately provide for them, and who talk about their elephants in familial terms – often as their 'children' – even when said elephant's welfare is sub-par. In many cases, these mahouts have owned or worked with their elephant for years or even decades, with their ancestors having raised elephants in captivity for centuries.

As Richard Lair explains, in many tourist camps 'outright cruelty is rare but indifference is rife', leading to 'unhealthy, poorly nourished elephants'.[76] Another study by conservation researcher Nick Kontogeorgopoulos notes that the welfare issues associated with elephants who work in camps are most likely caused by the decline in the 'quality' of mahouts, due to the decreasing social status of the job. As the industry has grown, the number of mahouts who have little experience either working with or caring for elephants has increased. In some of these cases it is not the mahout who owns the elephant, but rather a wealthier individual who pays the mahout a fraction of the income that is generated from the shows and rides in which both mahout and elephant participate. These hired mahouts might have little financial incentive to properly care for their elephants. Overall, the complex interdependency of mahouts and elephants in the contemporary tourism industry in Thailand is still a fraught symbiosis, yet, as Kontogeorgopoulos argues, 'given the absence of viable alternatives, tourism contributes to the welfare of domesticated elephants in Thailand in optimal, albeit imperfect ways'.[77]

* * *

Not long after my encounter with the two elephants in Chiang Mai, it became even clearer that there was a path I needed to follow in Thailand – a path walked by elephants. I had found evidence of them everywhere in the city; as well as those I had encountered in person, every market stall I visited displayed table upon table of elephant pendants and charms, bags and harem pants festooned with printed elephants, bracelets made from elephant tail hair and (usually faux) ivory rings, and elephant paintings and carvings. I even drank Chang Beer, the elephant-branded beverage that was popular with locals and foreigners alike. I saw many tourists wearing Chang Beer t-shirts bearing the logo of two white elephants on a green and gold background. Elephants also caught my eye on colourful posters displayed in shop windows and folded brochures offered by earnest touts, promoting Chiang Mai's numerous tour companies who offered 'elephant experiences' in the Mae Taeng region, an hour north of Chiang Mai. Just like the 'Majestic Elephant' pamphlet I had seen at the hostel, many ads depicted two smiling tourists sitting atop an elephant as its mahout, sitting astride the animal's shoulders or walking ahead, guided them through the jungle. Invariably, these elephants wore large, wooden benchseat howdahs decorated in carvings and perched atop thick folded blankets. Other ads depicted elephants performing in circuses: playing soccer wearing the colours of Manchester United or Liverpool; painting landscapes and flowers with brushes held in their trunks; throwing darts at giant bullseyes; or dancing for tourists in giant replicas of human clothing, including a lacy dress on an elephant calf.

One afternoon, on one of my daily walks around Chiang Mai's old city, I saw a poster quite different to the others, displayed in the large windows of a corner shopfront. A number of elephants roamed free through fields surrounded by jungle. Here, there were no howdahs, soccer outfits or paintings of flowers. Atop were the words 'Elephant Nature Park' in gold; above that was a logo of two elephants entwined, one small, one large – a mother and calf. I pushed open the door and walked into a pleasantly airconditioned room with walls similarly plastered in posters of elephants roaming in fields. A number of other tourists were milling around, reading information on the posters and chatting to several Thai people wearing t-shirts embroidered with the same logo of entwined elephants. I caught the eye of a woman across the room, sitting at a desk covered in brochures. She looked up and smiled. 'Sawadee ka!'

I returned the greeting and walked over to her. She wore a green nametag pinned to a red shirt bearing the elephant logo. Her name was Patty.

'Do you want to volunteer with elephants?' she asked.

I looked at the brochures before me. Along with pictures of roaming elephants were images of Westerners washing elephants in a river, cutting sugarcane with machetes and smiling at the camera, covered in dirt, as if they had laboured hard in the fields. My mind went back to the elephants on Doi Suthep and Ratchadamnoen Road who, in comparison to the elephants I saw around me, clearly lived in a different reality.

'Elephant Nature Park is an elephant sanctuary just an hour's drive north of the city,' Patty explained. 'We have a volunteer program for tourists. If you'd like, you could come to the park for a week and help look after the elephants. All the information is here in the brochures.'

I thanked Patty and with brochure in hand sat down in a chair by the desk. I was soon enraptured when I learned how I could help the thirty-odd elephants who lived at the park, all of whom had been rescued from situations in which their welfare was threatened – whether from begging on city streets, being employed in tourist camps or living in poor conditions in villages across the country. As part of a paid volunteer program, I could spend a week or more sur-rounded by elephants, staying in a bamboo hut and working every day to contribute to the running of the sanctuary. I could also get close to elephants without riding them or watching them perform. There would be shelters to clean, manure to shovel, food to prepare and property to maintain. The work involved would not be that different to my horse-related tasks back at home, just on a slightly larger scale. Manure would be heftier, fences would be higher, and preparing feed would be a monumental job. And rather than working with creatures I knew very well, I would get to know some who were still a great mystery to me, while also forming the basis for a PhD on animals and ethics in tourism. I made the quick decision to volunteer for a week and filled in the requisite forms. I paid Patty around US$400, which would cover my accommodation and food, contribute to the cost of elephant food and health care, and provide funds for future elephant rescue and rehabilitation. It would also help to cover living costs for mahouts and improvements and maintenance of the park's infrastructure.

The rescue of elephants – primarily by removing them from situations that are detrimental to their welfare – is a costly process. A Thai elephant is worth around one to two million baht, equivalent to US$30,000–60,000. Rescuing involves raising funds and negotiating to buy an animal that is usually the owner's sole income. This is complex not just because of the sum of money involved but because as long as elephants have value, rescue risks being a commodified practice for mahouts, who may view it as a source of income or even buy another elephant with the money from the sale. Yet purchasing an elephant is one way to ensure its safety and protection. In the case of ENP, funding from volunteers contributed to these rescues.

Paying to volunteer at Elephant Nature Park would differ from my previous experiences where I offered my time to work with animals and paid nothing to participate. Since the late 1990s, paid volunteering has become an increasingly common global phenomenon driven by the growing popularity of volunteer tourism. It is especially popular in Thailand, where tens of thousands of would-be volunteers flock yearly to work with animals and teach local children English, among other pursuits. Tourism studies theorist Stephen Wearing describes volunteer tourism as 'experiences that make a difference', ideally by directly contributing to the wellbeing of people, the welfare of animals and the conservation of the environment.[78] The concept of paid volunteering may seem paradoxical, but when funding is directed in these meaningful ways, volunteer tourism has the potential to provide tourists with unique experiences while also benefiting local communities.[79] It has therefore been viewed as a more ethical alternative to mass tourism that overcomes its colonial nature and provides mutual benefits for tourists and locals (and, indeed, animals).[80]

While it has grown in popularity since the 1990s, volunteer tourism has also been criticised for exploiting tourists financially while also failing to distribute funds to effectively benefit the intended human and non-human communities.[81] Indeed, I came across a couple of volunteer projects that left a lot to be desired during time spent in India, another volunteer tourism hotspot. In one case, I paid to volunteer on what was advertised enticingly as an 'animal rescue project' only to find that it didn't exist. Instead, I would be cleaning cages at a particularly depressing zoo, as had a young American tourist who had been scammed by the volunteer tourism organisation. Luckily, I had paid only a deposit and avoided losing US$1,800 on the sham project; the American tourist had not been so fortunate. But I also had numerous positive experiences volunteering across

Asia, which showed me that well-organised, financially transparent paid volunteer projects can successfully meet their aims by helping both people and animals. One of these was Elephant Nature Park, where I was introduced to Doc Ngern and her herd mates, and started to learn everything I could about Thailand's captive elephants.

Chapter 3

ELEPHANT NATURE PARK

When the minivan to Elephant Nature Park (ENP) picked me up from the hostel at 7am, it was already jam-packed with eight other volunteers, their luggage and, mysteriously, two plastic sacks full of bananas, each bigger than my already rather large thirty-litre backpack. I did not know it at the time, but bananas would feature a lot in my life over the next few weeks. The drive took over an hour, up then down then up again on winding mountain roads, the view from the bus windows a perfect vista of jungle and fresh blue sky dotted with wispy cirrus clouds. I chatted with the other tourists, sharing stories of our travels. Some of us were just starting out – only days or weeks into our travels, like me, and a couple from America who were on the first leg of a round-the-world trip. A quiet Swiss woman had been travelling for over a year, her weary dirt-stained backpack a marker of true intrepidness. My five-year-old backpack had done the hard yards, but it was pristine in comparison, its cheery pink-purple waterproof canvas betraying evidence of jaunts through Europe rather than epic treks through the forests, towns and cities of Southeast Asia.

Soon we drew through the large front gates of ENP, the minivan spitting up dust as it took a dirt road between bamboo huts and banana trees. It slowed as we reached a large two-storey wooden structure on stilts bordered on one side by a rushing river and the other by a herd of elephants grazing in lush fields. After offloading our backpacks, the other volunteers and I were immediately met by a duo of volunteer guides named Jack and Burm, who welcomed us to the park with enthusiasm and broad smiles. They shepherded us to a viewing platform that surrounded the structure, a place where over the days to come we would eat our meals and spend our evenings playing cards, chatting and drinking lethal Hong Thong whiskey. For now, we marvelled at the sight of so many elephants roaming before us in the fields, like we had wandered into a real-life Jurassic Park, where the dinosaurs were grass-eating pachyderms with no intent to harm us.

I spent those first moments on the viewing platform entranced, watching elephants amble through the high grass, pulling up plants with their trunks and stuffing them into their mouths. Occasionally one would trumpet, the sound booming across the valley and echoing off the verdant hills. More often, the elephants would emit high-pitched squeaks – unusual noises coming from such large creatures – or would slap the ends of their trunks against the ground, communicating through vibration. I watched an elephant rub herself against the trunk of a large tree for several minutes, evidently enjoying the feeling of the bark scratching her back. Two elephants dozed in the sunshine, their trunks intertwined. In the distance, elephants foraged for grasses and roots and ate fruit and sugarcane provided by their mahouts, who observed them as they roamed and were ready to direct them this way or that when they wandered too far. The mahouts were almost invisible among the fields and foliage, often squatting or sitting in the long grass or resting in the shade of wooden shelters strategically set around the park. The mahouts, the high concrete walls around the park's perimeter, the main building and the bamboo huts were reminders that the scene before me was a simulacrum of nature. But ensconced between fields and trees it felt so much more. It was like being on safari, witnessing wild giants roaming free among the grasses and trees.

The purpose of ENP was and still is threefold: firstly, to provide sanctuary for abused and injured elephants; secondly, to provide tourists with the chance to see them in a quasi-natural habitat and engender awareness of their plight; and thirdly, to provide employment, accommodation and safety for refugees escaping warfare and turmoil in neighbouring Burma, with male refugees being trained as mahouts while their families live on-site. The result is a lively, cross-cultural milieu in which the labour and funding from volunteers ultimately supports both elephants and refugee families. But the primary focus at ENP is on the elephants themselves, with mahouts performing a more silent role in the background, ultimately managing the movements of elephants and ensuring the park's smooth operations.

As well as the volunteers who stayed for a week or more, tourists also visited on day trips from Chiang Mai. During my first visit, around fifty tourists visited the park each day. The other volunteers and I stayed in bamboo huts in a small section of the park, away from the elephants but set among lush greenery by the banks of the Mae Taeng. We slept two per hut, living alongside geckos and a variety of insects, protected from the most irritating or dangerous by sturdy mosquito nets hung over our single beds. Still, sometimes the odd mosquito, an errant scorpion or a collection of ants would find their way into the nets, which we would beat thoroughly to ensure unwanted visitors were quick to leave. My British housemate Becky and I slept to the odd chirps and trills of gecko calls and awoke to the sound of distant rumbling and trumpeting as the elephants began their day. A frog lived in one corner of the bamboo bathroom and two cats – a friendly pair of tabbies with almost identical markings – watched us intently as we took bucket showers. One night we found a green snake coiled around the base of the toilet, forcing us to use our neighbours' bathroom until it vacated the premises the next afternoon and we could bucket shower in peace.

ENP had a well-organised program that taught us much about elephant welfare through talks given by volunteer coordinators and a number of videos that explained the welfare issues present in tourist camps. We also understood our place in the park well. We could watch the elephants and engage with them in small ways, such as by washing and feeding them, but here the movements of tourists were restricted rather than those of the elephants, unlike in camps. We could not go beyond the structures that contained us: the viewing platform, our huts and the main building, and stuck closely to our coordinators when out on walks around the grounds. Our activities were carefully structured to minimise disruption to the elephants' routines, and everything that we did – day in and day out – was focused on their welfare.

The other volunteers and I quickly became fast friends, bonding over our daily tasks and adventures, united in our new education about elephant welfare issues and equally awed by our experiences feeding, washing and watching elephants. We were all falling in love with these creatures while holidaying in a beautiful setting where we were actively making a difference. We spent our mornings collecting sugarcane and corn from huge fields, wielding machetes and carrying heavy bundles on our shoulders, often being bitten by fire ants and scalded by the sun. These tasks were difficult and tiring but ultimately satisfying when we saw the elephants dig into the feed with great gusto. Washing and dividing hundreds of kilos of pumpkins, bananas, pineapples and yams into elephant lunches and dinners was a monumental effort, rewarded by the experience of feeding the creatures. We all loved the feeling of their rough grey skin and the soft finger-like tips of their trunks that would take fruit and vegetables surprisingly gently from our hands.

Afternoons provided scope for different adventures, usually building and repairing the park's infrastructure, including fences, elephant shelters and volunteer accommodation. We spent one memorable afternoon travelling to a nearby village in the back of a truck, gleefully shirking the safety precautions of home as we rattled around the cargo bed like chickens off to market. In the village we collected huge bamboo logs, intended for fences and housing, and strapped them together with rope to form ten-metre-long makeshift rafts, which we floated on down the river to ENP. There, we dragged them with great effort from the current onto the sandy banks, before spending a relaxing afternoon watching elephants eating in the distance while we drank Chang Beer.

Each day we met new elephants and heard the stories of their pasts and their rescues. This is where I learned that as well as tourism, the legal and illegal logging industries were the source of many captive elephants' woes. Two elephants made a particularly strong impression on me. Max was a gorgeous, pale-grey bull with a gentle nonchalance who took bananas carefully from my hand. He was born in the forests of northern Thailand and worked in logging for many years before moving into tourism with his mahout. They then spent most of their days begging on the streets in the tourist areas of Bangkok, much like the mahout and elephant I had seen on Ratchadamnoen Road in Chiang Mai. One of Max's front legs had been badly injured when he was hit by a semi-trailer while walking with his mahout along a busy freeway. The injury caused his legs to stiffen abnormally and meant he would never work or beg again. Max's future looked particularly bleak when his mahout chained him outside a temple for years on end in an attempt to make some money from monks and other devout Buddhists, who made merit from caring for him. Luckily, Max was eventually rescued by ENP and loped around its fields until he died in 2009 due to complications with his legs.

Then there was Jokia – her name meaning 'eye from heaven' – who had also worked in the logging industry. Pregnant, she was forced to work through her labour and gave birth at the top of a steep hill. Her calf rolled down the slope and died from the tumble, after which Jokia went into mourning and refused to work. Her mahout, frustrated, used a slingshot to punish her, blinding her in both eyes, meaning she could never work again. After being rescued and sent to ENP she was befriended by an elephant named Mae Perm, who would guide her blind friend around the park, Jokia often with Mae Perm's tail grasped firmly in her trunk. Witnessing the friendship between the two elephants was heartening. Jokia's lack of value to the logging industry no longer mattered in this new world where she was valued by Mae Perm as a true companion in a tight-knit herd.

Stories like those of Max and Jokia were common among the elephants of ENP. There were those rescued from cruelty or malnourishment, from forced mating practices and overtly cruel training practices – all the outcomes of the tourism and logging industries. I also met several elephants with different health issues at the on-site veterinary clinic, including an older female elephant named Malai

Tong, a former logging elephant who had lost part of her hind leg after treading on a landmine. Many elephants have died or suffered similar injuries over the past few decades; injuries like Malai Tong's would never fully heal and needed ongoing care in the form of a giant daily footbath of antiseptic. Observing her work with the vet was fascinating: she calmly followed his directions and stood with her injured foot in the footbath for an hour or more, flapping her ears gently as he checked the damaged flesh. The vet explained that other elephants like her who had fully lost a limb were candidates for prosthetics designed at the Friends of Asian Elephant Foundation Elephant Hospital in Lampang, associated with the Thai Elephant Conservation Center.

The more I learned about these elephants, the more I wanted to undertake research into the intersections between elephant captivity and tourism. Days at ENP were spent half in a daze of wonder and awe, half in intense thought and contemplation as the enjoyment I felt volunteering with elephants met my academic need to prod and question and get to the bottom of the issue. At the same time, I found myself increasingly emotional about the elephants and their stories of suffering and rescue. Such emotions would ultimately guide the ways in which I recorded my observations over the years, driven by moral and ethical directions as well as a more 'scientific' approach, with its roots in elephant behaviourism and conservation science. My emotions also allowed me to attempt to understand the daily lived experiences of the elephants I encountered across all my fieldwork sites. As ecologist and ethologist Marc Bekoff explains:

> Lacking a shared language, emotions are perhaps our
> most effective means of cross-species communica-

tion. We can share our emotions, we can understand the language of feelings, and that's why we form deep and enduring social bonds with many other beings. Emotions are the glue that binds.[82]

My emotions of joy and sadness became ever more powerful through volunteering. Even after such a short time, ENP's elephants were changing my life in positive ways. I had fallen in love with ENP so quickly, having had the most amazing experience of any I'd had travelling. One afternoon, after I had finished my tasks for the day, I cooled off in the Mae Taeng River. The horizon was lilac and pink in the distance, the heat of the day dissipating while cool air rolled off the hills and into the valley below. Coils of smoke rose in the distance – the mahouts and their wives preparing dinner in their houses as their children, home from school, played and called to one another in the fields. The elephants were contained in their shelters overnight, fed their evening meal, their quiet rumbles and squeaks to each other carrying on the gentle wind. As I floated in moss-green water, the image before me crystallised and with it came the sad realisation that I would be leaving the park in just two days. Ahead of me were several more weeks of travel: up the mountain to the hippie town of Pai, further north to Chiang Rai and the Golden Triangle, then back to Bangkok for one more week working with street dogs. Plans had been made and hostels booked, but I was not yet ready to leave. As the current pushed me towards the bank, I decided to spend three more weeks at ENP.

The extra time at the park offered many new and exciting experiences. After a week of feeding elephants, I briefly became the 'manager' of the banana shed, sorting bananas into four different types: unripe, underripe, ripe and overripe. At 7am on my first day on the job, a flatbed truck with a large cage arrived at the park, filled to the brim with a literal tonne of bananas. The mountain of fruit would need to be transferred from the truck to a number of cupboards in the shed, a task that would take almost an hour.

'Form a chain!' I commanded a group of six volunteers, following the orders given to me the night before by the retiring banana shed manager, who had been promoted to veterinary assistant. 'Pass them down the line!' The first in the chain, a muscly American named Sam, hefted bag after bag of bananas off the truck, passing each five-kilo load to his neighbour, who then similarly hefted each bag into the arms of the next person, and so on down the chain. Finally, the bags came to me and, with one final heft, I packed them neatly into the appropriate cupboard, divided according to ripeness. Ripe and overripe bananas were high in sugar and more fermented, and could only be fed to older, larger elephants. Elderly elephants missing teeth could only manage ripe bananas but could not handle too much sugar, so their intake had to be regulated. Most elephants could eat underripe bananas, and the completely unripe bananas were stored in cupboards until they were ripe enough to be used. By the end of the week, my full education into elephant banana consumption had been realised, yet the fun and novelty of banana management had waned. I was covered most of the day in sticky, smelly fruit, my boots slimy with yellow-grey mush, my ENP t-shirt stained black from a disgusting combination of sweat and banana slime. It was several weeks before I could eat a banana without feeling nauseous.

The following week I spent a night in Elephant Haven, a hundred-acre plot of mountainous land several kilometres from the park. Six volunteers and two volunteer coordinators walked alongside five elephants, their mahouts and several of the park's dogs, who were rescued strays. It was a typically humid day as we headed out the front gate and down the quiet, winding main road, lined on one side by a sharp forested incline and the other by fields and wooden houses. We reached one of the small villages set along the Mae Taeng and crossed over the river, volunteers taking a narrow bridge while elephants and mahouts waded through deep water, still keeping dry the loads of food and barrels of water that would nourish us for two days. From the other bank we trekked upwards, following steep muddy tracks I decided were better navigated barefoot. Shoes were sucked off by viscous mud; feet at least could be retrieved – albeit with some effort – and mud provided an unexpectedly useful barrier between skin and thorny bushes. I tied the shoelaces of my boots together and hung them around my neck, heading further upwards with legs soon caked in soil, leaves and sticks.

For an hour or more we continued our ascent, the elephants ahead of us, gigantic grey behinds and swinging tails marking the trail, the pace quickening as the ground levelled slightly and we saw before us a basic structure hewn of bamboo and wood, where we would stay the night. Several of the park's dogs had made it before us and grinned at the slowpokes, tails wagging, as we rested, muddily and momentarily, before taking stock of our accommodation. As we wiped mud from our feet and settled onto the floor, cross-legged, someone procured Chang Beer from a backpack and we toasted to a climb well made. The elephants would roam overnight in the dense surrounding jungle, feeding and socialising. The mahouts cooked dinner for us on an open fire – fried chicken in the spiciest of sauces, stir-fried vegetables and sticky rice. As night fell, our stomachs full, the mahouts suggested we head into the jungle to find the elephants, guided only by torchlight and a few enthusiastic dogs. We trudged ever upwards, the mud still thick, drawn to the cracking, crunching sounds of elephants breaking and eating branches, and the crashing of their bodies through the undergrowth. The foliage was dense with prickles, spikes and sticky vines, and hidden roots and logs that tripped me up. I was soon convinced that I was covered in leeches; it was best to forget about this, I decided, and deal with the situation once back at the camp.

After tripping over a log and falling face first into a spiky bush, then backwards into a puddle of mud, I grew less enthused about chasing elephants and was content to let them disappear into the jungle. We returned to camp to tend to scratches and declare war on bloodsuckers. As I lay in bed that night, sleeping only in fits and starts on a mat on the floor, I felt a certain privilege. This was as close as the elephants would get to freedom and it was as close as we could get to them in what was essentially their terrain.

The next day, after a breakfast of pancakes, strawberry jam and peanut butter, we headed back into the jungle to find the elephants, happily guided by sunlight streaming through the canopy that illuminated the prickles, spikes and vines from the night before. The mahouts had brought them closer to camp; now we could see the grey boulders of elephant bodies between the trees, ears flapping and trunks swaying as they made a meal of their surroundings. Many of the trees around us were wrapped in thick ribbons of yellow-orange *saai sin*, the holy cloth of the Theravada monastic tradition. We had seen these the day before on our way up but could appreciate them more now that we were at a relative standstill. The cloth having been blessed by monks, tying *saai sin* to trees was intended to deter people from felling them. In his book *Forest Monks and the Nation*

State, J. L. Taylor argues that intrinsic connections between monks and the forest generates an animistic connection between human and non-human.[83] This form of spirituality approximates a kind of environmental activism. In blessing the trees of Elephant Haven, the monastic tradition worked alongside a contemporary movement for forest preservation and, in turn, the protection of elephants. I spent the morning wandering among the trees in quiet reflection, contemplating whether they would survive the outbreaks of illegal deforestation that we had learned wreaked havoc on elephant habitats.

In my final week at ENP I helped in the veterinary clinic, where I met a bull who had formerly worked in logging. His tusks had been stolen by ivory poachers, leaving large, weeping abscesses that needed daily cleansing. After logging was banned, like most captive elephants, he ended up in a tourist camp until being rescued. At the veterinary clinic, my role for several days was to flush the abscesses with a medicated solution using a large handheld pump. This meant inserting the nozzle of the pump as gently as possible to remove the infected gunk. This gave me the opportunity to peer into the bull's eyes, where I saw gentle intelligence and, I thought, appreciation for the care I was providing. By working with him, I learned a little bit more of what it was like to be a newly freed captive, safe from the perils of the logging and tourism industries yet still reliant on humans for care and protection. Despite all that he had been through, the bull appeared gentle and forgiving, enduring what must have been an uncomfortable process of medical treatment. My horses had somewhat prepared me for this role; I was used to cleaning wounds and mucky hooves and administering messy tubes of wormer – processes that my horses also quietly endured, and which similarly covered me with a variety of unpleasant substances.

I loved having the chance to connect with the bull in an intimate way. Moments of connection with elephants were the most profound and exhilarating aspect of my time at ENP, a feeling shared by my fellow volunteers. As well as feeding them, washing elephants in the river was one of our favourite activities. We would scoop water in small buckets and splash it over them before scrubbing them clean with thick-bristled brushes, at all times staying aware of the elephants' movements. But we also loved observing them from a distance, where we could see them socialise, roam, forage and play – four natural behaviours that contribute to good elephant welfare.[84] Ultimately, these behaviours best define the overarching interests of captive elephants, through which they express joy and feel social connection. Since 2018, ENP no longer allows tourists to bathe elephants; instead, they can watch them in the river and fields from viewing platforms. This shift away from tactile encounters has become more common in Thailand, as I will discuss in later chapters, and benefits elephant welfare by prioritising the interests of elephants over the desires of tourists.

My early observations of elephants at ENP set me up for my later research, where I tried to understand elephant interests by imagining life from their point of view. But it was difficult to engage in the sort of 'enlightened' form of anthropomorphism that ethicist David Fennell notes could 'break down the walls of speciesism' within animal tourism.[85] This is because, as theorist Donna Haraway argues, it is impossible for us to truly imagine what an animal might experience; indeed, Haraway believes that to claim to be able to do so is 'facile and basically imperialist'.[86] Further, as animal studies scholar James Serpell notes, we tend to view the lives of animals through the lens of our subjective beliefs, attitudes and values, which 'inevitably colour perceptions of the animals' welfare'.[87] If I was to attempt to understand the lived experiences of elephants, I would need to observe them as much as possible, as well as read books on elephant behaviour and talk to their carers about the animals' different histories, personalities and attitudes. I wanted to respect elephants by observing in a non-invasive way, recognising that they might not assent to their participation.[88] This often meant observing from a distance or with mahouts at hand when in closer contact.

The majority of my observations at ENP were of elephants happily wandering the fields in their herds, spending quiet days munching on grass and socialising. They also had access to forms of enrichment carefully designed by ENP. These included ropes strung from trees and giant tyres that the young elephants in particular enjoyed playing with, as well as an array of enrichment tools involving food, such as tyres and baskets full of corn, bananas and watermelons tied strategically to the top of fences to encourage foraging and play. The park's focus on positive reinforcement and treat-based training (primarily with bananas) allowed mahouts and other staff, including the on-site vet, to manage the elephants using gentle methods, such as target training, which teaches elephants to follow directions without using force. Positive reinforcement was complemented with desensitisation techniques that acclimatise the elephants to being touched and handled by the veterinary team. This means they willingly offer the team access to areas needing treatment, such as their ears or feet.

I have used positive reinforcement with my horses, including target training and clicker training using treats. Clicker training is a method whereby a clicking or kissing sound plus a treat is used as a reward for correct responses, and I've found it to be especially effective. I credit much of my horses' excellent temperaments and willingness to work and play with me to the positive reinforcement work I have done with them. I based some of my training on methods promoted by Andrew McLean, an Australian animal behaviourist who, after spending decades working with horses, turned his hand to introducing positive reinforcement for elephants across Asia. McLean developed the Human Elephant Learning Programs (H-ELP) along with Laurie Pond, which has been influential across Nepal, India, Burma, Thailand and Laos. As explained by the H-ELP Foundation:

> Positive reinforcement is when something the animal wants (such as a food or caressing) is given following the onset of a desirable behaviour. In positive reinforcement training, the trainer does his best to 'set up' the training so that the response is easily given.[89]

Behaviourists Gail Laule and Tim Desmond identify numerous benefits of positive reinforcement as a form of enrichment, including voluntary cooperation and reduced stress in husbandry and veterinary procedures, for addressing socialisation issues, and reducing excessive aggressive behaviour to group/herd members and trainers.[90] Further, as noted by cognitive scientists Justin Moscarello and Catherine Hartley, positive reinforcement has the potential to increase an animal's sense of agency because its past experiences become connected with positive rewards, thereby giving the animal more control over its environment based on its understanding of actions and outcomes.[91]

The forms of enrichment and positive reinforcement training at ENP certainly appeared to allow elephants to express their agency.

I observed the effects of these training methods on two young bull elephants, one born at the park, the other rescued at a very young age. Having never experienced punitive methods of training or life in tourist camps, both bulls – Hope and Jungle Boy – behaved quite differently to their older peers. I gained a clear sense of their personalities on display especially in moments of play, flinging tyres and rolling in mud while squeaking and trumpeting with what must have approximated joy in elephant terms. As Raman Sukumar explains, 'play is a common behavior among immature elephants', with many young elephants playing with each other by 'pushing with their heads, wrestling with trunks, mounting or rolling on [one] another (including in water), and chasing ... most frequently with age-mates'.[92] In a country where there is little scope for elephants to play with age-mates or even older elephants due to their captivity, ENP provided these young elephants with a start to life rather different to those rescued from camps. Rescued elephants appeared more reserved in their expressions of joy – perhaps because they had experienced little before arriving at ENP. However, it was clear to me that the older elephants at ENP experienced happiness through socialisation, with the physical touch of other elephants and vocalisations being crucial for herd bonding among elephants with similarly traumatic pasts.

These early observations provided me with a basic understanding of elephant agency and interests within a sanctuary context as a form of 'captive freedom'.[93] Elephant researcher Catherine Doyle suggests that sanctuaries are 'convinced that elephants do not belong in captivity' and are committed to providing elephants with 'space, natural environments, social opportunities, and autonomy'.[94] However, as animal studies scholar Elan Abrell explains:

> All sanctuaries must balance animals' freedom
> against concerns for their safety and wellbeing, albeit
> a relative freedom within the bounds of captivity …
> Indeed, despite these aspirations towards freedom,
> sanctuaries necessarily entail some degree of control.[95]

This was true of ENP, which was able to uphold the interests of elephants while also confining and controlling movements for the safety of elephants and humans alike.

Such forms of captive freedom would benefit all elephants in Thailand's tourism industry; however, because there is insufficient land available to rehome them in sanctuaries,[96] it is necessary to find other ways of offering elephants more freedom. Sadly, as conservationist John Seidensticker notes, 'almost no human-free refugia remain [for elephants], although we like to imagine there must be such places'.[97] Deforestation has not only destroyed the habitats of wild elephants in Thailand, but it has also reduced any available land on which captive elephants might be kept.[98] Conversations with the Director of the Thai Elephant Conservation Center (TECC) in Lampang suggested there may be up to 7000 rai (approximately 2750 acres) of land available across Thailand for keeping elephants in more natural conditions, including around 2000 rai (800 acres) in the TECC's surrounds. However, this land is unlikely to provide enough space for any significant number of captive elephants to roam, meaning they would still need to be closely managed and monitored.

Nonetheless, small-scale reintroduction or rewilding has been used in Thailand to integrate captive elephants into more natural habitats, a process whereby 'autonomous agents' are restored to the landscape.[99] To date, around 100 formerly captive elephants have been successfully reintroduced into three wildlife sanctuaries, where they are breeding well.[100] One of these is Doi Pha Muang Wildlife Sanctuary, Thailand's first elephant rewilding effort. The sanctuary was inaugurated in 1997 by Queen Sirikit through the release of three elephants, and now supports twenty. Released elephants have acclimatised, fending for themselves and moving deeper into the forest as time has drawn on, taking them further away from human communities, thus reducing the potential for human-elephant conflict. They have also reverted to their natural behaviours and established a recognisable herd structure.[101]

My early days encountering elephants at ENP were spent imagining freedom for elephants, mainly through their return to the wild. But I gradually learned that rewilding could not solve all the issues associated with the instrumental usage of elephants in the Thai tourism industry. Firstly, the process is expensive and prolonged – costing around US$31,000 per elephant – and can therefore benefit only a small number of Thailand's several thousand captives.[102] Secondly, food and water shortages associated with land degradation may encourage human-elephant conflict by forcing elephants to enter villages to find food.[103] Thirdly, it may be difficult to find elephants that naturally form cohesive herd units and can therefore coexist in a relatively small space.[104] This is in addition to the significant spatial issues that limit the capacity of available land to manage rewilded elephants.[105] Considering the large natural home ranges for Asian elephants (fluctuating between around 34–800 km^2 for females and 200–235 km^2 for males[106]), it is clear that a huge amount of space is needed for successful rewilding at scale.[107] One additional issue is the keeping of bulls, who must be carefully managed in rewilding situations due to their potential aggressiveness, nomadic nature and natural separation from familial herds of female and young elephants.

The reality is that Thailand's elephants are and will always be affected by humans. As ethicists Christen Wemmer and Christine Christen suggest:

> Most people want elephants to have a natural place to live on Earth, free of human disturbance. This was once possible, but no longer. Human activity and development are almost everywhere, and any concept of undisturbed nature is illusory. Ethical management is fundamental to the welfare of both wild and captive elephants ... Virtually all elephant populations are influenced by human behavior, or are at least subject to human management, that is, human decisions that bear directly on their welfare and survival.[108]

To borrow from environmental ethnographer Irus Braverman, it is clear that at a time when anthropogenic change has altered nature irrevocably, finding the means to develop effective, ethical conservation and welfare efforts for animals in captivity is essential. As 'alternative habitats', sanctuaries may not completely approximate elephants' 'natural' places of origin but provide some of the best conditions for elephants to experience socialisation, foraging, roaming and play.[109] My time at ENP certainly showed me how sanctuaries can offer elephants a greater experience of freedom within captivity. Soon I learned that there were other places across Thailand where elephants were also able to experience more agency, thanks to the work of ENP's founder, Sangduen 'Lek' Chailert.

Chapter 4

THE SAVE ELEPHANT FOUNDATION AND JOURNEY TO FREEDOM

Elephant Nature Park has played a crucial role in shifting the country's elephant tourism industry towards a more ethical focus. This has primarily been driven by Sangduen 'Lek' Chailert, founder of ENP and Thailand's influential Save Elephant Foundation. The significance of Lek Chailert's work has been felt not only in Thailand but also in neighbouring countries, such as Cambodia and Burma, for over twenty years. In 2010 she was named as one of six Women Heroes of Global Conservation. Thai people often have nicknames; Lek's refers to her height, *lek* in Thai meaning 'small'. I first met Lek during my stay at ENP in 2008 and soon learned of her powerful determination to save Thailand's captive elephants.

One morning, halfway through my first week at ENP, the other volunteers and I gathered in the large dining hall to hear Lek speak. This was an open room in the main building that looked out over the grounds of the park. A soft breeze blew through gaps in the slats of the walls, cooling us from the damp heat. In the distance were the sounds of elephants in conversation, their rumbles and squeaks resonating throughout the valley, between mountains, river and villages. We sat on chairs in a small circle, a troupe of dogs at our feet as the park's numerous cats climbed over us, our laps becoming their beds, our hands tools for petting and caressing. Lek entered the room, nodding and smiling. 'Thank you for being here,' she said, taking a spot in the circle. 'You are making a huge difference, just coming to the park. I thank you and the elephants thank you.' Discussion with Lek allowed us to dig deeper into elephant captivity and also learn Lek's life story, devoted to helping elephants. And so, we listened.

* * *

Lek Chailert was born in the small village of Ban Lao in 1962, home to members of the Indigenous Khamu tribe, in Thailand's mountainous north. From a young age she worked with her shaman grandfather to heal animals, including some of the elephants who lived near the village in logging camps. As a teenager she visited one of the logging camps and witnessed serious elephant welfare issues. This motivated her to dedicate her life to helping these animals. Lek was entrepreneurial, selling magazines on the streets of Chiang Mai to fund a project that would eventually become known as the 'Jumbo Express' – a mobile veterinary service that provides medical care to elephants while also working with rural communities to create new dialogues about human-elephant relationships. In its early stages, the Jumbo Express quite simply involved Lek travelling alone to the Thai–Burma border with medicine for logging elephants. Lek explained what those early years of activism at the border were like: days spent with sick and injured elephants whose owners were living in poverty and unable to provide them with health care. As well as magazines, she bought other items in bulk and walked from village to village selling her wares so she could afford to buy the medication. Over the years, Lek became a powerful voice for captive elephants in both logging and tourism, and soon became well known in the international conservation and animal welfare movement.

Lek founded Elephant Nature Park in 1998, in conjunction with Adam Flinn of eco-tourism organisation Green Tours. The large tract of land by the Mae Taeng River became home to several elephants brought to the sanctuary for a new life, with their numbers increasing over the years. Over the course of its development, ENP has generated the financial means to rescue and care for elephants by engaging tourists in the paid volunteer project, and has used the power of social media – including highly active Facebook and Twitter accounts – to promote ENP's work and improve the lives of the captive elephant population. As a result, ENP quickly became the most popular elephant welfare and conservation project in Thailand, with its volunteer program booked out several months in advance and dozens of tourists visiting daily.

The park's growing popularity was already evident in the differences I saw between my first visit in 2008 and second in 2011. In 2011, the bamboo huts and basic bathrooms had mostly been replaced with solid brick constructions and bathrooms with flushing toilets and hot showers. With these changes also came more structures that mediated tourist-elephant interactions. The old platform made of bamboo and wood from which tourists fed elephants was replaced by one made of cement to improve safety, and a solid steel guardrail had been constructed to better separate tourists from elephants during feeding time. Further changes included the construction of larger viewing platforms throughout the park and the expansion of the on-site restaurant. These changes were no doubt the direct result of tourists' increasing interest in the site, and funding from volunteers, day visitors and international donors. While ensuring the safety of the increased number of visitors, changes such as the guardrail and viewing platforms were indicative of a gradual shift in elephant tourism that purposely creates more distance between tourists and elephants, not just for the safety of the former but to give the elephants more space.

For the past twenty years Lek has travelled to northeastern Surin province to attend the annual Surin Elephant Round-Up festival, where she helps elephants in need. Surin is known as the elephant capital of Thailand but is a site fraught with serious elephant welfare issues. Many of these are the product of socio-economic dilemmas associated with deforestation and changes in agricultural practices. Back in 2008, I knew little about the place but for the arrival of a female elephant named Mae Bua Loy at ENP, whom Lek had rescued from Surin. Mae Bua Loy arrived at the park mid-afternoon on a truck that slowly arced its way from the front gate, around the main building and into the grounds to stop by the riverside where I stood waiting with other volunteers. Mae Bua Loy had made the twelve-hour journey from Surin along major highways and roads, through cities and villages, fields and forests. Park staff lowered the tailgate of the truck and Mae Bua Loy slowly inched out backwards. As her feet met the soft grass of the riverbank, she looked around, taking in the sight of the forest blossoming around her, the tumbling river and undulating fields. In the distance she could see a number of elephants grazing; several started to walk towards the truck, intrigued.

Mae Bua Loy stood still, evidently unsure of what to do. There was no chain on her leg or mahout by her side. It was up to her to decide what she would do next. After a moment of hesitation, she walked gingerly into the fields. Soon, she pulled clumps of long grass from the ground and chewed thoughtfully, surveying her new home.

Next, she wandered down to the river, where she collected dirt and loose stones in her trunk and flung them onto her back. She rubbed one foot against the other, spreading dirt and river water over her legs before stepping into the shallows, scooping up water in her trunk and spraying it over her back. By this time, an older female elephant named Mae Boon Ma had come to investigate the newcomer. Mae Bua Loy walked out of the water and over to the visitor, dripping with mud and tendrils of reeds. They both extended their trunks and caught each other's scent. Mae Boon Ma touched Mae Bua Loy's face with the end of her trunk, first gently her eyes, then her cheeks. Both ran their trunks along the length of the other's body for several moments, before lowering trunks and walking together off into the fields. Soon, Mae Boon Ma and Mae Bua Loy joined several other female elephants, and the little herd ambled further away from the river, the truck and those of us who stood entranced, watching them go.

Intimate physical touch between elephants is a key part of communication and herd bonding. As Indian ecologist and Asian elephant expert Raman Sukumar explains:

> Elephants actively communicate through a wide repertoire of tactile, visual, chemical, and acoustic signals. Several observers of captive and wild elephants have described the use of the trunk in a variety of contacts: reaching out to each other with extended trunks, entwining trunks, inserting the trunk tip in the other's mouth, placing the trunk over the back, caressing with the trunk, or just touching another with the tip of the trunk. Some of these contacts, such as making

trunk contact with the temporal gland or the genitals, are obviously to obtain chemical signals, but many others are purely tactile contacts. Placing the trunk tip in another's mouth, for instance, seems to be part of reassurance behavior under times of stress ... A calf may put its trunk into an elder's mouth to seek information about food. Leaning against or rubbing another's body is another form of tactile communication.[110]

I witnessed these behaviours daily at ENP as fascinating aspects of interactions within herds comprising small family-like systems. Having been rescued from different camps and villages, most of the elephants at the park were unrelated; nonetheless, they had developed strong ties with one another, akin to the bonds formed between herd members in wild elephant populations. Expressions of tactile communication were the foundation of such bonding, exemplified in the first moment Mae Bua Loy met Mae Boon Ma and followed her off into the fields, with the newcomer soon integrated into a family of elephants.

All the herds at Elephant Nature Park were partially created as friend groups, with individual elephants making choices as to whom to befriend. These groups were also curated by the park, which considered the personalities of different elephants to ensure they lived together peacefully. In the wild it is not unusual for elephants without a close familial relationship to bond with others within a herd, with herd relationships being naturally in relative flux. As ethologists Joyce Poole and Petter Granli explain:

Elephant families are composed of a discrete, predict-able composition of (mostly) related individuals, but over the course of hours or days, these groups may temporarily separate and reunite, or they may mingle with other social groups to form larger social units or aggregations ... Individuals who have no close relatives within their family still benefit from the same cooperative behavior.[111]

Such bonding is primarily the function of groups of female elephants, who form 'close and lasting social relationships [which] are remarkable in the context of their fluid social system'. This allows female elephants and their offspring to remain in an intricate network of sociality. This is why female elephants at ENP are chosen to live together, forming more stable groups than the male elephants, who in the wild by the age of around nine become less connected with the familial group, until they leave the group at around age fourteen and often form small bachelor herds. As Poole and Granli explain:

Newly independent males must acquire fresh skills to adapt to the society of males where body size and fluctuating sexual state determine interactions and relationships ... During the transition, young males' social activities center on getting to know age-mates, and playing with novel partners from outside the natal family.[112]

The complex reproductive and strength-based status of male elephants means that they cannot easily be herded together. This was reflected at ENP in the general separation of males from one another, with some roaming solo if not matched with other males or groups of females with whom they interacted well. The male elephants were also separated from others during periods of musth – the sexually active period in which bulls become aggressive due to hormonal changes relating to their physical need to copulate with females in mid-estrus.[113] As Sukumar explains, musth may have evolved as a means of signalling to other males their fighting ability, their resource-holding potential or intent to mate.[114] Bulls in musth commonly 'guard' females who have solicited the behaviour and usually mate with the guarding males. While musth plays a crucial role in elephants' reproductive behaviours, in a captive environment in which there are many female elephants, mahouts and tourists, males in musth need to be sequestered to avoid causing damage or injury.

Most of Thailand's captive elephants have never experienced herd life. Separated from their mothers at around two or three years of age, elephants live closely with humans but not so much with other elephants. They may see other elephants, be tethered next to one another in tourist camps or villages, but may never have the opportunity to interact as if in a herd. Herd life at ENP in a quasi-natural habitat, as with other sanctuaries and welfare/conservation projects, offers more freedom to captive elephants than elsewhere in Thailand.

Aligning with the growing interest in alternative forms of elephant tourism, Lek set up a new project in January 2014 called 'Pamper a Pachyderm', which was the first 'saddle off' program founded by the Save Elephant Foundation and involved two elderly female elephants retired from working in a tourist camp in Pattaya. Offering tourists the chance to interact with elephants without riding them, Pamper a Pachyderm has acted as a model for less intrusive elephant tourism by encouraging elephant owners to remove their animals from camps and support observational and gentle, tactile elephant experiences in more natural locations. This movement appears to also have influenced the owners of tourist camps, who are now 'more responsive to welfare concerns, and [the] need for elephants to express natural behaviors and forage for a variety of foodstuffs'. These changes have been supported by the 2014 Prevention of Cruelty and Animal Welfare Provision Act and the drafting of a twenty-year plan, the National Elephant Conservation Action Plan (2018–2027), 'which includes language related to establishing health care centers in four regions of Thailand, and conducting training courses on elephant health and welfare for camp owners, mahouts, and vet assistants'.[115]

When I interviewed Lek in 2015, she explained how some camp owners who were initially hesitant soon embraced this new form of elephant tourism. 'I went to some of the camps, and I told them how well we were doing, and that they could change and still be successful,' she told me. 'They had seen what we were doing for a while, but it took a long time to convince some of the camp owners to make the change. For example, there was one camp that offered elephant rides for thirty-five years, and they were interested but worried about the change, but we finally convinced them. It really was huge for them.

'We now have ten camps offering the Pamper a Pachyderm program, and all of them are doing well. They are all full every day. And it's working for them financially. They take in less people but charge more for the program than they do for rides, so they are making just what they would have used to. But now, instead of the elephants taking rides, they just go out walking in the forest a few times a day with by small groups of tourists who also wash them and feed them. These places are now so popular. I think some of the camps were surprised about this, but now they see that they can make a positive change for the elephants but not lose money.'

Other traditional camps not linked to ENP have also shifted to offer these types of experiences, but often combine them with bareback riding. This means that the elephants no longer wear a howdah; instead, tourists sit across their necks and backs, hanging onto a loop of rope. For example, popular Patara Elephant Farm in Chiang Mai – which used to be a traditional tourist camp – adapted to the desire for less invasive tourism practices by introducing an 'Elephant Caregiver for a Day' program, whereby tourists are introduced to individual elephants, taught about their behaviour and given the chance to feed them by hand. They can then ride the elephant bareback for a couple of hours, stopping off at a waterfall for lunch before riding them into the river and 'playing' with them. Other places have sprung up around Chiang Mai to offer similar experiences but expressly without riding, such as Elephant Jungle Sanctuary, where tourists can learn how to make traditional herbal medicines for the elephants as well as watching them wallow and play in mud pits. There are also now many sanctuaries around the country, such as Burm and Emily's Elephant Sanctuary, Boon Lott's Elephant Sanctuary, Tree Tops Elephant Reserve, Phuket Elephant Sanctuary and Samui Elephant Sanctuary, that only allow the observation of elephants. Overall, there has been a general shift away from 'anthropocentric' elephant camps – 'the purpose of which is to profit from tourist interest, but which do little to benefit welfare' – towards those that are 'ecocentric' – 'centered on concerns for elephant wellbeing', giving elephants 'more free time to interact with other elephants and more space to roam'.[116]

Evidence of the paradigm shift for elephant tourism also lies in changes to the imagery used to promote it in Thailand. In successive visits to Chiang Mai, I have noticed that posters and pamphlets picturing two tourists sitting on top of an elephant in a howdah, or images of elephants in circuses, are now less common. Instead, advertising material often shows tourists interacting with elephants in natural settings, such as in rivers and forests, washing, patting and feeding them, and riding them bareback. The growing number of 'elephant-friendly' alternatives bodes well for a future where captive elephants may experience more freedom. However, there is anecdotal evidence that camps wishing to emulate the sanctuary experience do not always have the elephants' best interests at heart. This is because they may encourage a large number of tourists to interact with the elephants, which can be dangerous to tourists while also causing issues for elephants, who may be crowded and stressed by the attention.

Sanctuaries like ENP rely on the participation of a new wave of tourists who are arguably more empathetic and compassionate towards elephants. These outcomes can be understood as an 'ethics of care', which 'encourages engagement with sympathies towards the wellbeing and integrity of animals, individually and collectively'.[117] My time at ENP taught me how volunteer activities – from cleaning shelters to cultivating, collecting and preparing food for elephants – encompassed this concept. An ethics of care can best be understood, in the words of animal studies theorist Lori Gruen, as 'view[ing] other animals as beings with whom we are in relationships, and it is within these complex relationships that animals command our ethical attention'. As Gruen further explains:

In order to respond ethically to the needs and interests of other animals, ethical agents need to develop empathetic skills allowing them to understand the experiences of another, as well as to situate those experiences in a larger social, political and economic context.[118]

As found in a study by Madyson Taylor and colleagues of volunteer tourism and elephants in Thailand, tourists commonly engaged in an ethics of care by 'witnessing abuse, questioning moral responsibility, connecting with elephants, and advocating for improved conditions'.[119] My own experiences and education at ENP were certainly built around these themes, and showed me how choosing to spend time, money and recreation working directly with elephants could influence their welfare through empathetic responses.

Stemming from both my personal experiences and observations, I started to understand how ethical care for elephants was connected to the emotions felt while volunteering with elephants. While my own emotions certainly guided this work, so did those of the tourists and sanctuary/welfare project operators I observed and interviewed, whose affective responses to elephant suffering motivated demands for better treatment. As animal studies scholar Adrian Franklin contends, such emotions are often the product of undoing destructive binaries (human versus non-human) out of concern for animals, constituting a transformative process that can have both moral and regulatory outcomes.[120] As I found, the ethical elephant tourism movement improved elephant lives as much through rules and policy as through affective and moralistic responses towards the treatment of elephants. These included the beliefs and feelings that people such as conservationists, Western tourists, Thais and Indigenous mahouts have about elephants. This deeply emotional terrain has profoundly reshaped the world of Thai captive elephants. For example, these elephants are increasingly viewed by tourists as beings with their own interests, and learning about captive elephants at sanctuaries and other more ethical tourism sites appears generally responsible for this shift. The education programs and online resources made highly accessible at these sites, along with the actual day-to-day experiences of living, working with and observing elephants allow tourists to get to know elephants and experience the emotions that come with these encounters. This in turn catalyses another shift in which tourists learn about tourism's impact on the animals' welfare.

In 2011 I interviewed three volunteers at ENP, asking one question on which they elaborated: 'What have you learned during your time at Elephant Nature Park?' As Michael, visiting from South Africa, explained:

> Coming here and working has taught me a whole lot about elephants and what we can do to help them. I just feel so glad to have done something that is good for elephants and not go to one of those camps or tourist places where they treat the elephants badly.

An Australian tourist named Kim explained that she had learned about the lives of captive elephants in tourist camps as a result of her stay:

> Most people just don't think, oh, what has that elephant had to go through, I mean what has happened to it to

make it able to give rides to people. I saw elephants painting in Phuket and I thought, that's weird. I knew something was strange about it, but it was not until I came here that I realised what was actually going on.

For Meredith, another Australian, ENP allowed her to differentiate herself from other tourists:

It's good to feel like you're doing the right thing by elephants and that you're not doing what everyone else is doing, like riding elephants or whatever. I do feel proud of being able to say that I have done something different and something that is better for elephants.

The three tourists all indicated that they would take ENP's message home with them. As Michael explained, 'I will tell my friends not to ride elephants.' Kim similarly said that she 'would make sure that people know what elephants go through', while Meredith noted that 'people just need to learn that [watching elephant circuses] is wrong … it's bad for the animals'. It was evident that all three volunteers had learned not just about general welfare issues, but also about the very specific problems associated with elephant tourism. It was tourists such as these who, through their involvement with ENP, could contribute to the shift in elephant tourism in Thailand not just by becoming informed, but also by asking other tourists to change their behaviour.

* * *

Following my second visit to ENP, I headed further north to volunteer on another project run by the Save Elephant Foundation called 'Journey to Freedom', based in remote villages in the Mae Chaem district, northern Thailand. The program began in June 2010 when a handful of volunteers and volunteer coordinators from ENP walked two elephants from tourist camps back to their former home. Located in a mountainous area, this region is home to people from the Indigenous Karen tribe, who practise traditional elephant husbandry and are commonly known as one of Thailand's hill tribes. The elephants were originally owned by Karen people, but leased to mahouts working in elephant camps as a means for the villagers to make an income. In his extensive anthropological study of mahouts of various Indigenous tribes in Thailand, Joachim Schliesinger describes the longstanding relationships between the Karen people and their elephants:

> Traditionally, the Karen have been famous for hunting and training elephants. [They] are the largest group of elephant keepers in Thailand. Until quite recently almost every Karen village along the border with Burma had one or more elephants ... The Karen consider their elephants as members of the household and regarded having an elephant as not only an important source of income for the owner but also a symbol of status within Karen society.[121]

The Karen were one of the main tribal groups involved in the legal and illegal logging industries and were therefore profoundly affected by the logging ban, leaving tourism as one of the only options for their survival. Deforestation in Mae Chaem has adversely impacted the Karen villagers' ability to feed and care for their families and their elephants. Further, the logging ban also prohibited the clearing and burning of land to create swiddens for crop cultivation, which led to shorter fallow periods, meaning the fields could not recover between crops, leading to a decline in fertility.[122] Faced with the multiple issues of unemployment, elephants to feed, and lower land production, Karen people turned to tourism. Some mahouts sold or leased their elephants to the Thai Elephant Conservation Center in Lampang or to tourist camps in places like Chiang Mai, with some Karen travelling with their elephants to work as mahouts at those locations. Since the late 1990s, ecotourism has also become a form of income for Karen mahouts and their families, whereby tourists visit Karen villages to participate in forms of cultural tourism, such as hill trekking with local guides or volunteering within the community to teach English at local schools.

Journey to Freedom was akin to cultural tourism with a specific focus on keeping the integrity of Karen culture despite the presence of tourists and providing villagers with a source of income from volunteer tourism. When I visited, I spent around US$400 to work on the volunteer program, passing through two small villages before arriving in Ban Mae Satop, where the program was primarily based. Tourists stayed in basic huts that were owned by the villagers, with most of the tourist funding going to support their livelihoods. Each day, three other tourists and I walked with the elephants and their mahouts through the forests and spent time collecting food for elephants. The latter lessened the workload of the mahouts, meaning they could spend more time performing tasks such as harvesting rice and corn to feed the village. The volunteer coordinator on the program during the time, Chakkrapong 'Jack' Chaiyakarn, was a wealth of knowledge about elephant welfare in the Mae Chaem region, and several years later acted as interpreter when I visited elephant camps around Chiang Mai. He explained the aim of Journey to Freedom succinctly: 'You pay to walk with the elephants so they don't have to go to the tourist camps to work. Instead, they can stay in the village and you can stay here with them, and see a little bit of what it's like to live here.'

Along with the other tourists, I stayed outside Ban Mae Satop's main hub, permitted to visit for one week only to restrict outside influence. The program only operated in the dry season, as in the wet season the steep and winding dirt roads that were the only access to the village flooded and were susceptible to landslides. Even in the dry season, the village was difficult to reach. The drive took over four hours in an all-terrain vehicle, which struggled up and down the many ravines, shaded in dappled sunlight that filtered through the canopy.

As we arrived in Ban Mae Satop, several small children ran towards the truck, jumping up and down and grabbing my hands excitedly. I laughed as they helped me heft my backpack onto my back, for they were not much bigger than it. The children followed as Jack led us towards a smattering of wooden houses sitting in a clearing in the forest. The villagers had come out to greet us; several men quickly grabbed our heavy backpacks and carried them up a steep wooden ladder and into our accommodation, a wooden structure half-open to the elements at the edge of the village, which perched on stilts like the Karen's own houses. The stilts offered protection in an oft-flooded area and the space under each hut was used to house animals such as chickens and pigs in pens, and even small cattle and buffalo. I discovered I would be sleeping on a rattan mat on the floor, covered with a hand-sewn mosquito net. It was not the first time I had slept on the floor during my travels and I had worked out a strategy for protecting my hip bones and spine from the uncomfortable arrangement. This simply involved bundling all my clothing under me like a lumpy mattress and hoping it stayed put if I tossed and turned in the night.

During the evening, after the villagers left us to settle in, we sat at a large wooden table, playing cards and chatting while eating dinner the locals had prepared for us – stir-fried vegetables, rice, cobs of corn blackened from fire, plates of bananas and slices of pineapple, most of which were harvested in the village and nearby fields. The two American tourists, Jeff and Rebecca, had brought along their iPad and were playing a game called Fruit Ninja by the fire, which involved slashing through an array of fruit bouncing vertically across the screen using one finger, without cutting the occasional bomb and ending the game. It seemed pointless until I had a turn and found it to be both highly addictive and strangely soothing. Interested in the strangers and their technology, two young Karen boys came to join us by the fire, eager to handle the iPad and see what was captivating us. Jeff showed them how to play the game and they were quickly immersed in it, laughing uproariously as they slashed through bananas, pineapples, apples, strawberries and more. It was a virtual parallel to mahouts I had seen at ENP who cut up food for the elephants by throwing pumpkins up in the air and chopping them with a machete, with neat pieces falling back into baskets on the ground. Over the next week I would see Karen people engaging in the same novel process of elephant food preparation and pondered the strange coincidence of a form of entertainment from outside the village mirroring one of the daily activities within it.

Jack asked the boys about the technology they owned. They had mobile phones to play basic games, make calls and listen to music, and were now motivated to save up for iPads after playing Fruit Ninja. It was apparent that Karen youth were keen to access new technology that would connect them to the outside world. I discussed this with Jack, who explained that Karen children increasingly wanted to go to college and university outside the village and Mae Chaem, with their parents supporting the idea. This would give their children a chance to earn more money while allowing their families to keep their elephants at home.

* * *

The next day, we undertook the first of many daily walks with the elephants, along perilously bumpy dirt roads that wound deep into the valleys and fields below the village, meeting at streams that glittered in the sunlight with some of the clearest water I had ever seen. The elephants were masters of climbing up and down those steep roads; volunteers were certainly less so. Down was tricky enough, but the way up was barely tolerable. I found myself asthmatic and red with effort on many of the upward climbs and was always happy when a villager somehow navigating the rough ravines by motorbike ferried me back to the village. Two of the elephants we walked with were a young male and female, whom the villagers hoped would eventually mate. The female had been subjected to forced breeding in her earlier life and had killed the calf. The mahouts hoped that she would now become happily pregnant because her health had improved dramatically, and she was bonding well with the male. Though we trailed the pair at a distance due to the presence of the bull, on other days we also walked with two females who we could get closer to and feed giant cucumbers and watermelons by hand. These elephants had also been retired from tourist camps and were evidently enjoying life back in their traditional home, where they had natural food to graze on and no work to do.

On several days we worked with the villagers in the fields, harvesting rice and corn. I enjoyed having the tourist gaze reversed as the villagers laughed at our pathetic attempts to wield rice sickles, and the hilarity that ensued when I slipped on a muddy slope and fell into the irrigation trough. Every day we cooked our own lunch, using ingredients sourced locally. We spent hours cutting cane and grasses for the elephants, ending up covered in scratches from thistles and bites from ants and other bugs. We showered using buckets, pouring freezing cold water on ourselves to clean off the day's mud and dust. We used squat toilets that were often home to snakes and large spiders, and went to bed every night after the sun set, exhausted but content.

One day, on our way down another treacherous hill, we met twin baby elephants who had recently been born in the village – a rare and auspicious event, as twins occur only in one percent of births.[123] Their mahout proudly stroked their heads as the twins' mother stood behind him, half-asleep in the cool shade. He said a few words to Jack, who explained to us the significance of their birth: 'Twins are very powerful for the Karen people. There was a blessing and peace ceremony when they were born, and the villagers took their birth as a sign of good fortune.' Perhaps that fortune referred to the new way of life the Karen's elephants had experienced since the inception of Journey to Freedom, and the new income stream offered by low-impact, sustainable tourism that brought money into the village and kept elephants at home.

As well as offering a stable income for mahouts, Journey to Freedom provided funding even when tourists were not in attendance, meaning the villagers received a regular income all year round. This has helped the Karen of Ban Mae Satop to rebuild their traditional relationships with their elephants in a more ethical tourism setting that tackles welfare issues while respecting cultural traditions. Importantly – as I will discuss in the chapters to come – such a project undoes what environmental activist Vandana Shiva terms 'biopiracy', which disavows connections between people who are politically underrepresented and the non-human world. As Shiva explains, people from non-Western cultures, and especially Indigenous groups, have specific ways of 'relating to and knowing' the non-human world, but their views are often ignored by a Westernised approach towards managing the environment. To follow Shiva, if we are open to learning from Indigenous people, we may better understand the cultural significance of their relationships with non-human species.[124] Recognising the validity of such forms of 'local' or 'Indigenous' knowledge requires us to let go of Westernised, ethnocentric cultural belief systems, instead becoming open to new ideas and theories about relating to the non-human world.

My experiences with Journey to Freedom showed me firsthand how a sustainable, community-based volunteer tourism project could help tourists learn about Indigenous elephant practices. This occurred in part by engaging in daily activities focused on elephants, and through cross-cultural contact via intermediaries like Jack, whose translations provided access to fascinating information about the lives and culture of the Karen. Through Jack, I learned the villagers were pleased with the changes the project had brought to their village, while retaining their cultural integrity. 'They are happy here and don't need things from the outside world,' Jack explained. 'They say that as long as rice is on the table, they are happy.' Further, the Karen did not want their elephants to go back into tourism. The owner of the twins was especially adamant. 'He's worried because so many people want to come and see the twins and he doesn't know their intentions,' Jack told me. 'We can help protect them by keeping them here with the Karen.'

By offering the Karen incentives to keep their elephants at home and care for them in more traditional ways, Journey to Freedom was a model for elephant tourism that benefited both humans and animals in an often fraught relationship. Lek Chailert has stressed the importance of involving mahouts in decisions made about their lives and those of their elephants. As demonstrated by Journey to Freedom, she takes a strong focus on working in villages alongside mahouts to improve the lives of captive elephants. When I talked with Lek, she explained why this focus was important, particularly considering the limited space available at ENP.

'I want to work with the people,' she said. 'I don't want to take the elephants away from them – that's not my dream. I'd rather train mahouts and show them how to better care for their elephants. One day I won't be here, but mahouts can still look after their elephants.'

Lek explained how she had worked with a mahout in another remote village in Mae Chaem to bring his fifteen elephants back home from zoos and camps so they could instead roam the forests. 'He brought three of his elephants to ENP and he saw the elephants roam free, having mud baths,' she explained. 'He had tears in his eyes, watching them. He quickly decided he wanted to bring them back to the village because he had never seen his elephants so happy. This meant a lot to me. He said it had opened his heart and he wanted them back.'

Lek's words highlight the importance of involving mahouts in efforts to improve elephant welfare. In investigating mahout lives and histories, we can learn much about elephant captivity and what it would mean to find more natural habitats for Thailand's elephants. I took these ideas with me as I bade farewell to Ban Mae Satop and the truck rumbled us back to Chiang Mai, where I would board a bus and head to my next destination for the most influential part of my journey. This would involve further immersion into the world of Indigenous mahouts and a deeper understanding of the mutual plight of captive elephants and their people.

Chapter 5

THE SURIN PROJECT

I did not sleep well on the thirteen-hour bus trip from Chiang Mai to Buriram, tossed to and fro as the vehicle traversed the steep and winding mountain roads. By the time I arrived in Buriram, my body was a pretzel of aches and pain. It was just after 6:30am and the dimmest light of the morning sun had just appeared above the horizon, shimmering through a cloud of red dust. Semi-delirious, I was met at the bus station by Josie, a young English biologist who had worked for a year as a volunteer coordinator on the Surin Project, an elephant welfare initiative that operated in the small village of Ban Ta Klang, about an hour from Buriram. With an effusive greeting, Josie swept up my backpack and loaded it into the back of a flatbed truck, where it settled quietly on a bundle of sugarcane. The driver of the truck, wearing a battered New York Knicks cap and a checked shirt, hung his head out of the window and gave me the thumbs up and a broad smile.

'Sawadee ka,' I said as I returned the gesture and clambered into the back of the cab.

Josie took the passenger seat and as the driver took off, she turned to me and asked, 'How was the bus ride?'

'Terrible,' I sighed. 'I haven't had much sleep at all.' Yawning, I looked out at the waking streetscape – awnings pulled up to expose small shops and restaurants; food vendors pushing their carts up against gutters to set up for the day; and children in uniform tumbling out of houses and small blocks of apartments, bearing enormous backpacks and shrieking unnecessarily loudly for the time of day. Morning had broken, but all I wanted was to be in bed, preferably one that did not rock and rumble.

'The ride's rough,' Josie agreed, 'but if you feel like it, we're going to get straight to work after breakfast, and you're welcome to join.'

I smiled through another yawn. *Bed*, I thought resolutely. *Sleep.* 'Okay!' was what I said. 'Sounds great.'

'Excellent,' Josie replied. 'Now, I just have to warn you.'

'About what?' I asked, slightly worried.

'Well, I know you've just come from ENP and I want to make sure you're prepared. Do you know much about the project?'

'A bit. I got the idea it's not quite like ENP. That it's not a sanctuary. That it's working with people and elephants in a village.'

'That's right. It's definitely not a sanctuary. Some people are shocked by it.'

'By what?'

'The conditions. For the elephants. It's not the nicest.'

I nodded. I had gathered as much from the website, but I was not quite sure what to expect. 'Yeah, I thought it would be a bit different.'

'It is. You'll see as soon as we get there. It's a place where elephants really need help. The people there do the best they can but it's not enough. You'll see things you don't agree with and things that look really cruel. But we try to understand what life's like for them and help them find ways to improve their elephants' welfare, rather than only criticising them.'

I reflected upon this as we left the shops, restaurants, food carts and schoolchildren behind and headed out to the irrigated rice fields, the truck zooming along a narrow road fringed on both sides with swathes of luminous green. Very few trees could be seen; the landscape was rice fields from horizon to horizon. We shot across a small concrete bridge over a tumbling red-brown river, coloured so due to the terracotta-hued dirt that contrasted with the vibrant fields and filled in the spaces between the rice plantations. Soon we entered a small village, a collection of wooden huts on stilts and whitewashed brick houses lining a potholed road. Chickens and dogs scattered as the flatbed trundled through.

Josie turned to face me and smiled. 'Almost there!'

More rice fields followed, then not far along appeared another small village composed of brick-and-mortar houses and wooden huts, many on stilts, set along several narrow cement and dirt roads also running wild with stray dogs, chickens and roosters. A sign by the roadside announced in Thai and English: 'WELCOME TO BAN TA KLANG ELEPHANT VILLAGE'. A few more turns and we reached a huge fence made of stone bollards painted a dull salmon colour. Here, the truck pulled through a gate and rumbled through potholes and large piles of fresh elephant dung, still steaming. Ahead was the source, mahout sitting atop, a hook over his shoulder as the pair strode away from us.

We passed a young bull, chained to a tree by both front legs. He rocked from side to side, swinging his trunk back and forth, trying to reach some sugarcane just out of reach. Soon the truck stopped by a wooden house on stilts, under which a group of Western volunteers sat at a couple of old linoleum-topped tables. 'We're here!' Josie called, as the driver turned off the truck and jumped out of the cab. Grabbing my backpack, he ran up the steps of a neighbouring house – my home for the next two weeks. Tethered to its side was an enormous elephant I learned was named Fah Sai, meaning 'clear skies'. During the day, this was her home, too.

For those gloriously hot and dusty days I worked with Josie and other volunteers to clean elephant shelters, prepare elephant food, and build fences and other infrastructure, my money going towards elephant upkeep and mahout wages. After that short stay, I wanted more, and would return to Ban Ta Klang six more times, spending many months volunteering and, for a stretch, working as a volunteer coordinator. The Elephant Village became my second home – the place I thought about and wrote about for years, where my passion for captive elephants really came alive. It might seem strange, coming from the beauty and nature of ENP and Ban Mae Satop, to choose to call second home a place rife with elephant welfare issues. But Ban Ta Klang taught me so much about how we can help captive elephants, while also immersing me in a fascinating culture.

Working on the Surin Project was fascinating from the start. Like ENP, it was founded by Lek Chailert, who in 2009 – in cooperation with the Zoological Parks Organization of Thailand and the Surin Provincial Administrative Organization – developed a project for improving captive elephant welfare by providing financial support for mahouts and a model for volunteer tourism based around observation and gentle tactile experiences. The mahouts themselves, including an inspiring and passionate man named Sarot Ngamsanga, also played a crucial role in its inception, along with elephant conservationists Jeff Smith and Alex Godfrey, the latter who provided great insight into the running of the project during my first visit. The project was based within the Surin Elephant Study Center (SESC), a thousand-acre property that comprised much of Ban Ta Klang.

The SESC provided housing and an income for mahouts as well as shelter and food for around two hundred elephants. It also employed elephants and mahouts in a small-scale tourism venture based on shows and elephant riding.

The SESC aimed to promote the culture and traditional elephant practices of the Guay, a marginalised Indigenous tribe who have lived in the province of Surin for hundreds of years. (They are also known as the Kuay, Kwi, Kuy and Gwi, each a different intonation of the same name.) The Guay are Thailand's original 'elephant people' – guardians of ancient knowledge of living and working with elephants. They historically lived in seclusion in Surin's once dense forests, where elephants and humans communed spiritually and culturally for almost a thousand years. I knew nothing of the Guay on my first visit, but their fascinating relationships with elephants would become the focus of my research and the reason I returned to Ban Ta Klang time and time again.

The Guay's elephants are 'household' elephants, a term coined by conservationist Richard Lair to describe the animal's peculiar status.[125] Originally from California, Lair has lived in Thailand since 1980, working tirelessly to protect captive elephants. In 1992 he led the development of the Thai Elephant Conservation Center (TECC) and the associated National Elephant Institute in Lampang in conjunction with the Forest Industry Organization. As well as writing the influential book *Gone Astray: The Care and Management of the Asian Elephant in Captivity*, Lair has made a profound contribution to captive elephant management through the 2005 publication of the *Elephant Care Manual for Mahouts and Camp Managers* (with Preecha Phuangkum and Taweepoke Angkawanith) and his long-term conservation and welfare work with the TECC. As such, Lair has had extensive experience working with mahouts and understanding their cultures. His conception of household elephants perfectly befits those of Ban Ta Klang, who live with or near their mahouts and their families. Household elephants are usually chained up by the side of the house under a shelter, or are kept otherwise nearby. Their mahouts purchase sugarcane, napier grass, fruit and vegetables to be fed by hand, and sometimes take the animals to graze on a range of plant species, including banana trees and bamboo, in fields and forests nearby. These household elephants are very much part of the family, and the mahouts' close relatives, including children, play an active role in all facets of elephant care. Ceremonies involving elephants are core to family life, and all generations take part in blessings and other events in which elephants have spiritual significance.

During my fieldwork, the majority of Ban Ta Klang's Guay population worked in the burgeoning local elephant tourism industry. This included providing infrastructure and support for the SESC, which attracted hundreds of (mainly Thai) tourists a day who came to ride elephants or watch them perform, to visit local markets, and to try local food. The SESC's premise was similar to that of camps that provide entertainment for tourists, but its aims were more complex, with plans to renew Guay culture and keep families in traditional social structures while also providing for their elephants. This had interesting implications for both people and elephants in Ban Ta Klang.

The SESC was a strange place. Its entrance from the main road opened up onto lush green gardens complete with orchids, lily ponds and shady trees. The main office lay beyond, a squat white building set behind two enormous, white-painted cement tusks that rose up out of the ground like twin pillars. By the side of the office sat a sacred wooden platform with a roof and three sides, known as the Pakham Spirit House. It was an important part of the Guay's strong spiritual traditions, which revolve around the auspiciousness of elephants. The spirit house contained what is known as *pakhamchang* – a length of rope used for capturing elephants fashioned from buffalo hide. The Pakham Spirit House was used in spiritual ceremonies, where candles were lit, offerings were made to the spirits, and prayers were sung to protect villagers and elephants from harm. The spirit house also contained various offerings used in ceremonies, such as trays of flowers, incense, rice wine and various fruits.

Behind the SESC's main office was a small museum dedicated to Guay elephant culture, with numerous images and anthropological treatises that informed my early understanding of the history of Ban Ta Klang and the cultural practices of the Guay. The SESC's central tourist attractions were located beyond these buildings: a small market selling clothing festooned with elephant iconography, trinkets such as elephant keychains, elephant hair rings, and idols made from faux or real ivory cut from the tusks of captive elephants. While it is illegal to sell products made from ivory taken from wild elephants in Thailand (usually via poaching), it is legal to sell ivory cut from the tusks of captive elephants. Mahouts will cut the tips of the tusks off for this purpose; this eventually grows back. The market also sold a selection of drinks and ice-creams for tourists to enjoy while watching the small circus show on-site. The circus operated twice a day – at 11am and 2pm – and attracted several hundred Thai tourists and a far smaller number of Western tourists every day. These tourists arrived in huge buses that obnoxiously blasted loud Thai pop music as the vehicles trundled down the main road.

Before the start of each circus show, a similarly obnoxious

speaker blared a tinny recording of a song once played on an instrument fashioned from buffalo horn. This used to mark the start of the traditional elephant hunt, where Guay men would go into the forests and capture young elephants to train. The song signalled for tourists to take their seats in one of the stands that surrounded a small circus ring, where the elephants performed. The speakers went on to blast the latest popular Thai pop hits while the circus master boomingly announced each performance about to take place. The circus took the same form most days. First up were two young elephants who entered the ring with their mahouts astride, holding hoops with their trunks. They spun the hoops and nodded their heads along to the music, before retiring to an area outside the ring, right near the blaring speakers. Next, another young elephant was brought into the ring, her mahout carrying a handful of darts. The elephant would throw the darts at a balloon tethered to a pole at the opposite side of the ring. Each burst of the balloon was met by the wild cheers of the audience and the enthusiastic yells of the circus master. The dart-throwing elephant would then retire, with another elephant entering the ring to kick soccer balls into a small goal, followed by another who painted a picture of flowers on a piece of paper attached to an easel. Finally, all the elephants were brought back into the ring, and tourists invited to purchase bananas and sugarcane to feed them, or to have their photo taken with them. The circus often concluded with a small tourist child being held up by an elephant's trunk for the ultimate photo to the cheers of an enraptured crowd. To the left of the circus ring, elephants were chained up, waiting for tourists to ride them. Those tourists clambered aboard the animals from huge mounting blocks and were taken on a ride around the SESC for about half an hour. This journey through an unusual landscape allowed tourists to observe the daily lives of mahouts and their elephants.

Behind the façade of the office, its gardens and its circus, the SESC was a rambling, shambolic landscape of wooden houses, elephant shelters, piles of manure, concrete and dirt roads, and large stagnant dams. There was also an ancient elephant burial ground, where the bones of over a hundred elephants were interred over the decades and centuries. These were marked with cement blocks shaped like tree trunks cut off at the ground, topped by large concrete brimmed hats that were intended to provide the bones with shade and protection. Elephants were not buried here right after they died; rather, they were buried in a field for several years, after which their bones were dug up and moved to the cemetery.

While many things have changed since I was last in Ban Ta Klang, during my fieldwork, mahouts lived either out in the village or within the SESC itself. Some of the houses in the SESC were traditional wooden abodes on stilts, with room for a kitchen underneath and an elephant in a shelter to the side. Others lived in small shacks of wood and scrap metal, their elephants also kept at the side or nearby. These houses were surrounded by dusty red soil and scrubby bushes and trees, which in the dry season gave the appearance of scorched earth. There were physical signs of elephants everywhere: trees and branches crushed underfoot, huge footprints in the sand, and piles of fly-blown manure. The sounds of elephants in conversation echoed out across the grounds – loud trumpets, high-pitched squeaks and deep, guttural rumbles.

As in tourist camps, elephants in both the SESC and Ban Ta Klang more broadly were chained up most of the day and all night, so they could not wander and cause conflict in the village. While the majority lived under tall wooden shelters topped with straw roofs or corrugated iron, a significant number did not, and were exposed to the sun for most of the day. Some of these elephants were on longer chains, with access to a dam to cool off, but were socially isolated, far from the circus and office in a hinterland of scrub and red dirt. None of the elephants had ongoing access to a natural food source; all were mainly reliant on their mahouts for the provision of grass, sugarcane, fruits and vegetables. Most were lucky if their mahouts had time during the day to take them off their chains and walk with them through the property and down to the dams and river. These time limitations were usually the product of the mahouts' employment in the on-site circus and riding venture, and/or other work to support their elephants and families.

The Surin Project incentivised mahouts to spend more time with their elephants by providing them with an income paid by volunteers. While the SESC paid a decent wage, it was hard for Guay mahouts to make ends meet, and paid volunteering offered significant financial benefits. It also meant their elephants had time off their chains, with their mahouts spending part of the day walking with them around the SESC and through the village and local fields, accompanied by volunteers. These walks attended to their welfare and interests; in the wild, elephants walk some eighty kilometres a day and develop physical problems if they don't move.[126] In captive settings, providing elephants with activities such as walking may allow the animals to exert choice and control.[127] In the case of the Surin Project's elephants, walking activities promoted choice and control around socialisation – with elephants choosing companions they preferred to walk with. It also offered some choice and control around foraging, with elephants being offered a selection of forest plants or the remnants of field harvests, such as rice stalks and husks. The latter were left behind after harvest season and were purchased from farmers by the Surin Project as complementary feed to sugarcane, grass and fruit. While still monitored and controlled by their mahouts, on these walks the elephants were better able to exert some form of agency, certainly more than if they were chained up, working in the circus or giving rides.

Over the course of my visits, the Surin Project employed an average of twelve mahouts at any one time, who were bound by certain rules. While at first there were some bulls on the project, later only mahouts with female elephants were permitted to join. Males were too unpredictable, causing issues when near one another and near volunteers. (Like the Surin Project, camps across Thailand have a proportionally larger number of female elephants than males due to the females' docility.[128]) Secondly, mahouts followed a strict daily schedule from Monday to Saturday, beginning with collecting elephant food in the morning (sugarcane and grass, complemented with fruit and vegetables) and walking with the elephants and tourists during the day, before returning home at night for the final feed and chaining up under shelters. Thirdly, mahouts were not allowed to use hooks with their elephants. This final rule was one that some mahouts in the village were unwilling to follow, hooks being considered by many as necessary tools for elephant control. While some mahouts I talked to believed that just holding the hook was enough to stop an elephant from misbehaving, others suggested that it protected mahouts from danger due to blessings performed as a part of spiritual traditions. Despite their concerns, the mahouts who decided to join the project and eschew the use of hooks appeared to manage without them very well, and I discuss some of the hook-free training I observed later in this chapter.

During my fieldwork I saw on a daily basis how the project helped mahouts and improved elephant welfare. Volunteers came from around the world to clean out shelters and enclosures, taking dung and the remnants of grass and sugarcane to spread out on fields around the village to fertilise crops. We helped mahouts with their daily work, building new shelters and harvesting sugarcane. We washed and prepared elephant food and planted and irrigated fields of prickly, dense napier grass. We also assisted in a small-scale refor-estation project, planting native species like bamboo to rejuvenate some of the arid areas. In the afternoon, we followed the mahouts as they walked with their elephants along paths through scraps of scrub and forest, to muddy dams where the elephants wallowed and social-ised, or down the long main road to the Mun River, where, wading in, we fed the animals cucumbers and yams by hand, cooling off in the murky flow.

We stayed in houses on stilts made of wooden slats with thick gaps that let the bugs in, but the breeze as well. The houses lined a common road; this was a thoroughfare for mahouts riding or walking with elephants, locals whizzing by on scooters, food vendors selling ice-creams and fruit from carts pulled by motorbikes, and dogs, chickens and roosters running wild in the dust. Like the locals, vol-unteers managed with simple facilities. There were no flushing toilets, no hot water, and we quickly became used to cold bucket showers and sharing bathrooms with frogs and sometimes centipedes. Our bedrooms were simple – a mattress, fan and invaluable mosquito net the only furnishings, along with a few strategically placed nails and hooks in the wall to hang clothing. Invariably, the smells and sounds of elephants would creep through the gaps in the slats and perfume the night. Dreams of the forest were common, but so were nights of broken sleep when trumpeting and rumbling matched the howling of dogs and the strange midnight cackling of geckos.

* * *

My days as a volunteer on the Surin Project were some of the best of my life. When I returned to Ban Ta Klang for the second time in 2012, I had been through some harrowing months where my health had suffered greatly. This threatened to up-end the research, and the fieldwork I intended to undertake that year appeared less and less likely to happen. But I was committed to my PhD and convinced my father to come with me to Ban Ta Klang as my research assistant and general provider of moral support at a time when I was not strong enough to travel on my own. He loved Ban Ta Klang, the elephants and mahouts, though he tired of the heat and stayed cool in the shade when we went on long, hot afternoon walks in the forest or out across the rice fields.

At home, my father renovated run-down houses; in Ban Ta Klang he built us benches in the two-level shelter on stilts looking over what we called the Enclosure – a large, fenced-in patch of land with a giant lily-studded dam where the elephants wallowed in the afternoons. We could sit on those well-crafted benches and dangle our legs out over the dam while we watched the elephants tumble together in the water, spraying and splashing each other and duck diving under, coming up streaming brown and green, wearing lilies like crowns. My father had seen me in the depths of illness; now, with his help and the life in the village, I was getting better and finding laughter again. He ensured I fulfilled my research plans, taking observational notes every day, which we would dissect in the evening while sitting on the balcony of our house eating fresh lychees and mangosteens. As well as the observational research, I planned with Ocha Buddee – one of the volunteer coordinators – to undertake some short interviews with mahouts about their views of the project.

Ocha was Thai and had worked on the project for years, growing close to the mahouts in the process. He helped me immensely by interpreting and translating these early interviews, and I learned about how the project had helped the mahouts financially, which had had great benefits for their elephants' welfare. The four mahouts I interviewed were Nithipat, Sripachan, Huey and Pol, who explained how they had been offered roles with the Surin Project as it became a force for alternative elephant tourism within the SESC, providing them with a salary that did not require their elephants to work in the circus or taking rides. I asked them about the biggest differences they had experienced while working on the project.

As Nithipat explained, 'I can afford to care for my elephant, and I have made extra money so my children can now go to school and university. The biggest thing that the Surin Project does to help me is by paying for the grass and sugarcane.'

The case was similar for Sripachan, Nithipat's cousin and one of the few female mahouts in Thailand, who shared the role with her husband. 'The money from the government was not enough to support my family,' she explained. 'The Surin Project helps because we get extra money, and they buy the food for us. Sometimes we don't have enough food, especially in summer when it's so dry, and it's very hard for us to survive. Sometimes we have no money but working on the project means that we don't have to worry about food for the elephants. I hope that I can stay here working on the project so I can save enough money to send my oldest daughter to uni.'

Huey also experienced similar benefits. 'As well as helping me with my elephant, the other reason I joined the project was to pay for my children's education – to send my son to university. The best thing is that the project supports my family, and what has made the biggest difference for me and my elephant is the food the project provides.' He also explained how life at the SESC had improved the welfare of elephants, including his own. 'Compared to the elephants who are street begging, the elephants here are much healthier. Before, when she was begging, she was quite skinny. Now she has more food, and she can walk in the forest during the day, and at night she can sleep somewhere much better than on the streets.'

In Pol's words, 'The biggest difference that the project has made is by providing elephant food. The money they pay me also helps my family a lot. I'm single and I have to look after my parents while I'm still not married. So I have to make sure I have enough money for myself and enough for my parents, too.'

What was significant to me was that the Surin Project had mutual benefits for the mahouts, their families and their elephants. Firstly, the mahouts and their families could stay together because the mahouts did not have to live in tourist areas to make money from begging or from working in tourist camps. Secondly, the Surin Project provided enough money and elephant food to free the mahouts from long working hours, thereby giving them more time to look after their elephants and to spend at home with their families. Thirdly, the project appeared to make a significant financial difference. This had a direct impact not just on the welfare of the elephants but also on the mahouts' families, with the desire to send their children to school and university and provide for ageing parents being common interests. These initial interviews provided me with the foundation for my later, and much longer, study of the Guay and their elephants.

* * *

After conducting the interviews, my father and I sat on the balcony of our house, looking out over the grounds of the SESC and the muddle of houses, shelters and elephants. The day had been hotter than ever, but for the first time during our stay the skies unexpectedly broke, sending a torrent onto the red dirt below that splattered the dust and turned it to mud. Elephants in the distance trumpeted at the change in weather while the children who lived across the road whooped as they jumped in the puddles, their legs soon coloured ochre. In the midst of the moment, I felt a deep sense of belonging and a newfound happiness. The rain soon stopped, and the cool smell of wet earth caught my nostrils, the damp carrying with it the scent of the forest. Somehow, the simplicity of rain breaking the heat had changed something in me, and I felt connected to Ban Ta Klang and the people and elephants around me.

The sense of connection drew me back the following year, now in good health. The connection had been unexpected in some ways; I had loved ENP and Ban Mae Satop, with their beauty and freedom for elephants. But Ban Ta Klang had captivated me for other reasons, for the beauty there was rough around the edges. What I had grown to love was the feeling of working at something, helping where the most help was needed and finding answers to questions about longstanding problems with no simple solutions. By volunteering, observing and researching, I was learning about life in the village and the experiences of those around me, from other volunteers to the mahouts and the elephants themselves.

During all of my fieldwork trips between 2012 and 2014 I was blessed with the company of two volunteer coordinators who soon became close friends. Kirsty and Wills Sandilands, a Scottish couple in their late twenties from the Shetland Islands, were funny, intelligent and kind, and their passion and love for elephants shone through in everything they did for the Surin Project. Having volunteered as part of a round-the-world trip in 2011, they were invited back to work as volunteer coordinators and happily took on the job, living in the small village for two years and keeping mahouts, elephants and volunteers happy during that time. They had initially been inspired to volunteer with the Surin Project after their experiences travelling in Asia, where they saw other animals mistreated for the sake of tourism.

'We'd seen a lot of elephants being treated badly in Nepal and India, and we actually rode elephants in Nepal, which was a horrible experience,' Kirsty explained. 'It made us think, "Why are we doing this? How can we help?"'

'We didn't want to support anything that was bad for any animal, just for the sake of tourism,' Wills continued. 'And Kirsty really wanted to find something that was good for elephants.'

'I did some research,' Kirsty said, 'and found Elephant Nature Park. They were fully booked, so instead we came here. We absolutely loved it; it's one of the best things we've ever done.'

'When we arrived, we got on so well with everybody – volunteers, mahouts, the coordinators at the time,' Wills continued. 'There are a lot of good places we've visited, but we were especially drawn back here. We went through China, India, Australia … But all we wanted to do was come back to Ban Ta Klang.'

Kirsty had been a primary school teacher back home and

Wills had worked as an electrician. Their mix of practical skills and know-how made them the ideal pair to run the Surin Project. They were passionate about educating volunteers to teach them, in Wills's words, 'about why elephants are here, what the mahouts' lives are like, and how we can help them both. Educating volunteers is important to us because, for many travellers, riding an elephant is on their bucket list, which is a massive thing that helps the industry along. And it's amazing how little information they need to change that view. Everybody who comes here that I've spoken to about it really would prefer to see elephants in the forests, off the chains.'

Wills and Kirsty were also passionate about working with the local community and had set up English programs for the mahouts' children, with the eventual aim of passing on the running of the project to the Guay villagers. Ultimately, as Kirsty explained, 'We want volunteers to see things from the mahouts' point of view. They have lived here all their lives, and have worked with elephants all their lives, so you can't just come in and tell them what to do. The project aims to keep the culture the same, as much as possible. You just want visitors to be able to come here and have a taste of their culture.'

Wills and Kirsty's extremely well-organised schedule made every day an equal mix of work, fun and learning. On our walks they would teach volunteers elephant facts of all sorts and kinds. What is the difference between Asian and African elephants? The first are shorter than their African cousins, with much smaller ears and a trunk with only one tip (their cousins have two). Elephants perspire, but can you guess from where? From around their toenails, of all places. And why do they cover themselves with mud and dust? To keep the insects away and the sunburn at bay. I could never have guessed that these animals communicate over hundreds of kilometres through seismic vibrations, but thanks to Kirsty and Wills the volunteers and I were adding to our knowledge every day.

They also encouraged volunteers to closely observe the fascinating behaviours of the elephants on the project, wherever we were on a particular day – whether walking through the forest or rice fields, or watching them from afar in the Enclosure. Enormous Fah Sai had a sweet and gentle nature, and had once been runner-up in an elephant beauty contest. There was something about Fah Sai that emanated peace, and whenever I had the opportunity to look into her eyes – when feeding her or washing her in the river – I felt I could see in their depths humour and great intelligence. Fah Sai had a rolling gait and what looked like a serene smile on her face, giving her the appearance of being unconcerned with the world around her. It could pass her by with its worries and noise, but she would take it all in her stride. I observed her closely on our walks, especially her profound friendship with one of the other elephants, Euang Luang – 'golden lotus'. They would often hold each other's trunks as they enjoyed their time off their chains together in the forest. Their friendship was beautiful to observe, and in those moments I could imagine what life would be like for them if they could roam free together in a herd, able to pick and choose what they wanted to eat, communicating with each other, and building a relationship unique to them.

Fah Sai's temperament also appeared to influence the behaviours of other elephants on the project. She was often up ahead on walks, setting the pace for the others as an imposing but peaceful presence. She also appeared to be less bothered when there was a disturbance or perceived threat, such as a dog suddenly appearing noisily from the undergrowth or a motorbike backfiring nearby. While some of the other elephants would signal distress by slapping their trunks on the ground, bellowing, and forming tight-knit groupings for safety, Fah Sai seemed to be less stressed and more likely to continue walking while still remaining on alert – head raised and ears spread to face the threat.

Another elephant named Wang Duen ('crescent moon') had orange-hued skin and was best friends with her two shelter mates: Nong Lek, meaning 'little girl', and Neua Tong, a type of lily. They would play together in the dam in the Enclosure, splashing each other with glee and muddily climbing over one another amidst the reeds and lilies. Wang Duen was large and quiet, while smaller Neua Tong was more demonstrative. Whenever she was separated from her friends – such as when both were taken away to be washed by their mahouts and she was left alone in their shared shelter – she immediately showed impatience and distress, trumpeting, swinging her trunk, pacing, and pulling against her chain until one or both returned. Her behaviour reminded me of my two horses, who suffer from separation anxiety and pace their paddocks whinnying at a high pitch when one is taken away from the other. Like my horses, captive elephants appear not to cope well without herd mates in proximity, and on being reunited also behave similarly: my horses whinny at a lower pitch, running towards each other and touching noses, while Neua Tong and other elephants I have observed greet each other by uttering deep rumbles, trumpeting, ear flapping, and caressing each other – all signs of social bonding.[129]

Of the three herd mates, I particularly liked Nong Lek, whose diminutive size made her easily approachable. I spent many lovely, hot afternoons with her and her mahout, Suchad, in the forest. One afternoon I sat in the shade with the other volunteers, watching Nong

Lek scratch herself with the rough pointed end of a sturdy length of grass held firmly in her trunk. She discarded it occasionally to reach up into the trees to rip off the odd branch or two, or daintily select from a choice of leaves. It was always fascinating to watch the elephants use their trunks with such dexterity – whether for scratching, eating, throwing dust and dirt on their backs, or splashing water from the dam or river – demonstrating their species' particular adeptness at tool use and environmental manipulation.[130]

On another afternoon, Nong Lek wandered over to where I was sitting and put the end of her trunk on my water bottle, which was almost full. I opened the lid carefully and she cupped her trunk. I poured a little bit of water into it. She raised her trunk to her mouth and sucked the water down. I repeated the process until all my water was gone, and the other volunteers then did the same. When she realised we had no more water left, Nong Lek wandered off, leaving us parched in the shade. She ambled over to where Wang Duen and Neua Tong stood munching on sugarcane; her friends greeted her with trunks outstretched and rubbed them against Nong Lek's eyes and face, as if to ask her what she had been doing.

Behind my house lived an elephant named Sai Fah – with quite a different temperament to Fah Sai and Nong Lek. One evening, as I prepared for bed, listening to music on my phone, I heard a loud crash above me on the tin roof, then moments later, another. When I poked my head out the window to see what was causing the racket, I caught sight of Sai Fah, some five metres away, flinging a large chunk of sugarcane towards the house. It smashed against the roof, sending dirt raining down onto my head. I yelped and retreated back into my room as another chunk of cane slammed against the roof. 'Okay, okay!' I muttered, running to my phone and switching off the music.

That seemed to solve the problem. The next day I told Kirsty about our interaction. 'She's very opinionated!' was her reply. 'Her name means "thunder", after all.'

Sai Fah's thunderous nature was certainly evident on many of our walks, where she was always up ahead, safely away from the volunteers, briskly ripping branches from trees and flinging away the remnants once she had eaten the best bits. Her mahout, Dao, needed to constantly manage her behaviour – making sure she stayed with the herd and did not get too far away from him in the dam – giving him a more difficult job than Fah Sai's mahout Thong Dii, for instance, whose elephant was less strident in terms of her opinions. These moments of proximity to elephants – of experiencing their personalities, their likes and dislikes – provided further insights into their experiences of agency within captivity. I could imagine Sai Fah in the wild, bossing around her herd mates and flinging branches at anyone who dared to make noise while she was trying to sleep, just as I could imagine Neua Tong and Nong Lek as social youngsters, and Fah Sai as a calm, maternal peacekeeper.

***

Life in Ban Ta Klang was always a balance of fun, work and sadness. The latter was almost a constant, the product of seeing elephants on a daily basis in unhappy situations. But I could also see how the Surin Project and the SESC were making substantial, beneficial changes for elephants and mahouts. Some of the most meaningful experiences came from interactions with mahouts, with the project placing a special focus on exposing volunteers to the lives and culture of the local Guay people. At the start of every week, new volunteers were inducted into the project via a traditional Guay welcoming ceremony, conducted by a local shaman. Volunteers were encouraged to learn each of the mahouts' names – along with those of their elephants – and had many chances to observe their remarkable skills in handling their elephants. We would watch each mahout as he rode his elephant into the dam, dexterously moving around on top of the elephant as the animal splashed and rolled in the water. In 2014, when I was working as a volunteer coordinator, I shared my knowledge with the volunteers about what the mahouts were doing when they were working with their elephants, explaining how each mahout constantly talked to his elephant using vocal commands and language that made sense only in the specific context of their individual relationship. This encouraged the volunteers to closely observe the individual relationships, while also prompting the mahouts to demonstrate various aspects of their skills for the observers.

As well as working alongside them, volunteers had many chances for social interactions with mahouts. Every Saturday was set aside for the Mahout Olympics, in which tourists, mahouts and volunteer coordinators competed in a number of games. Small teams comprising members of each of these groups would take turns playing games invented by the mahouts, such as Elephant Poo Ten Pin Bowling, or an inventive game known as 'Thai Whispers', which involved a Thai or English phrase being passed along a line of people until the phrase was either successfully relayed to head mahout Sarot Ngamsanga or, more often, revealed to be completely indecipherable, much to the hilarity of the native speakers of either language.

Friday night was always cause for a party, held in the wooden structure overlooking the Enclosure where we normally ate meals and took part in Thai language lessons. Together, volunteers and mahouts cooked food and played games, sharing rice whisky, Chang Beer and laughter. The mahouts would auction off the perfect souvenirs, made by them: colourful elephant footprints created by painting the bottom of elephant feet and asking them to step on a large piece of thick artist's paper; bags hand hewn from local silk; t-shirts with elephant logos, decorated with the mahouts' and elephants' names; and machetes in sheaths fashioned by hand.

The small community that formed between mahouts and tourists was made possible by the shared goal of improving the lives of elephants. This community was forged through undertaking daily tasks together, whether it was learning the best way to cut sugarcane with a machete, helping mahouts wash their elephants, or being shown how to clean an enclosure without being tackled by a playful elephant calf. I learned how to dig up tree stumps and carry large branches back to project headquarters with the help of a mahout, precariously balancing the branches on our shoulders as we bumped along dirt roads on a motorbike. I helped mahouts build fences and shelters, plant and water trees and fields, dig irrigation channels, and cut down swathes of elephant grass – all in the burning sun. After undertaking some of these tasks, I was so sweaty, scratched, bruised and muddy that I felt like I would never be clean again. The volunteers and I coined the term 'Surin legs' to describe the state of ours after weeks or months of work. Marked with red scratches and blue and yellow bruises, Surin legs were badges of honour. One day, after helping mahouts build a shelter high enough to house enormous Fah Sai, my arms ached so thoroughly that I was not sure I could work on the shelter again the next day. After a cold bucket shower and a solid night's sleep – despite the almost constant barking of dogs and crowing of roosters throughout the night – I arose sore but refreshed and ready to work again.

My observations of and interviews with volunteers showed me that they became educated about mahout culture and elephant welfare through these experiences. For many of the volunteers, the community focus was one of the things they enjoyed most about the Surin Project. As my housemate Nicola explained, 'This project really offers you a chance to work so closely with the community and the mahouts. You really get to see them really enjoy their job and enjoy your company as well as volunteers. So it's really nice to kind of work really closely with them and get to know them. We really have a laugh together and it's really good fun.'

In Laura Ann Hammersley's description, volunteer tourism can lead to the creation of 'relationships of understanding' that allow tourists to work with local communities without assuming that the volunteers themselves are 'to be the providers of change, knowledge and skills'.[131] The Surin Project was able to create these relationships by introducing Guay culture and imparting the mahouts' knowledge of elephants to the volunteers, while also educating them about the difficulties the mahouts faced in caring for their animals. When I spoke to former Surin Project manager Alex Godfrey, he succinctly described this process as 'pushing local community values onto the volunteers', rather than the other way around. 'Tourists have to see what mahouts are working with,' Alex explained. 'One of our biggest things is letting people come here and making them understand that this is the way it is, why this is working this way, why the culture is that way, and not making any excuses for it either. We make them understand the whole bigger picture.'

Working with the volunteers themselves was an incredible experience, and when I took on the role of coordinator I really got to know the inside operations of the Surin Project. I became fast friends with many volunteers and enjoyed the daily hijinks we would get up to during our afternoon breaks, when the heat was more unbearable than ever. We were obsessed with the 'Ice Truck Man', as we called him, who travelled around the village with his refrigerated truck and bags of ice. He would bring us several bags each day, which we would stash in the large ice box that also held snacks bought from the local market, where they were protected from both the heat and the project's four dogs.

'I want to marry the Ice Truck Man,' sighed my housemate Nicola one afternoon as we sat in the shade, fanning ourselves with giant banana leaves.

'Same!' I agreed. 'I want to live in his ice truck.' We burst into fits of giggles.

Complaining about the heat was one of our favourite pastimes. On many days the temperature never dropped lower than 30°C and usually topped 38°C. There was nothing you could do but deal with the heat and everything that came with it. We dressed in modest clothing for cultural reasons, with our shoulders and knees always covered, which also protected us from sunburn but often felt stifling. By the end of a long day of work and walking, or bathing in the murky river, our clothes would be disgusting and would need to be washed in a bucket and hung out to dry in the gusty, hot wind. One day, while walking in the forest, we came across a large truck spraying water out over a new plantation of trees, part of a local reforestation project. We pleaded with the driver and he turned the giant hose on us, drenching us from head to toe. He would also have made a suitable husband in scorching Ban Ta Klang.

The heat would break at night, and when the cool air finally crept through the slats in our houses, we circulated it using our rickety electrical fans and got a good night's sleep. That was, of course, if no one in the village had decided to hold an excessively loud party, which happened on more than a few occasions. 'Do they need to hire the largest subwoofers in existence?' Emily, a volunteer from New Zealand, screeched one night as a karaoke party went into full swing across the other side of the village, just as we were heading to bed. Even though we were at quite a distance, our houses shook from the bass, and we migrated with other volunteers to another section of the SESC, but still could not escape the din. The next day, when the party was still in full swing, we learned it was to celebrate one of the men entering monkhood, something most men in Thailand do at one point in their lives. We were more tolerant of the noise after learning this, until on the third day of the party Ocha informed us that the mahout would only be part of the monastic tradition for two weeks. Immediate wishful plans to destroy giant subwoofers were concocted, but luckily that night was the last of the party.

Some of the grand plans for the elephants failed in a spectacularly funny way, such as providing them with a crop of watermelons volunteers had painstakingly grown in a field just outside the village. For over six months under the blistering sun, we had tilled and irrigated the field using buckets of water and a heavy hose full of holes, motivated by the vision of feeding the elephants fruit we had grown especially for them, lovingly and sweatily, by hand. Watermelon Day came and we plucked the crop of around sixty and placed them in baskets to be ferried back to the SESC by truck. The elephants awaited us, brought to project headquarters by their mahouts to enjoy the feast. As soon as the baskets were placed before them, the elephants tucked in, scoffing watermelons like popcorn. Two minutes later it was all over – six months of work gone in a flash.

It would be the last time we cultivated watermelons.

There were less hilarious moments that involved a vivid awareness of the challenges of managing bulls in the village, specifically two incidents that tested the speed and tenacity of myself and other volunteers. Captive bulls retain many of their wild traits and can be anything from unpredictable to downright dangerous. When placed within the confines of a village – among houses, shops and schools – a bizarre ecology that straddles wildness and civilisation develops. This can give rise to some unusual and sometimes frightening situations. One morning, after I had finished cleaning the large shelter shared by Wang Duen, Neua Tong and Nong Lek, I walked across the road to Fah Sai's with my rake over my shoulder, as I did most days. Headed in my direction over a small rise was a bull with huge, thick tusks, and his mahout. The tusks had been cut off at the ends; instead of two points, they were flat, and thick as two small logs. Abruptly, with a deep trumpet, the bull rushed at me with ferocious speed, his head held high with ears and trunk extended. Too scared to scream, I leaped sideways behind a tree as fast as I could. Grasping onto the tree and my rake for some sort of comfort, I marvelled, heart pounding, as the mahout somehow managed to take back control just before they drew level with my tree. The once charging bull now walked sedately as his mahout guided him towards his shelter. I now know that what had happened was a mock charge;[132] the bull had stopped on his own accord, while his mahout – evidently aware of the mock nature of the behaviour – had barely batted an eyelid.

Several weeks later, I was sitting with three young volunteers in the shade after a long day of planting saplings, enjoying cold drinks and snacks as a huge bull and his mahout walked along the main road towards us. It was early evening and lots of the villagers were outside, relaxing, talking and laughing, mingling around some of the houses further down the road. Suddenly, the bull elephant gave a guttural roar, shaking his head and trunk with violence, hitting his mahout and flinging him upwards and through the air. With a groan, the mahout crashed into the side of one of the houses, then fell in a heap. The villagers screamed as the tusker charged through them, sending them running and tumbling in his path. I saw in an instant both the bull's madness and the determined manner in which he was heading our way. I yelled at the volunteers to run and hide in my house, just nearby and well placed off the ground. We streamed up the wooden stairs and slammed the door behind us. We peered out through the gaps in the wooden slats to see the elephant nosing around the front of the house. If he had wanted, he could easily have broken the house apart; what would not break if hit by four tonnes of enraged animal? Luckily, the bull soon turned away and charged off into the large grassy clearing across the road. Here, he stopped for a moment, then bolted towards houses on the other side of the clearing. We heard people scream and other elephants trumpet in fear, but the elephant passed straight by them, barrelling off into the distance.

I cracked opened the door to our house and peered out. Walking towards us now were nine mahouts. Two carried a length of chain between them. Four carried over their shoulders long, thin wooden poles with machetes tied to their ends. These, I realised, were makeshift spears. The remaining three held hooks. The mahouts set themselves up at various places along the road and under a large shelter on our side of the clearing, waiting for the bull to reappear. They did not have to wait long. Soon, the enraged bull charged back over the clearing, trunk tucked in, head up as he pounded towards the large shelter. As he reached the shelter the bull soon slowed down but shook his head ferociously. The mahouts quickly formed a half circle in front of him, the four with spears striding out from their positions, weapons raised. Two threw spears, hitting the bull in the chest. Another threw his spear at the elephant's torso. Blood streamed from the wounds, and the bull further slowed his pace. Soon he stopped completely and stood still, blood coursing.

The mahout with one end of the chain sidled up to the bull and threw the length around his neck, then attached this to a chain around the elephant's front left foot, while his partner kept the other end in hand. Another mahout clambered up onto the bull and sat across his neck, hook held aloft. Kicking his legs against the sides of the bull's head, he guided the animal into the cement and steel shelter, where he could be contained. The mahout positioned the elephant against one of the shelter's strong cement poles as the mahouts on the ground raced over to chain the bull's foot to the pole, and to use the other end of the chain to loop around the other foot to hobble him. The elephant was now subdued, faced with his recapture.

Later I learned that the bull was in musth and was taken to one of the shelters further away from the main part of the centre, where he would be chained up until his period of musth was over, his wounds from the spears treated and monitored. Luckily, the mahout who had been thrown by his bull was not seriously injured. After a day in the hospital, he returned home, limping, bruised and bandaged, but ready to get back to his elephant. What I had witnessed in this spectacularly terrifying moment was the 'wild animal in chains' of Richard Lair's description. The bull was undeniably a captive, his autonomy curbed by human control. This was a fascinating and disturbing example of the underlying tension that can exist in some mahout-elephant relationships – often between men and their bulls.

While musth was responsible for the second bull's behaviour, the former was perhaps expressing his dislike of my rake, which no doubt could be mistaken as a weapon – perhaps of the sort that had once been used against him. These incidents represented the complex consequences of keeping elephants in captivity, and bulls in particular. In the second case, I was shocked and somewhat horrified by the use of force to control the bull, but after working in Ban Ta Klang over the years, I knew that incidents like this were rare and that I had been unfortunate to witness one of such ferocity on the part of the bull, and as punitive on the part of the mahouts. Perhaps once a year a bull would become enraged and charge through the village, and the mahouts would need to act quickly to avoid potentially fatal outcomes.

These episodes raised many questions in my mind about wildness and captivity in a world where elephant freedom is curtailed due to both the landscape in which they live and situations in which they pose potential threats to humans. I became more interested than ever in understanding elephant captivity in the village and the nature of interactions between mahouts and their elephants. After numerous trips to Ban Ta Klang and around fifty hours of interviews, I gained great insight into the fascinating culture of the Guay mahouts and their unique elephant practices, and helped open a channel of communication with the world outside the village by recording their stories.

Chapter 6

THE GUAY MAHOUTS
OF BAN TA KLANG

Over the course of my fieldwork, I grew close to Sarot Ngamsanga, the broad-chested mahout with a brilliant smile and infectious laugh who guided our daily walks and kept us safe when any of the elephants made a rapid change in direction. From him, I learned more about the role that the mahouts played in their elephants' lives. Sarot worked hard on his English and loved to make hats out of palm fronds and giant leaves he would bestow on laughing volunteers. He would wear his own trademark cowboy hat every day, and we nicknamed him the Guay Cowboy. Sarot had been instrumental in setting up the Surin Project, working with environmentalist Jeff Smith to establish connections between the Save Elephant Foundation, the Zoological Parks Organization, the Surin Provincial Administrative Organization and local mahouts. Sarot was involved in all aspects of the Surin Project, committed to building and maintaining the project's infrastructure while also coordinating mahouts and elephants, and engaging with volunteers.

In the early days of my fieldwork, Sarot's young elephant Nun Ning acted like his jealous girlfriend. With ears flapping and trunk swinging she would make it quite clear that he belonged to her, and anyone who wished to talk to him would do so at a distance. They would walk hand in trunk through the patches of forest, chatting in a cross-species language foreign to volunteer ears. When we would walk to the river, Nun Ning would amble into its depths and Sarot would follow her in and lovingly scrub and wash her.

I experienced Nun Ning's possessiveness any time I talked to Sarot about my research on our walks, where she would come up and bump me out of her way with her belly, before sidling up to Sarot and glaring at me. Whenever I would spend time with her in the river, it was with caution, for she would duck dive in the water with adept speed, suddenly rising up and splashing me thoroughly before striding off purposively, leaving me dripping from head to toe. Sadly, between my trips of 2013 and 2014, Nun Ning – whom Sarot leased from an owner in northern Thailand – was taken back by her owner and put to work in a tourist camp. This was not an unusual upset to mahout-elephant relationships, with a study showing that a significant proportion of elephants are owned by private owners (22%) or camps (32%), in comparison to mahouts (37%).[133] This separation was devastating for Sarot. Yet while we once discussed raising money to buy her back, he said, 'If I had that kind of money, I would give it to my children for school. That's more important.' From then on, his role on the Surin Project was as head mahout, his enthusiasm and passion making each day informative, fun and exciting. He dearly missed Nun Ning but was focused on doing whatever he could to ensure the other elephants on the project were cared for.

I also observed the unique nature of the relationships between other mahouts and their elephants. Fah Sai's mahout, Thong Dii, had owned Fah Sai since she was a calf, and they had developed a strong relationship over the years, evinced in the ways they effortlessly communicated. Unlike most mahouts, who rode their elephants into the dams and river, Thong Dii could stand on the banks as Fah Sai took to the water herself, gleefully rolling in its murky depths before coming back out when Thong Dii asked her. This particular relationship was founded on the skills that Thong Dii had developed as a result of his lifelong commitment to mahoutship, passed down from his father and his grandfathers before him. Like the other mahouts, Thong Dii was also remarkable in his physical abilities and tactile communication skills with his elephant. All the men on the project were – to borrow from Richard Lair – 'superbly conditioned athletes able to move around or on top of elephants with the skills of an Olympic gymnast'.[134] Each displayed such prowess during their daily interactions with their elephants, showing their unique capabilities of manoeuvring up onto their elephants from the ground, often assisted by their animals' cocking one knee as a stepping stone to the top, or even jumping from one elephant to another while in the dam, caring for a pair at a time so a fellow mahout could keep dry.

What I witnessed was more than simply physical prowess, for the men were also skilled in verbal and non-verbal communication with their elephants. As anthropologist Pittaya Homkrailis explains:

> The Guay have also developed a special language for speaking with elephants. For example, 'how' is 'stop', 'duen' is 'step back', and so on. The Guay have also developed a special sensitivity to elephants' sounds. The long 'paeew' an elephant makes when it is signaling it is in deep fright, for instance, tells Ta Klang villagers to be immediately prepared for it to run amok and possibly cause injury. The body language of elephants can tell a lot too. If an elephant

stops waving its ears suddenly when a stranger approaches, the beast is signaling its unfriendliness. It could even attack the intruder.[135]

There are other sounds that mahouts interpret during their interactions with their elephants; as well as the long-ended 'paeww', the same sound accompanied by the elephant hitting the end of its trunk to the ground signifies a desire to chase – such as towards an irritating dog – while a lower-pitched 'uum' signifies a lesser level of fear or discomfort. A mahout can also recognise a variety of body language cues that intuit him to the animals' needs or experiences. For instance, an elephant who rests its trunk on the ground may be sleepy or sick, while a relaxed elephant will wave its ears and tail continuously, and one with a tense trunk may be angry and ready to attack.[136] My observations showed that each mahout and elephant engaged in a form of two-way interspecies communication that was unique to their specific relationship, founded on the ancient elephant traditions of the Guay and passed down through the generations.

Having already learned how the Surin Project benefited Guay mahouts, my second series of interviews delved deeper into the mahouts' lives and culture. I was interested in finding out whether working on the project affected the mahouts' autonomy. I already knew from several mahouts that they lost some of their independence in tourist camps, and wondered if they had more freedom within the volunteer tourism program. While acknowledging the rules and regulations that guided the project, including work schedules and the ban on the use of hooks, Sarot and several other mahouts – including Thong Dii (Fah Sai's mahout) and Dao (Sai Fah's mahout) – explained how their ideas were used on the Surin Project. This allowed me to glean how involved they were in some of the decision-making processes, and whether their involvement might influence the future of Guay culture and mahout-elephant relationships. These conversations took place in the Enclosure, where the mahouts and I sat in the shade watching the elephants graze among the trees before us, picking at branches and munching on piles of sugarcane strewn across the ground. The men explained they had developed two major parts of the Surin Project's weekly schedule. The five-acre Enclosure, with its expansive dam and patchy vegetation, was built at the mahouts' request. As Sarot explained, 'This was important to us because we wanted somewhere the elephants could go and swim and socialise. They can eat all the branches and leaves from the trees, and we can let them have their own time here, off their chains.'

The mahouts also asked for the Surin Project to organise the long walks that took place every Wednesday and Friday, in which we accompanied the elephants through fields and along roads to the Mun River, where volunteers would join the mahouts and their elephants in the water. As the mahouts explained, these walks allowed them to change the elephants' environment, and better replicate the traditional ways in which elephants foraged, because the elephants could eat the variety of plants that grew along the river. We then discussed the problem of deforestation, and the mahouts had many ideas about how to reforest some of the areas within the SESC. Along with us volunteers, the mahouts had been working on small-scale reforestation projects both inside and outside the SESC, mainly focused on planting small native shrubs and trees along water sources. They had focused on plants that were favoured by their elephants and hoped that over five years or so, some of these areas would be dense enough to allow elephants to forage. However, it was evident that this aim might be difficult to achieve. As Sarot explained, 'Sometimes people come and cut the trees down. There's nothing to protect them, no policy or anything else.'

I was interested in understanding whether the mahouts felt that their relationships with their elephants had changed since they joined the project, particularly because they could no longer use bull hooks. Sarot explained that while most mahouts had once used them, the key to training their elephants was a combination of positive and negative reinforcement that could operate with or without hooks. 'If a mahout asks his elephant to lift her leg and she does it correctly, he gives her a reward, like a banana or some sugarcane. But if she does something wrong, like he tells her to lift her leg but she doesn't do it, then he might use the hook to tell her that she has done the wrong thing. You can poke the hook into her leg and she will lift it.'

He showed me how he would tell Nun Ning that she had 'done the wrong thing' without using a hook. We both arose from our spot in the shade and wandered over to Nun Ning, who was eating sugarcane nearby. I kept my distance, knowing she did not like me getting too close. Sarot ran his hand down her front left leg, tapping the back of her knee while using voice commands to ask for a response. She responded by lifting her leg, so he immediately stopped tapping, patted her and gave her praise. 'Now I will ask her to move away from me.' He held his hands up before her and gave the command '*toi*', which means 'go back' in Guay. Nun Ning looked at him, looked back at the sugarcane, and continued eating. 'She's naughty,' he laughed. '*Toi*,' he said again, raising his hands higher, and she ambled back a step. He patted and praised her; this was enough to satisfy him. 'Yes, it's harder without the hook,' he said. 'It takes more time; they can be naughty and sometimes do what they want and not what you want.

But they also know that you are their family and that you have the food, so usually they will cooperate.'

What Sarot had shown me was combined reinforcement: positive reinforcement and negative reinforcement used together. In contrast to the former, negative reinforcement is a method whereby the removal of pressure is used as its own reward, to indicate that the animal has done what was asked of them. In this case, tapping Nun Ning's leg and stopping at the moment of response confirmed the correct behaviour, with pats and praise constituting positive reinforcement. My own work with horses relies on this combination, and certainly not solely on positive reinforcement, which has its limitations especially when it comes to riding. My legs against my horse's sides or my hands softly on the reins are signals to move forward or to slow/stop, with the release of that pressure immediately after the command has been obeyed signalling to my horse that he has responded correctly – negative reinforcement in action. It is essential that negative reinforcement is done with a light touch, and when these pressure-release commands are combined with treat-based clicker training, for example, a dual method for training develops that is highly effective, forging cross-species communication. According to trainers with H-ELP, 'combined reinforcement motivates the elephant to efficiently trial new behaviours while the positive reinforcement amplifies the reward'.[137]

In their experiences working with elephants at zoos, John Lenhhardt and Marie Galloway found that combining positive and negative reinforcement was highly effective, and also noted that negative reinforcement – to be distinguished from punishment – in some ways mirrored social dominance in elephants, allowing the trainer to manage the animal. They also argue that it was possible for a trainer to use a hook as part of this combined training method while eschewing aggressiveness on the part of the trainer. As they explain:

> Given the current concern over use of the elephant hook, or ankus (also sometimes referred to as a guide), we feel we must emphasize again here that negative reinforcement is not the same as punishment. Negative reinforcement encourages the repetition of a behavior and punishment is used to extinguish a behavior. Negative reinforcement removes something in conjunction with the performance of the desired action or response. The use of an ankus (as a stimulus) to cue a behavior can be an example of negative reinforcement. Negative reinforcement is intended to have an impact on the immediate behavior – the behavior just then taking place. It allows for the desired behavior to be positively reinforced.[138]

The authors also explain that trainer-elephant relationships based on social dominance develop when the former establishes trust and confidence with the elephant, eventually leading to the animal accepting the human's presence and directions. This allows for free contact management, whereby the trainer can directly interact with the elephant. However, as they note, the social dominance method is much more difficult to implement with bull elephants; the natural sociality of females appears to benefit the training process.

As I would learn from other mahouts through our interviews, training elephants was an ongoing process, with the relationship between mahout and elephant certainly being reinforced during their daily interactions to maintain trust and confidence. They described how they would use the hook on the sensitive parts of an elephant's body – usually just behind the ears – as a means of directing the animal, just as they would use their feet and legs in the same area to give commands when riding. They also stressed that as well as positive reinforcement, patience was crucial to all aspects of the training relationship. As a mahout named Boon Ma explained, 'Elephants are very sensitive and intelligent, so they understand everything that you are doing. You have to be very patient with them. It could be easy to get angry at them, but that can make things worse. I want to make sure I have a happy elephant; it keeps us both safe. I make sure I take my time and work out how to talk to her so that we understand each other.'

Inevitably, the matter of cruelty came up, with the mahouts noting there was a number of mahouts in the SESC who were using methods they did not agree with, including the punitive use of hooks. They felt sad that the elephants were already suffering due to a lack of freedom and that cruel training methods only worsened their lot. They connected these issues to the need to train elephants more quickly for the tourism industry, but felt it was not their place to interfere with other mahouts' training methods. According to the mahouts, this seemed to be a particular issue with younger mahouts who had not grown up following old traditions of training based on combined reinforcement. It was evident that the mahouts I had befriended – who worked with elephants using more gentle methods – were the ideal candidates for welfare-positive tourism ventures like the Surin Project, but that further outreach was needed in the village to shift attitudes towards training more broadly.

These early discussions about training led to later interviews, with the Guay mahouts on the Surin Project offering to share not just their knowledge about elephants and training, but also stories about their lives, culture and traditions. Ultimately, these stories would reveal much about the changes that had occurred over the century in Ban Ta Klang, all of which had affected mahout and elephant lives alike, including the ways mahouts trained and cared for the animals.

* * *

Over the course of centuries, Thailand's mahouts brought elephants from the wild into captivity. Mahout-elephant relationships can be understood as a process of co-evolution, whereby – in the words of environmental geographer Jamie Lorimer – elephants and their ecologies 'bear traces of multimillennial histories and multinational geographies of movement, captivation and conflict'.[139] Mahouts from the Guay tribe certainly co-evolved with elephants, and both were and still are affected by the changing natural environment around them. Today's Guay mahouts live in what was once a fertile valley bordered by two rivers, which was significantly affected by deforestation. They are a marginalised group due to both their indigeneity and the ecological crises that have impoverished them culturally, spiritually and socio-economically. Such impoverishment has been reinforced by what is arguably their 'animalised' status. In the past, the Guay's work with elephants positioned them as reverent – engaged in mystical, ancient traditions with charismatic, intelligent and magical creatures. But today, they are more likely to be demeaned due to their involvement in the same practices, which are often perceived as cruel, dirty and unappealing. Indeed, as conservation researchers Liv

Baker and Rebecca Winkler argue, 'the occupation of mahout is now considered one of the lowest jobs in Thai society'.[140]

Mahouts who participate in cruel practices may do so because they do not have strong traditions and have not been exposed to techniques to adequately control their elephants without force.[141] Cruelty by mahouts can also be connected to a lack of education and a life of poverty, which ultimately impact on their ability to care for elephants. Such behaviour may tar outsider perspectives of all mahouts, despite differences in their training methods and skill sets. As a whole, the culture of mahoutship may be considered highly problematic in the rapidly changing contemporary landscape of elephant tourism, which is shaped by emotional responses to the treatment of elephants. Under this lens, mahouts are often viewed as perpetrators of cruelty who we elephant lovers can blame for the animals' woes.[142] Such beliefs and responses are the product of imposing ideals from the Global North onto cultures and communities in the Global South.[143] Within this idealised view, elephants are beloved charismatic megafauna in need of protection. As Lair argues, '[t]he elephant, perceived as a long-treasured "household elephant" in most Asian minds, might often be viewed as an abused "captive elephant" in contemporary Western eyes'.[144] It is important to acknowledge that these ideals may further marginalise Indigenous elephant people.

In tracing the reasons why negative perceptions of mahouts are common, I found that tourists' fascination with and reverence for elephants may also impact the wellbeing of Indigenous mahouts like the Guay. The perceived necessity of returning elephants to 'the wild' is arguably based on the idea that humans have no place in the elephants' world, a product of the conservation discourse that, as environmental biologists Arturo Gómez-Pompa and Andrea Kaus argue, suggests 'there is an inverse relationship between human actions and the wellbeing of the natural environment'.[145] This has the effect of positioning the people who live and work with elephants as interfering with nature, rather than having firsthand knowledge of the multispecies world they cohabit that might contribute to conservation and welfare efforts.[146] It may also lead to mistrust and prejudice if and when tourists believe elephant people to be unjustifiably cruel without having any real knowledge of mahoutship culture.[147]

Ultimately, tackling welfare issues associated with elephant captivity requires us to address practices that harm elephants while also championing those that protect them. It also means simultaneously attempting to conserve natural and animal worlds from damage inflicted by humans while acknowledging that it may be impossible to separate humanity from those worlds. The complex interdependence of mahouts and elephants, combined with contradictory practices of care, control and cruelty, make it difficult to find easy solutions to these issues. However, investigating the factors that have contributed to these myriad problems can provide insights into how to reshape contemporary mahoutship to uphold rather than violate elephant interests.

My interviews with and participatory observations of Guay mahouts from three generations allowed me to explore how deforestation and associated socio-economic factors have impacted mahoutship. The work of anthropologists and historians writing in English and in Thai provided me with initial insights into Guay culture, as well as historical and scientific corroboration of the mahouts' stories. One such anthropologist is Peter Cuasay, who describes the Guay fittingly as 'an ancient and magical minority people' for whom the 'capture and keeping of elephants is a central tradition, an indigenous knowledge system, and a sacred collective undertaking'.[148] Cuasay notes the difference between 'elephant Guay' and other Guay peoples, noting that elephant Guay – locally known as *Guay Aijiang* – are just one part of a broader Indigenous group. As Bhumijit Rueangdej explains in his detailed history, the Guay likely migrated around 1200 BC from India to northern Cambodia, northeastern Thailand and southern Laos.[149] Today's Thai elephant Guay are a smaller group bound together in the Mool river basin, the flatlands surrounded by the Chi and Mun rivers in Surin province.

While there was once a Guay Kingdom, it was eventually merged with the Khmer Kingdom around the fourteenth and fifteenth centuries. Forced to enter the Laotian army, in the seventeenth century many Guay headed west across the Mekong River from Laos to settle in 'free land' in northeastern Thailand. The migration was also precipitated by natural disasters such as flooding, and newly migrated Guay were often invited to live with those who had been in Thailand for some time. One of the primary drivers of migration was also a desire to move closer to prime elephant capturing spots, with elephants having already been an important part of Guay life for several centuries. Thailand's Guay were traditionally isolated from the rest of the country and known as *Khmer Pa Dong* – 'Khmer jungle people'. During the Rattanakosin Era (1782–1932), the Khmer Pa Dong region was combined with the Kingdom of Siam, yet the Guay's isolation and the difficult topography of their region meant they could not be integrated into the country's labour system. Instead, the Guay were engaged in a system of tribute – sending lac resin, fragrant wood and other forest products to King Rama III and his predecessors instead of engaging in work for the kingdom. As

Rueangdej notes, this could be the reason why the Guay are also known as *Suai* – meaning 'tribute'.[150]

As Pittaya Homkrailis explains, the elephant Guay's 'magic' relates to their unique spiritual beliefs, which are at the intersection of Buddhism and Hinduism, with animistic elements that link daily life with the spirit world.[151] Shamanism is central to their culture, and shamans call upon the spirits in protection and ordination ceremonies named *Pakham*, which were traditionally performed before the tribesmen went into the forests to capture elephants.[152] This is what gives the Pakham Spirit House in the Surin Elephant Study Center its name. As Yasothara Siriprapakorn notes, the Guay's traditions can be connected to the auspiciousness of elephants in Buddhism and Hinduism, with three elephants – the Great Elephant Palilaika, Sawat Khunchorn, and Airavata – all being potent symbols of power and prestige within those religious traditions.[153] As I would find, there were very specific practices associated with Pakham that stretched back centuries and were just important to the Guay's contemporary lives as they were in the past.

Due to CITES legislation banning the movement of elephants across borders, the Guay can no longer hunt elephants in their natural environment, yet they still practise the rituals associated with the hunt to maintain their connections with the spiritual realm. In his fascinating book *Ta Klang: The Elephant Valley of Mool River Basin*, Homkrailis includes detailed information about historical elephant captures, how captive elephants have been bred from wild ancestors, and how the mahouts train their elephants. His work demonstrates the traditional status of the Guay as most certainly an elephant people, living as much in a human world as one at the frontier of the animal world, where they inhabit a cross-species zone. As Homkrailas explains, the Guay's magical animist traditions guide their own form of elephant science, which 'includes indicators or marks of good and bad elephants, the art of elephant riding and mantras and spells used with elephants'.[154]

Joachim Schleisinger has also written at some length about the Guay, discussing the tribe's past as revered elephant keepers and their relationships with mahouts from other tribes within Thailand. He also outlines the history and day-to-day practices of the Guay specifically as they relate to elephants. Schleisinger notes the necessity of providing records of their elephant practices as their culture declines:

> [Because] the Kui have no written script and … can no longer hunt wild elephants in their traditional habitat, such knowledge of traditional customs will vanish after the deaths of the last *krubas*, who are all very elderly.[155]

Like Schleisinger, my concern is that the culture of the Guay will disappear if it is not recorded because the skilled generation is growing older and increasing numbers of young Guay people are moving away from Ban Ta Klang and the elephant culture. This concern is matched by one for the increasingly precarious socio-economic status of the Guay, which will affect their cultural longevity and financial security, as well as their elephants' survival. As heritagist Pattrapon Vetayasuporn explains, the 'life of Thai elephants and Gui mahouts are in [an endangered] situation. To prolong and even survive [they] need a proper solution … to preserve traditional spirit and generate income for daily life'.[156]

Cuasay presents an interesting perspective on how the Guay's relationships with elephants have changed over time. He describes the men as agents of transformation 'who translated the wild into the tame while moving elephants from woods to workplaces'.[157] Historically, the Guay captured and trained elephants for the rest of Thailand, starting with their use in war and leading to their contemporary roles in tourism. However, as criticism has grown of their practices, Guay mahouts today find themselves in a different social position. As Cuasay explains:

> The Kuay bear the stigma of negative wonder for their association with elephants. Hanging on the elephant body like so many question marks ... they absorb the marginality the discipline of spectacle removes from the public experience of the Asian elephant. The uncanny remainder of the modern imaging system is seen in turn as primordial ethnic identity: the Kuay are, at last, perceived as being, by nature, marginal people.[158]

As previously discussed, such marginalisation has meant that mahouts are easy scapegoats for the woes of Thailand's captive elephants.[159] However, because as Cuasay notes, care for elephants ultimately relies on the 'underling, the often poor and usually "tribal" or ethnically marginal mahout',[160] it is important to involve these mahouts in ventures aimed at improving captive elephant welfare while avoiding their further marginalisation. Importantly, Indigenous knowledge and ancient traditions could be used to positively reorient aspects of mahoutship culture that have been corrupted by the use of elephants in tourism.

My aim in writing about the Guay aligns with that of Homkrailis: to 'lead both local and foreign readers to a better understanding of the heirs of the Thai elephant-raising culture', particularly in light of the fact that 'this segment of Thai heritage is fading'.[161] Recording the mahouts' stories captured some of their ancient systems of knowledge for preservation, and by staying in the heart of the village, living in a number of different houses over the years, and getting to know the community I was fully immersed in Guay culture. Inspired by the work of Srichandrakumara, I set out to become more than the 'casual observer' who 'look[s] on at the silent and methodical actions of the men engaged in [elephant husbandry] … quite unaware of the extraordinary rites and ceremonies which have to be observed and of the complexity of their nature'.[162] My immersive research allowed me to picture with increasing clarity what life was like in Ban Ta Klang before deforestation affected the region and mahouts and elephants alike. I learned how macrocosmic changes in Thailand's cultural fabric have had devastating consequences for these mahouts, who are small players in its socio-cultural and economic systems – on the fringes of mainstream Thai society. As Cuasay describes, the Guay today are 'a marginal underclass with a dislocated culture, seemingly out of place and out of time',[163] affected by the institutions that have bound them to the ebbs and flows of national industries: logging, agriculture and tourism being three of the most influential.

As previously discussed, my introduction into the world of Guay mahouts occurred via my friendship with Sarot Ngamsanga. As well as expressing his desire for me to record the Guay's life stories, Sarot stressed that the history of Ban Ta Klang and its mahouts is often ignored in the broader narrative around mahout-elephant relation-ships. When I undertook my first interview with him, he explained that the typical logging-to-tourism story did not apply to the Guay, something I did not yet know. 'There were no teak forests here,' he told me. 'It wasn't like up north, with all the valuable wood, and we didn't have loggers come in here with their elephants to cut it down and take it all away. There was some good wood, but deforestation here mainly happened because of the development of roads and rice fields.' Historical differences such as these were important to record, and Sarot guided me through interviews that focused on life before and after the forests disappeared, starting with stories from the oldest generation – the elders known as *krubas*.

Chapter 7

THE KRUBAS

In Ban Ta Klang, I met five Guay krubas who had worked with elephants for decades. While they had retired from the job, they remained connected to elephant culture by conducting spiritual ceremonies and ordinations. As the few remaining men in Ban Ta Klang who had participated in elephant hunts, they were the last of the shamans still alive in the village – a position directly connected to their status as elephant catchers. The krubas were Ta'Ma Supnak (aged 72), Ta'Nui Salagnam (aged 80), Ta'In Saendee (aged 82), Ta'Mew Salagnam (aged 86) and Ta'Peng Yeeram (aged 88), with the prefix 'Ta' denoting respect. The krubas were wiry men who dressed in a mix of modern and traditional clothing: t-shirts or long-sleeved shirts paired with wrap-around *pha nung* (sarongs) fashioned from dark red and green silk with black or gold foundation thread. These sarongs were handwoven by the women of the village, who practise a traditional form of sericulture – the cultivation of silkworms and spinning of silk on traditional wooden looms. With their unparalleled experience with elephants, the krubas were the most respected and revered men in Ban Ta Klang, especially Ta'Peng, who in his life had captured fifty elephants – the largest number of any mahout in the village – giving him a particular status of importance among the Guay.

The krubas spent much of their days sitting on a covered wooden platform in the Surin Elephant Study Center, right near the main office and the Pakham Spirit House, talking, resting and making handicrafts like elephant hair amulets and decorative wooden sheaths for machetes. Once at the edge of the forest, the platform and Pakham Spirit House sat on sacred ground, where ceremonies were undertaken for centuries that called upon the spirits who lived in the forest for blessings and ordinations. This was a place of the utmost spiritual significance for all villagers in Ban Ta Klang. Despite the numerous changes around them, the krubas still felt intrinsically connected to the site. Two of the interviews with them were conducted while we sat in the shade of the platform, protected from the midday sun, on my lunch break from volunteer duties. Further interviews were conducted with Ta'Mew, Ta'Peng and Ta'In separately at their homes in the village.

I had built trust with the Guay community over the course of my fieldwork trips. After befriending Sarot and conducting my preliminary interviews – alongside my Thai interpreter and fellow volunteer coordinator Jureerat 'Pum' Boonwan, who was highly knowledgeable about Guay culture – what was effectively a 'snowball' technique introduced me to other mahouts who were keen to be interviewed about their lives and experiences. From the krubas I gained a wealth of information about Guay culture and modern history, told through narrative storytelling. Ta'Mew in particular provided in-depth accounts of the Guay's elephant hunts and captures over the course of two lengthy interviews.

When the krubas were young, Ban Ta Klang sat in a clear area surrounded with dense forest. The forest was intersected by streams and the powerful Mun and Chi rivers, swarming with fish, and hidden among the trees were numerous species of birds as well as a variety of mammals, including native cattle (such as buffaloes and bantengs), leopards and wild dogs, and reptiles such as snakes and chameleons. The krubas lived with their families in simple wooden houses on stilts with straw roofs. The roofs would be rebuilt at the end of every rainy season before they grew too wet and heavy, and collapsed. To the side of each house was a tall wooden shelter used to house elephants; the animals would spend their nights there hobbled with rope or chain. The villagers kept chickens and buffaloes and cultivated small fields of rice for food as a form of subsistence farming.

During the day, the mahouts would release the elephants into the forest. There were plenty of crops that grew wild that the elephants loved to eat. The mahouts would often let the elephants roam free, but sometimes would loop a length of chain or rope around the leg of one of the elephants; sometimes they would attach the end to a tree, but more often they would leave it loose. The elephant would still feel something pulling on their leg, which was enough to keep them from wandering too far. The rest of the elephants would graze around them, staying close to their herd member. The mahouts did not worry about them wandering off into other villages and causing problems because there was so much food available. But they would hang big wooden bells on rope around the elephants' necks so they could always hear where they were, even when they travelled off into the depths of the forest. This meant they could go and find them before nightfall and bring them back to the village.

The forest was home to all the spirits and ghosts, who lived there among trees so tall and thick that the canopy blocked out the light. During the day, especially if you had an elephant to ride on, you could go safely through the forest without fear. Sometimes you would see something that looked like a person walking through the forest, but it would be a ghost – perhaps of an ancestor. Ghosts were everywhere, and while it could be scary to see them, most meant no harm. But there were also evil spirits out there, especially at night, when the forest was terrifying. Then, you would feel your skin crawl if you went anywhere near the dense mass of trees, so everyone made sure they were at home, safe in their houses after dark. Interestingly, Ta'Peng explained that once he achieved the status of shaman he was no longer scared of ghosts in the forest. He had his own spiritual presence and felt more powerful than any of the bad spirits that might have been out there.

The mahouts lived in proximity to elephants and interacted with them from quite a young age, as early as five or six years old. But each of the mahouts learned to work with and train elephants somewhat later – Ta'Ma, Ta'Mew and Ta'Peng at fourteen years old, Ta'Nui at thirteen and Ta'In at ten years of age. Their grandfathers and fathers showed them how to ride, care for and communicate with elephants. Though they were immense and powerful, the young mahouts were never really scared of the elephants. As Ta'Mew explained, 'Our fathers would tell us not to be afraid, and that nothing bad was going to happen because the elephants would take care of us.' Learning to ride an elephant was exhilarating once you knew that you were safe and that the creature would not harm you. Elephants they rode at that age were usually older females, perfect for learning on. Later they could progress to younger elephants and bull elephants, the latter being the hardest to train and control.

The elephants had been in their families for years or even decades, and were treated as somewhat of a family member or pet. They would sometimes use them to carry heavy items like sacks of rice and would ride them out into the forest or between neigh-bouring Guay villages. All the elephants were either caught from the wild or were the direct descendants of wild-caught animals, with elephant captures occurring along the Cambodian border, where wild elephants roamed the jungle. All the men in the village took part in these captures, learning from those with decades of experi-ence. The journey to the border alone took fifteen days each way on top of the hunt itself, and the mahouts needed to carry as much rice and other foodstuffs as possible to ensure they returned to the village before anything ran out. They would also hunt wild boar and deer, and might sometimes pass a village on the way there or back where they could buy more food. For the most part, they saw no one; it was just thick jungle the whole way to the border and back. But they would always know exactly where they were going, all the best places to camp, and the best sites for clean drinking water to ensure they did not get sick. This was mainly the responsibility of the head kruba, who was the fount of wisdom and directed the hunt, though all the mahouts had shared knowledge about the processes and practices involved. With no written language, this was the result of generations of mahouts creating an oral record of the stories of the hunt as well as a mental map of the area. The head kruba was always in charge, however, and the other mahouts had to pay attention to him and abide by several rules. The head kruba always ate and slept first, and would take the lead when the group headed out into the forest. The mahouts were not permitted to change their clothes for the duration of the hunt. Contravening any of these rules would bring bad luck, and the hunt would fail.

The mahouts would use a variety of tools to capture elephants: primarily a rope of buffalo hide known as *chuek batr* and extensions to it used to secure the elephant, including the *kaen narng* (a bamboo 'lock') and the *tham*, a rope tied around the neck of the elephant and reinforced with thorny spikes to subdue the animal. The hunt was difficult but rewarding. When the mahouts left the village, they would ride out on older, well-trained elephants who would help them corral and capture younger elephants. A 'decoy' elephant would be used to attract its wild cousins and would be tied to a tree using a rope called *sai yong*. A trumpet fashioned from buffalo horn called *sanaeng kel* would be blown to mark the start of the hunt, to communicate among mahouts about the movement of elephants, and to ensure no one was lost or endangered while living in the forest. The brash, tinny recording that played at the Surin Elephant Study Center before the start of the twice-daily circus is a recording of the *sanaeng kel* tune that used to mark the beginning of the hunt.

The mahouts wanted to capture young elephants because they would be easier to train. 'We never took the really young ones,' Ta'Mew explained, 'because we would have to wait years to train them. They were just too small and needed to stay with their mothers. They still needed milk and would die if they were separated. They had to be able to survive by themselves. So we wanted to catch slightly older elephants – around four or five years old. We didn't mind if they were female or male; we would take anything that we managed to catch, they just had to be small.' Larger elephants were usually too powerful and would not be easy to take back to the village, so any the mahouts caught would be released, though the captured elephants would also need to be large enough to have someone sit on their backs.

Capturing elephants was a dangerous occupation. Men were often injured falling from elephants, into holes or over rocks and branches, suffering cuts, gashes and sometimes broken bones. These injuries were treated by herbal medicines that the mahouts concocted from a variety of local plants. Recipes were passed down generations like the mental maps of the forest. Another common problem was punctured feet, caused when either an elephant or a mahout stepped on a sharp root or stick. It would be near impossible to pull out, but herbal medicine applied to the wound would draw out the root or stick while another medicine would heal the wound, stopping any bleeding and chance of infection. The mahouts also made a variety of medicines from wild elephant dung and urine. Due to the diversity of natural food the elephants consumed, their dung and urine had medicinal and antiseptic qualities and were especially helpful for infections when mixed with fresh water. The Guay even used this medicine for ear infections, with just a small amount inserted into the earhole, while headaches were treated by inhaling a mix of elephant dung and leaves placed over coals and covered with a cloth. The men would collect wild elephant dung and urine to take back to the village to be used to make herbal medicine at home. The dung was important spiritually and would be used for a variety of ailments. During the hunt, malaria also took its toll, the forest being the perfect breeding ground for mosquitoes. Many men succumbed to the disease and there was no herbal treatment. The best they could do was to light fires so the smoke would deter the insects. There were also tigers in the forest, though they did not pose much of a threat, being scared off by the sight of so many people and elephants together.

Before they left the village, the mahouts would call upon the spirits to protect them. They needed to know it would be safe to go into the forests and that they would be successful in their mission. 'There is a special language in which we speak to the spirits,' Ta'Mew explained. 'It is not a language used between humans. It is only a language the Guay use to speak to the spirits. We call it the ghost language.' To get their protection, the mahouts would conduct a ceremony at the Pakham Spirit House, asking the spirits for their permission to undertake the hunt. 'If they said no, you couldn't go,' Ta'Mew continued. 'Something would go wrong.' This spirit or ghost language is unique to the Guay and contains coded words only understood by mahouts and the spirits themselves. These words would describe all aspects of the hunt, such as the elephants that were suitable for capture. The decoy elephant was *taneeya*; a male elephant was *dteeo-deaa moom*; and a sacred elephant was known as *krupakam*. When using the ghost language or communicating in Guay, it was essential for the mahouts to speak quietly so as not to scare wild elephants away.

The site in the SESC where the Pakham Spirit House still sits was the Guay's centre of spiritual communion for hundreds of years. The coil of Pakham rope – also known as *chuek batr* – that sits dustily in the Pakham Spirit House was the traditional tool used to capture elephants. Made from buffalo hide, the Pakham rope ends in a lasso, and has special significance. 'You could only catch elephants with the Pakham rope,' Ta'Ma explained. 'Today, the Pakham rope is just a memory from the past, but once it was used on every hunt and was an important part of our culture.' To capture elephants, two mahouts would sit astride one large elephant, with one on her neck, where he could direct her to chase the younger elephant the mahouts wanted to catch. The other mahout would sit further back on the elephant, holding a length of Pakham rope, ready to lasso the young elephant around one of its hind legs once the animal had grown tired from running.

'It was always two men per elephant,' Ta'Mew recalled, 'so, if we had twenty men, we could catch ten elephants; if we had forty men, we could catch twenty, and so on.' If they were lucky and had enough men, the mahouts could catch up to fifty elephants in one hunt, conducted over two or three months. Sometimes, one mahout and his partner could catch two or three elephants themselves, while other men might not catch any elephants at all. Once lassoed, the elephant would be tethered to a larger, trained elephant. This would be the captured elephant's new 'friend' and would be used to teach the youngster how to behave. The young elephant would stay tethered to the big elephant while the group travelled back to the village.

Once home, the mahouts would leave the young elephants tethered at the edge of the forest for a week or more. They wanted them to slowly acclimatise to the noise and activity of village life before starting training, because elephants could panic at the sight of so many people, houses and other animals like dogs and buffaloes. 'At first, we would hobble a young elephant's front and back legs, so she couldn't run away,' Ta'Mew recalled. 'We would bring her delicious food like pineapples, bananas and sugarcane, and she would start to like us.' It was rare for them to have such things in the forest, and the young elephant would become tamer as a result of receiving these yummy snacks. 'We could then hobble her just by the front legs, once she came to know she would get food from us and that this was a good place to stay.' A spiritual ceremony would be conducted to make sure there were no evil spirits that had followed them back from the jungle before the training began.

Basic training for riding would take around two weeks. First, the mahouts would train the youngster to have someone on her back, using the elephant's larger friend to help. They would bind the youngster with rope to the friend – neck to neck – which would stop her from moving around. They would then climb atop the larger elephant and slowly move onto the smaller one, first by putting one foot on the youngster before moving inch by inch onto her back. 'Usually, the little elephant would try to shake you off,' Ta'Mew explained, 'so it was better to do it very slowly. One leg, then the next. Always touching them so they know that you are there. Eventually, you would get two legs over the elephant's back.' The mahouts could get hurt at that stage of the training, so having the quiet, well-trained, older elephant to help, along with other experienced mahouts, was essential.

'It depends on the elephant, how long it takes to train them,' Ta'Mew explained. 'It might take about two or three months to complete all the training. We would just keep the young elephant connected to the older one. Slowly you could make the rope between them longer and longer and keep practising until the youngster just let you do it. You just had to be very patient.' After they were able to sit on the younger elephant's back without being thrown off, the mahouts would then start to train her to move left and right and to go forward and backward. 'You used your legs and feet against the side of the elephant's head to teach her which way to go,' Ta'Mew said. 'You also used verbal commands.'

Ta'Mew also explained that the elephants were considered part of the mahouts' families. 'It was important not to have any favourites, like children. You have to treat each elephant equally. If you like one elephant best, and not another, then they won't like each other. It's important to treat them the same.' The krubas also explained that while some contemporary training practices were the same as the old days, mahouts today rushed training, when it was better to be patient and have the training take longer. Each explained how they watched the older Guay men train the elephants using patience. They were not sure about training methods in other parts of the country. 'We sold elephants to the people up north,' Ta'Mew recalled. 'The training they did there was probably different because they were using them for logging, and we weren't because there were no teak forests here. We made money to support the village by selling elephants. But we kept many elephants for ourselves because they are so important to us spiritually.'

In the late 1950s, the forest along the Cambodian border became more dangerous. Khmer rebels patrolled the area, and the mahouts would pay them money to have access to their traditional hunting spots. On one hunt, tragedy struck. 'For some reason, the Khmer people started to shoot at us,' Ta'Mew explained. 'We ran as fast as we could, but some of our people were killed or injured. Soon we couldn't go near the border at all as it was much too dangerous. Not long after that, it became illegal to hunt elephants at all – they called it "poaching" – so that was the end of the practice.'

After that, hunting practices began to decline and Guay culture changed irrevocably. 'We asked the Department of National Parks if we can go hunt them in the wild again, so we can keep the tradition alive,' Ta'Peng explained. 'There are many in the national parks and they are breeding, so we think there are enough for us to take some, but the department said no. We want there to be another kruba to take on our role, but we have to accept that the tradition has ended.' At one stage, a Guay mahout captured a wild elephant and brought it back to Ban Ta Klang, hoping to keep the culture alive. It stayed in the village for several years until it was confiscated by the authorities and taken to the Thai Elephant Conservation Center in Lampang.

'We hunted elephants,' Ta'Mew explained, 'but we didn't think of ourselves as poachers. Poachers kill elephants and take their tusks. If they had to, they would kill a whole herd just to get to a bull with big tusks. They would kill the bull, too, and cut off both tusks, right to the base. If you have your own bull elephant, and you want to sell ivory, you just cut off the tips of the tusks. They grow back. You can legally sell things made from the tusks of captive elephants, but not wild elephants. That's because they just kill the wild ones. They don't even care that the tusks will grow back. They only care about the money.'

It had been around thirty years since the krubas rode elephants. They told me they were now too old and it was much too far to fall with fragile bones. The world around them had changed, and though they still felt close to elephants, the culture was quite different. In some ways, life in modern day Ban Ta Klang was easier than it was in the past. The krubas described the massive floods that inundated the village during the wet season, making life extremely difficult. These were the result of an inefficient drainage system in the basin of Tung Kula Ronghai, some fifty kilometres north of Ban Ta Klang. The villagers would cultivate fields away from the main channels of water, but sometimes crops would be destroyed and the villagers would go hungry. Houses sometimes collapsed and the only road through the village – a deep gully dug in the ground by waterflow – became a quagmire. While Ban Ta Klang was once a large village with a thousand families or so, many people left the area as a result of the floods and damage to the rice fields. They found new places to live in other provinces, such as Chanthaburi and Sakon Nakhon.

Those who remained in Ban Ta Klang were often hungry, with much of their daily lives revolving around collecting enough food to survive from the fields and forest, whether this meant rice farming, hunting or fishing, or collecting fruit, berries and herbs. But apart from these problems, there were many parts of the old life that were better. There was a strong sense of community and camaraderie between villagers, and no need for money as everything was exchanged in a bartering system. People were happier, and the isolation of the village protected the local culture. The krubas also believed it was much better for the elephants back then. 'They could just live in the forest around us, eating everything they could,' Ta'In explained. 'There were so many trees that they loved to eat, and they would also eat the bark and roots from trees. It was a healthy, natural diet.'

Today, the krubas still have strong personal connections with the spirits. As shamans, their main role in contemporary Ban Ta Klang is to conduct blessings and ordination ceremonies and commune with the spirits, largely as a group. As Ta'Ma explained, 'Anyone can hire us to call upon the spirits for good luck.' This includes people in Ban Ta Klang and those from neighbouring villages, who often want both krubas and elephants for ceremonies. As it was in the past, the Guay still visit the Pakham Spirit House to talk to the spirits, burn incense, pray and receive blessings. This was and still is a place where the spirits converge and locals make offerings in the spirits' names – an array of food and drinks the spirits seem to like, including orange juice in small bottles, parcels of sticky rice, and bunches of lady finger bananas.

'The spirit house was built in a very special and significant place, between a triangle formed by three huge trees that we called *sam phinong* (three brothers),' Ta'Nui explained. 'These were some of the biggest and oldest trees in the village, with rich, dark bark and tall, straight trunks.' Some people in Ban Ta Klang have their own small Pakham spirit houses, with pieces of the Pakham rope in them, but many villagers go to the SESC to be blessed by the krubas at the main

Pakham Spirit House. 'A lot of the time, people who want to be blessed are wishing for good luck, health or success,' Ta'Mew explained, 'but sometimes they just wish for money. It's up to them. It is just our job to call upon the spirits.'

The krubas discussed how the value of elephants had changed over the decades. 'We think it's crazy!' Ta'Ma explained. 'When we sent trained young elephants north to work in logging, we would sell them for about two thousand baht [US$60]. Now elephants cost a million baht [US$30,000] or more. They have a different value because of tourism.'

Ta'Peng had worked at the very first camp in Pattaya when elephant tourism was in its infancy in the 1960s, along with around thirty other Guay mahouts and their families. After the hunting practices declined and they were no longer able to sell elephants to the northerners, this became one way of making money outside the village. At first, the camp only offered rides but eventually there was a shift towards circuses as a way of attracting more tourists. This paralleled a general shift around the country from more traditional, village-based mahout-elephant relationships to those within tourism contexts.

The Surin Elephant Round-Up was an important tourism venture that provided mahouts with an income outside the village. Now a huge festival that attracts several hundred mahouts and elephants and thousands of tourists to Surin city in November every year, in its early days the round-up was quite a simple affair. The krubas shared an interesting tale about the first round-up, which occurred in 1955, and its connections with the first wave of elephant tourism in the area. This event was not an organised festival but a gathering of over a hundred men and elephants in an old airport in Tha Tum district.

A photo was taken of the large gathering of mahouts and elephants sitting and kneeling together on the ground. 'You'll see that photo anywhere you go in Surin, a picture of many, many elephants and mahouts,' Ta'Ma explained. This was the first photo of the Guay and their elephants to reach the public in any significant way. The event was evidence that the forest was home to many elephants and the people who lived with them. This marked the beginning of a big change in Ban Ta Klang and Surin province more broadly, whereby people outside the village learned that there was money to be made from elephant tourism.

But the biggest change to the world of the Guay and their elephants was deforestation. What was once thick jungle was cut down gradually over many decades. A new road was built through the village in 1982, filling in the gully that had once kept the village fairly isolated. The road meant that outsiders could now come through the village and cut down the trees for various uses. This was exacerbated by further land clearing by both people outside the village and the Guay themselves, who, after the cessation of hunting and selling elephants to the north, were growing increasingly more crops to survive. This meant that much of the surrounding land was cleared and redeveloped as rice fields. More recently, those fields have also been affected by the lower level of the Mun and Chi rivers, with the lowlands – once moist from groundwater – now drying out, the removal of trees causing erosion and aridification. As Ta'In explained, 'There are not many old trees around here anymore. One of the only ones that still exists is one of the three brothers, the three tall trees that once grew around the Pakham Spirit House.' The other two were felled after growing weak from having elephants chained to them, a product of changes in the village that meant elephants could no longer roam more freely.

As it shades the Pakham Spirit House, the sacredness of the last tree brother deters anyone from cutting it down.

As the krubas explained, everything around the tree and the spirit house changed irrevocably. 'Now it's just a busy built-up landscape, whereas it used to be beautiful,' said Ta'Mew. The krubas said that the spirits hated the big tour buses, the motorbikes, the loud music and the noise created by the circus at the SESC. Some of the spirits were still there but many had moved away to where it was quieter. Despite the noise, the krubas were happy that the SESC was set up in 2005 as it brought mahouts and elephants home from tourist camps and rejuvenated Guay culture as a result. 'Before, the village was empty and really quiet,' Ta'Mew recalled. 'Everyone was in the camps.'

After mahouts returned to work at the new SESC, the village became busy again. 'It's good that the centre opened up,' Ta'In explained. 'Now, everyone is home and there are lots of jobs to do, so we can earn some money. People always want blessings. But we still have problems here with the elephants because there is never enough food and water.'

The krubas were hopeful that the Guay's elephant-keeping traditions would persist despite ongoing changes and environmental problems. As Ta'Mew explained, the younger generations still believed in the spirits and some would continue to care for elephants into the future. Yet, while their sons were mahouts, there were fewer people in the youngest generation who wanted to work with elephants. 'A lot of the kids, they want to leave the village and go to the big cities,' Ta'Ma explained. 'We try to keep the Guay language alive here. It isn't written down, so it needs to be kept alive by speaking. The children learn it in school. We also make sure they know about the spiritual beliefs. They don't care about the traditional clothes now. We still make and sell traditional silk clothing here, but not many people in the village wear it anymore. Now everyone just wears Western clothes.'

Ta'Mew commented on the ways the elephant culture was passed down the generations. 'They need to watch and learn, and constantly respect the knowledge of those who are older with more experience.' However, he believed that a lot of the knowledge of the hunts would gradually fade away after the krubas died. 'No one can use the knowledge because we can't catch elephants anymore, so no one is very interested in learning.' While the krubas still conduct all the important ceremonies within the village and those that neighbour it, this aspect of the culture also risks disappearing. They conduct these ceremonies as a group, but as each kruba moves from this life to the next this group will reduce in numbers until no one is left. To keep the strong spiritual connections of the Guay intact, the younger generations will need to find a way to continue ceremonies and related traditions in the absence of their spiritual leaders.

During the course of our interviews, I tried to imagine what Ban Ta Klang had looked like when the Guay were still isolated, before the noise of the circus and trucks and the endless dry heat had set in, replacing the quiet coolness of the forest. I pictured how their elephants had lived, roaming and grazing, while the spirits and ghosts of their ancestors wandered among the trees, watching over daily life and elephant-human interactions. The interviews had introduced me to a fascinating world and culture, and from here I was able to trace changes that had occurred in the village and beyond over the past eighty-odd years. I had also met and spoken to mahouts who were either the sons of the krubas I had interviewed or others of the same generation, including men who had worked in camps for many years.

A further series of interviews would reveal much more about life in Ban Ta Klang before and after deforestation, and why the loss of the forests precipitated the move towards tourism as the primary source of the Guay's income, with a profound impact on their elephants' welfare.

Chapter 8

THE NEXT GENERATION

The mahouts I interviewed from the next generation were Sarot Ngamsanga and his friends Thong Dii Salagnam (Fah Sai's mahout), Lord Insamran and Boon Ma Salagnam, who were between 45 and 52 years old. Each was keen to fill me in on the next stage in the history of Ban Ta Klang and surrounding Guay villages, including neighbouring Ban Chinda, where Sarot was originally from. My extensive interviews with these men gave me great insight into the rapid changes since the krubas' time due to deforestation, how their livelihoods and culture were directly affected by this critical environmental crisis, and why they had to turn to tourism to survive. Before we covered the topic of deforestation, the men reminisced about their childhoods and teenage years over a number of conversations. This involved interviews within the SESC – either at the Surin Project's headquarters or while watching elephants in the Enclosure dam – and a series of dinners at Lord's house in the village. The mahouts would talk openly, often for two or three hours at a time, over ample meals of meat and fish, vegetables, chili and rice, usually cooked over a traditional stove or which I would buy already prepared from the local market. In facilitating these conversations, I was aware of how fortunate I was to have the mahouts open up and talk with me. Their willingness to share was a product of both the trust that had developed after my many visits to Ban Ta Klang and numerous interviews I had conducted, along with their desire to share their stories with people outside their village, province and country.

When the mahouts were children, everything they needed still came from the forests, just as it had when the krubas were boys. There was natural food not just for elephants but for humans too. Traditional medicine came from the forests, and every family could catch fish from the surrounding rivers, trap crickets to fry with salt and pepper, and collect wild-grown foods like bananas, young bamboo and tamarinds. They grew crops and rice in small fields cleared in the forest, kept chickens and pigs in pens, and grazed water buffaloes, who would wallow in the streams that intersected the village. The forest provided the Guay with wood and giant leaves to build houses, roofs and fences, and to create fires for cooking, staying warm and keeping mosquitoes at bay. It also offered ample grazing for elephants, with access to a range of foods such as napier grass, bamboo and wild fruit, plus a range of shrubs, roots and twigs. By dispersing seeds in their manure and clearing land, the elephants created a more productive ground layer, keeping the land fertile and ensuring biodiversity.

The four mahout boys were close friends and loved working with elephants. Like the krubas, each had learned the skills of mahoutship from their fathers and grandfathers. While they were also exposed to aspects of elephant husbandry from a very young age – at just four or five years old – it was not until they were about nine or ten that they became more involved in the daily practices of elephant-keeping. Then, they enjoyed watching their fathers and grandfathers work with the elephants and would follow them as they rode into the forest or travelled to surrounding villages. Soon they would learn to ride elephants, and they spent many afternoons after lessons in the small village school riding down to the river to let the animals graze in the forest, using the same method of hobbling as the krubas – with one elephant's leg chained or tied to keep the herd in one place. All they could think about at school was spending time with their elephants. Often, they would hide from their teacher in the morning, keeping an eye out for each other in the hope they could avoid going to school and spend time in the forest instead, but they would usually be found out and dragged along to school by a less than impressed teacher.

Nonetheless, the mahout boys had ample time to spend with their elephants. In the early evening they would pack a small lunchbox of rice, meat and vegetables and head down to the spot where the Mun and Chi rivers connected, a distance of about three kilometres through lush forest. During the wet season the river coursed with a multitude of fishes, and the mahouts would sit on the riverbank talking and fishing while their elephants roamed around them, munching away on rampant vines, low-hanging canopy and tree roots. The young mahouts would find delicious fruit to eat in the forest – some to eat themselves and some to take home. They would also search for particular natural remedies, such as a tree bark that could be used as a topical treatment to clean cuts and avoid infection, both for people and for elephants. 'We would stay out in the forest all afternoon and head back before nightfall,' Sarot explained. 'If you got lost or tired, you would always be okay. You could just close your eyes and pat your elephant, and she would take you straight home.'

The village was a fun place to be a young mahout. 'We got up to a lot of mischief,' Thong Dii laughed. 'We would fool around and do pretty silly or even dangerous things. Sometimes six or seven of us would get on one elephant and ride around like that. We would fall off all the time and just laugh about it.' Almost every aspect of daily life revolved around elephants, and the boys were excited to participate in all cultural traditions, from ceremonies to training. 'Some of the work we did was to prepare elephants to sell to the north,' Lord explained. 'We just did some basic training to get the elephant used to having someone on its back, just the usual commands for riding or sometimes lifting things. The ones we kept were like our pets, friends or family, but the main reason we had them was for spiritual reasons. They were important for all our ceremonies.'

Thong Dii reminisced about one particular ceremony that was of great importance to the Guay. 'When an elephant was around three or four years old, we would conduct the elephant naming ceremony,' he explained. 'We would tie a piece of paper with a name on it to a banana tree, then several others to other trees, surrounding it in a circle. The young elephant would then pick a tree to eat, thereby choosing its name.' The names related to the weather, the elements, flowers, fruit and auspicious items, just like the elephants I had met on my journey, whether it be Doc Ngern's silver flower, Fah Sai's clear skies, Sai Fah's thunder or Wang Duen's crescent moon.

Ordinations held on elephant back were used to bless men about to join the monkhood, while elephants were also used in wedding ceremonies and funerals. Burials were conducted in an area of forest named *Chang Leung* – where the men of the krubas' generation would rest after capturing elephants. Chang Leung still comprises part of the Surin Elephant Study Center, including the land in the Enclosure. Like the krubas, the younger men also saw many ghosts of their ancestors in the area, who looked very different to when they were alive. 'Some of the ghosts had very long hands, and others very long feet,' Thong Dii explained. 'We often needed to come here to collect water very early in the morning; we would always come as a group or with elephants as it was much too scary to see ghosts when you were alone.'

When the mahouts were very young, each house in the village was surrounded by trees, with quite a distance between each family's home. Most houses were open on one side, and sometimes the families felt exposed to the elements, especially at night. The elephants played an important role in protecting the villagers from ghosts, bad spirits, snakes and tigers. As Sarot explained, 'When you had an elephant chained to the side of your house at nighttime, you were always safe.' As well as using them to carry sacks of rice and riding them to nearby villages, the mahouts sometimes travelled by elephant to Surin city. During all their travels, the elephants' protection meant the mahouts could battle through the forest without fear. 'When you rode your elephant, you could go anywhere,' Thong Dii explained.

Before the first dirt road was built through the village in 1982, riding elephants was one of the main ways that the villagers travelled around the area. At that stage, it was especially difficult to leave the village during wet season, when the only way in and out – the deep gully through the village – would course with thick, deep mud. 'In many places the gully was four metres deep and about three metres wide,' Sarot explained. 'Our houses lined one side of it with the forest on the other. There were spots where you could walk up and down where it wasn't so deep, so if you wanted to go to the other side, you would have to go to one of these spots and cross over. The funniest thing was that when people rode their elephants down there, it looked like they were hovering above the ground, because you would just see their torso and head moving along. The whole of the elephant's body was down there in the gully!'

When the village flooded, life was very difficult. Usually, the villagers would have enough food in storage to last through any wet season. But if the rains came early, the fields would be inundated, and the crops could die before the residents had a chance to harvest them. 'There were times when I was just so hungry,' Lord remembered. 'I would just think about food all the time. I couldn't concentrate at school because I was so hungry. I had a little pencil – we all did – and a piece of chalk and we would write notes in class on it. I remember one flood season, sitting in school, so hungry, and smelling the pencil. The wood smelled so good! Almost good enough for me to eat it. I didn't but that's how desperate I was, that I would almost eat my pencil.'

Until recently, the area around Ban Ta Klang had always flooded but, as the krubas had also explained, the situation was sometimes so dire that Guay families left to find new lodgings in drier areas. 'You'll find Guay people now throughout Surin who are related to us by ancestry, but who don't have elephants,' Sarot noted. 'They left when the flooding got really bad. It was so bad that it was enough for them to want to forget the elephant culture. We understand why they left, but we could never do the same. Without elephants, we don't have a purpose.'

The Guay's land management practices allowed the villagers to live a fairly subsistent lifestyle with little outside economic influence. The mahouts recalled the bartering system that was primarily used. 'We would share everything,' Sarot explained. 'We exchanged food, such as fish and vegetables, without needing money. Each month there would be one or two ceremonies and festivals, and everyone would come together to help out. If there was an ordination ceremony for a monk, we would take our elephants and the abbot of the temple

would conduct the blessing for free. Everyone was happy to participate because it was a good thing for the community, and also good
for the next life – for reincarnation.' The abbot was once considered
the head of the community, with the temple being the central place of
communion. The villagers would pay their respects here and receive
benefits, whether these were related to the rice and crop growing
seasons or good luck and health for family members. There was also a
strong culture of traditional medicine in the village, with treatments
made from forest resources serving the Guay's needs.

After the abbot died, things started to change, with money
becoming more important than unity among community members.
The ceremonies were still conducted by the new abbot, but villagers
were now encouraged to pay. While people from neighbouring
villages had long been involved in the ceremonies, they became more
interested once it was easier to travel through the forest due to the
development of the dirt road in 1982.

'The elephants brought great spiritual benefit to people,' Sarot
explained. 'Thai and Guay people believe that elephants are sacred
beings, and you can get good luck from touching and feeding them.
It's very good luck if you pass under the belly of an elephant, so a lot
of the villagers would want to pay us to do that. Another thing that's
good luck is to pour water over an elephant's ear. If you collect the
water and wash yourself in it, you will have a lot of good luck, and if
you are sick, the water will cure you.'

The mahouts managed all interactions between their elephants
and visiting villagers to ensure the safety of elephant and human
alike. The villagers were willing to pay good money for the blessings
and, as a result, the rate charged by the temple and mahouts soon
increased. What the mahouts termed a 'social tax' also surged, with

families needing to pay large sums of money to others for weddings and other events of importance. Money became more important than spirituality, while at the same time the worsening floods were making it harder to survive with a subsistence lifestyle. The clearing of land around the village by the Guay increased the amount of space where they could grow rice and fibres to sell locally to make cloth and other materials. This deforestation process, while small-scale at that time, would eventually spiral out of control, and not entirely due to the Guay's agricultural practices.

As well as growing rice, crops and fibres, the Guay needed to make an income from other sources outside the village. After finishing school between the ages of fourteen and sixteen, many young men left the village to move to other towns and cities to find work. Sarot moved to Bangkok to work as a labourer, sending money back home to support his family. After three years of this life, he moved back home to harvest rice in the fields surrounding Ban Ta Klang and nearby Ban Chinda, where he was joined by Thong Dii, Lord and Boon Ma, who had also left the village to earn an income for their families. Soon, it would be time for them to take on one of the most important roles in the village: taking elephants to nearby villages and provinces to offer ceremonies and elephant rides to other people. This was a ritual that occurred after the rice harvest in November, just before the dry season set in. In the wet season, there was plentiful food in the forests for the elephants, but in the dry season, food became scarcer. The greenery in the usually rampant forest grew thin, and the small remaining grazing areas would become contaminated with manure. 'Elephants will not consume plants that have been defecated upon, so they could not graze in this area,' Lord explained. 'At this time of year, we would need to leave the forest to rejuvenate.'

The income made in the outside villages directly related to beliefs surrounding elephants, including the traditional ceremonies of passing under elephants and washing in elephant ear water. The young mahouts would also sell amulets fashioned from elephant tail hair and small Buddhas or rings carved from ivory cut from the tips of their elephants' tusks. These were popular with other villagers, as were the elephant rides. At that time, the traditional howdah was a wooden construction set upon five or more layers of thick bark cut from nearby trees, with a large piece of buffalo hide stretched across the makeshift saddle pad. According to the mahouts, this was gentler on the elephants' backs than more modern steel howdahs and human-made supports.

'People would love travelling for a short while through the forest on the elephant's back,' Thong Dii remembered. 'And there would always be girls – lots of girls – who loved to see us. The girls always wanted to know when we were coming to the village. They would bring our elephants food and give us treats, too. It made us feel very special. We would always have our favourite girls in each village and would be pleased to see them every year.'

The villagers also brought the mahouts gifts of banana trees, sugarcane and grass to feed the elephants. They would proffer the remnants of harvest yields for which they had no use, but which the elephants happily devoured. The mahouts could also graze their elephants in the forests around these villages, which were still thick with vegetation after the wet season, having no elephants to make a meal of them. They would stay at the edge of the village so the elephants could eat while they slept. 'We would tether or chain one of them,' Boon Ma recalled, 'but we never worried about them running away because there was so much food. They could eat all night and day, and there would always be more food for them.'

'We'd stay out there with buffalo hides over our heads,' Sarot chimed in, 'sort of like handmade tents that were just enough to give us shelter. It was often quite uncomfortable and there were lots of insects that could sting you, like mosquitoes, ants, centipedes and scorpions. The centipedes and scorpions were the worst. They'd climb into your clothes and sting you everywhere. They were so painful and they could make you very sick. We had to be careful not to get them in our clothes or we would be miserable.'

There were also plenty of snakes in the forest, some who would invade the mahouts' camp and startle them during the night. Most of the snakes were not venomous but on occasion a deadly king cobra would slither into the camp, putting the mahouts on high alert. They would corner it and quickly kill it with a machete; it would be a tragedy if elephant or human alike died from one of their bites. If it was dry, camping in the forest was quite pleasant, but if it rained it was miserable and hard to sleep. 'We couldn't light a fire so we'd be cold and wet, but the elephants would be happy,' Sarot explained. 'It was a difficult life but we enjoyed travelling and exploring new places.'

'We travelled hundreds of kilometres on foot over the years, through forests and along roads, finding places to stay along the way,' Thong Dii remembered. 'All of us spent four months every year for six or seven years living like this.' The men would return home every April, just in time for the village's harvest ceremony and the start of the new rice growing season. But as the years went on, the area experienced a major ecological change. While Ban Ta Klang and its surrounds have always flooded in the wet season and become more arid in the dry, periods of genuine drought were becoming more common. The river level would drop, the ground would crack and crops would fail, meaning the villagers would have to re-sow their fields, wasting resources and time.

An even more significant change occurred in the early 1990s, when the dirt road through Ban Ta Klang was sealed with bitumen and cement. For a while, the villagers thought the new road might make life easier. The floods would no longer isolate them and they could travel to the city by moped to buy food from the local markets if their crops failed. But as Sarot explained, 'The road was the worst thing to happen to Ban Ta Klang.' Now anyone could come through the village. Trucks and cars came rumbling through, bringing outsiders who cut down the trees, making quick money selling them for lumber, paper or furniture. The Guay cleared even more land for rice and other crops as their subsistence lifestyle dwindled. Within a few years, almost the entire forest had been destroyed, and the once quiet village became scorching hot and vociferously noisy. After that, the Guay's culture changed very quickly and their elephants' welfare suffered enormously. 'There was nowhere for the elephants to roam or anything for them to eat,' Sarot explained, 'and it was dangerous for them to be loose with all the traffic coming through the village. We also needed to stop them from roaming around and destroying all the rice fields. So we had to start chaining them up and feeding them by hand.'

The Surin government became aware of the Guay people's financial struggle. They devised a plan to plant eucalyptus in various areas around the village and buy the wood back from the Guay if they tended to the trees.[164] The eucalyptus was to be used for wood chips and paper. It offered an income but the venture made the land even more arid and used so much water that the river level dropped even further, rendering the land increasingly infertile. Now the need to buy elephant food became even more urgent. The Guay had to work the rice fields more intensively and also develop new areas to plant and upkeep fields of napier grass and sugarcane to feed their elephants. This was a long process with limited yield, which took up the better part of each day to tend to. Soon the mahouts were working up to eighteen hours a day. They would arise before dawn then drive out to their own fields or to those of local farmers whose produce they had bought and would have to harvest, which would take around an hour or two. They would return home to feed their elephant and then take the animal down to the river to bathe. After this, they would start work in the fields or on local construction sites. This meant chaining their elephants up under their shelters and leaving them all day.

Late in the afternoon, they would return home, exhausted, where they had a short time to rest before either riding their elephant back down to the river or bathing them with a hose under its shelter. By this time, night would have fallen and they would have some time to spend with their family, eating dinner and chatting, before it was time to go to bed before starting the routine again the next day. The mahouts would provide the basics of care for their elephants, but much of the passion and love for spending time with the animal just for the sake of it had gone. The disappearing forests were symbolic of a new stage in mahout-elephant interactions in Ban Ta Klang and its surrounds, and relationships in a tight-knit community were now affected by serious economic and environmental changes.

Elephants suffered greatly as a result of deforestation. Not only were they chained up for almost all of the day, but they could also no longer socialise, had very few chances to wallow or forage, and became more aggressive as a result. Their health also declined. Now primarily eating food produced by humans, elephants were denied important nutrients, which led to physiological changes. As Sarot explained, 'Elephants are much smaller than they were in the past. Their reproductive ability and health have declined.' The animals also suffered emotionally due to their social isolation and the stressful conditions of living in a built-up environment, which also made it harder for females to become pregnant or carry pregnancies to full term.

The mahouts also found that other aspects of their traditional lifestyles with elephants were changing. Much of this was the result of new money associated with ceremonies and the increased social tax. Some ceremonies ceased to occur, such as the one naming young elephants using banana trees. 'Now they usually just give a name at birth,' Thong Dii explained. Traditional medicine also became less important. The villagers would travel to see doctors outside the village, which cost money and therefore warranted an increased income. A further issue occurred once Ban Ta Klang became more accessible, when Surin locals who were not Guay became increasingly interested in making money from elephants. The first Surin Elephant Round-Up in 1955 had introduced the Guay's elephant culture to the outside world, and the new road provided opportunities for people to come to the village to look at the animals. Soon enterprising individuals realised there was a way to make money from elephants, and a small tourism industry developed in Surin.

The new interest in elephants led to some intriguing scenarios. In one case, Sarot and Thong Dii were both asked to take part in an elephant swimming race, organised by a major television station as part of a boat festival in nearby Tha Tum. 'There were ten elephants swimming at once, ridden by famous actors,' Sarot explained. 'It was rainy season, so plenty of water was in the river. It was a strange thing to be part of. Both [his elephant] Sai Bua and Fah Sai were in the river with the actors sitting on their necks – without any mahouts. We stood on the riverbank and gave the elephants commands. There was a large crowd that cheered as the elephants swam along the river, while the actors posed on their backs. Sai Bua won and Fah Sai came in third! We had trained them to swim for half a month. Elephants already know how to swim but some of them can be scared. The best way to teach them is to have a more confident elephant in the front with a mahout on its back. The other elephant will follow; she will touch the tail of the one in front with her trunk.'

Sarot had also regularly been involved in the annual Don Chedi Memorial Fair, a two-week festival held in Suphanburi province in late January. In mid-December, he and Sai Bua would walk to Suphanburi from Ban Ta Klang with other mahouts and their elephants – a journey of about 400 kilometres. Before their day of departure, the krubas would choose an auspicious day to perform a ceremony to protect the men and elephants on their journey. At the festival, the mahouts would participate in a mock war on elephant back to commemorate the 1592 victory of King Naresuan the Great of Siam over the Burmese troops, led by Phra Maha Upparacha, the Burmese Crown Prince. The royal duel that took place between king and prince led to the Siamese Kingdom regaining sovereignty from Burma. The demonstration was similar to those held at the Surin Elephant Round-Up every year, in which each of the mahouts I interviewed had participated in their youth.

The popularity of elephants as forms of entertainment also meant that men with little experience purchased the animals to make money begging. For decades, the Guay mahouts had been making their yearly dry season trips to the surrounding villages, but other people had now realised they could make money from these villagers, too. As Sarot explained, 'The potential money people believed could be made from elephants attracted people who didn't have any history with elephants and didn't know how to look after them properly. They just wanted to get into elephant tourism quickly.' Soon men with no real experience were buying elephants, training them using intimidation, and taking them to the villages the mahouts used to visit, where they would demand money and food. They were considered pests. No one wanted to be blessed by these men and no one wanted to ride on their unruly elephants. The Guay mahouts soon found it was no longer viable to travel to the other villages. People would hide in their houses rather than running out and greeting them. 'This is why the image of the mahout is so bad,' Sarot explained. 'Some people take advantage of their elephants. They give us all a bad reputation.' The Guay mahouts connected the behaviour of these men to the demands of tourism, explaining – like the krubas – that such demands were encouraging training methods and practices that were detrimental to elephant welfare, changing the practice and culture of mahoutship in a negative way.

While some villagers would still offer harvest remnants to feed the elephants, these were no longer free. As Sarot explained, 'They put a price on something that was once worth nothing. You couldn't get banana trees or leftover corn stalks or rice husks for free. You had to pay.' Now there was not only less natural food for elephants, but a source had been lost that they had relied on during the dry season. Mahouts were working harder than ever but were still somehow poor, and their culture and traditions fractured as the day to day of their lives with elephants changed. Despite its difficulties, a deep nostalgia for the past set in, when the Guay's lives centred on living with elephants in a more tranquil world.

Due to the lack of available elephant food, Guay mahouts had to discover different ways to make money and feed their elephants. Many left Ban Ta Klang in the late 1990s and early 2000s, travelling with their elephants to large cities where they could make money begging or in tourist camps. At that time, the tourism industry was growing rapidly due to the influx of unemployed logging mahouts and elephants from the north, as well as a greater demand from foreigners as the country became one of the biggest tourist destinations in Asia. As such, there was significant economic motivation for Guay mahouts to leave Surin for tourist camps in Pattaya, Phuket, Chiang Mai, Ayutthaya and Chiang Rai. This was the next stage of the mahouts' stories, which was shared with me by Sarot, Thong Dii, Boon Ma and Lord one afternoon under the shade of one of the elephant shelters. As we watched elephants demolish a pile of freshly cut sugarcane, the mahouts explained what happened once the forests were all but gone and they were forced to leave their ancestral villages with their elephants.

Chapter 9

AFTER THE FORESTS DISAPPEARED

In 1995, 27-year-old Sarot decided to head to Bangkok with his six-year-old bull elephant Jan Jao ('the moon') – a journey of 300 kilometres. There, amidst sprawling highways, malls, hotels and bars awash in neon and grit, he would take his chances in street begging. He was leaving his family behind, but his village Ban Chinda, like neighbouring Ban Ta Klang, had been stripped of all its natural food for Jan Jao and his mother Sai Bua ('lotus flower'), the family's two household elephants. Sarot hoped he would quickly earn enough money to support his family in his new venture. His friends Thong Dii and Boon Ma had also recently left home, heading to camps in Pattaya and Phuket, but Sarot preferred to try his luck in Bangkok. Other Guay mahouts who had taken their elephants there spoke of good money from Thai people and Western tourists who loved elephants. With Jan Jao in tow, he hired a truck and made his way to the city.

Sarot's new home was a makeshift camp under a noisy overpass on the outskirts of the city, where he lived in a tent among other Guay mahouts in their own shelters. The elephants lived in the same lot, chained so they could not wander, and there was some grazing available in the form of grass. The men would cook food over campfires or bring home packages of rice and meat bought from food vendors on their daily travels into the city. They would buy sugarcane, grass and fruit for the elephants from markets on the outskirts or head out to some of the fields further away to harvest their food.

Every morning Sarot and Jan Jao would head into the city. They worked well as a team, taking care of one another and keeping each other company. Together they would stride along the roads to reach the congested heart of the city. Sukhumvit Road was their destination, a wide, diesel-soaked carriageway that linked the city's entertainment hotspots of Nana, Ekkamai and Thong Lor. Small lanes known as *sois* branched off from the main road like circuitous vines, their fruit the bars, clubs, restaurants and shops that tempted locals and tourists alike. Here, Sarot could find plenty of people who wanted to have their photo taken with Jan Jao. He could buy parcels of pineapple and bananas for cheap from the markets and sell a pinch of them for twenty baht a pop to locals and tourists. They would feed the fruit to Jan Jao, earning Sarot a fair profit.

Street begging in Bangkok could be perilous. Elephants or mahouts were sometimes hit by cars and trucks or electrocuted by low hanging wires. Sarot was careful, giving vehicles a wide berth and using his keen senses to check for danger and avoid it as best he could. Street begging was also repetitive and stressful, but Jan Jao was a tolerant elephant. He would endure camera flashes and enthusiastic pats from wide-eyed Thais or Western tourists. Sometimes the bar and restaurant owners liked him hanging around. An elephant could bring luck and also patrons. But some did not like him at all and would shoo him away. Others would threaten to call the police, who were cracking down on Sarot's particular sort of occupation. Then he would take Jan Jao elsewhere, back along the main road until he reached another soi.

Sarot grew concerned for Jan Jao, who had developed stereotyp-ical behaviour and was worryingly thin. The whole experience was wearing them both out. He decided to head home, but things were the same as when he had left, with no elephant food and no way of making an income. Friends who were working in elephant camps in other parts of the country would call to tell him how great the work was – there were plenty of tourists, lots of money, and the camps would take care of accommodation and all the elephant food, as well as providing meals for mahouts. One friend at a camp in Pattaya was particularly convincing, so Sarot used all his savings to book a truck to take him and Sai Bua to the coastal resort city, a hundred kilome-tres east of Bangkok, leaving Jan Jao at home with his family. Sarot would arise early every morning to feed Sai Bua grass and sugarcane from trucks that would arrive twice a day, before taking tourists for hour-long rides around the camp. 'Life was not too difficult, but not easy either,' he told me. He was making decent money, Sai Bua had plenty of food, and Sarot was much better off financially than in either Ban Ta Klang or Bangkok. But there were not always enough tourists, meaning that his income could be limited because he relied on commissions and tips for each ride on top of his usual salary.

After a few months, Sarot moved on to another tourist camp, this time in Hua Hin, a seaside resort in the Gulf of Thailand. A friend had promised him he would make far better money, but this did not eventuate. 'I worked a long time without payment, always asking when I would get some money, and while they always said "soon", I never received anything. For that reason, I decided to move again.'

Over seven or eight years, Sarot and Sai Bua worked in five different elephant camps. It was costly to hire a truck to move from camp to camp, but the promise of better money or conditions would be his incentive time and time again. Overall, this period of employment benefited Sarot and his family financially; sometimes he made up to 70,000 baht (around US$2,300) a month. But the work also took its toll. 'I really missed my family,' Sarot told me. 'Life in the village was difficult, but I had the support of the community.' Sarot also missed the spiritual traditions and Guay culture, where elephants were more than just tourist attractions. He wanted to go home but there was nothing there for him: no source of income and no food for Sai Bua. It was better to keep working and hope that one day things would change.

Meanwhile, over in Japan, Thong Dii was training elephants at a popular zoo. He had been headhunted for his unique skills by the zoo's owner, who had observed Thong Dii while he was working at an elephant camp in Samphran, forty kilometres west of Bangkok. While all the young mahouts were skilled in mahoutship, Thong Dii had a particular talent, borne out of many opportunities to work with different elephants. He had been caring for his family's two elephants – including Fah Sai's mother – since he was in primary school and had had equal experience with gentle females and more aggressive males. In the eyes of the zoo owner, he would be perfect for the role, which also involved managing elephants and other animals on TV and film sets. 'I even worked with lions and tigers,' he explained. 'You see teeth and claws and you want to run. But I learned how to do it. You had to not show fear. You had to believe you were in control, and you'd be okay. I also sometimes worked with horses. In some ways, they are like elephants. They are both sensitive and respond well to body language. But horses get more scared of things and you need to use a lot more control to make them trust you. Elephants are more likely to trust you if you are a good mahout. And elephants are smarter than horses. A horse that's scared is much harder to settle down than an elephant, so I had to learn how to communicate with the horse to make him trust and follow me.'

Thong Dii had travelled overland to the zoo with two elephants in tow, a journey of a month and a half that involved hiring a truck to Chiang Rai, then taking a boat across the Mekong River to Laos, followed by another truck to Shanghai, and one final boat to Yokohama. Lord had followed not long after with his own elephant Yuki – Japanese for 'snow' – after also being headhunted for his skills, while Boon Ma also joined his friends to work with a variety of animals. Lord had previously been working at a camp in Pattaya, the same camp that his grandfather, kruba Ta'Mew, had once briefly worked at decades earlier. At that time camps were very basic, mainly offering rides and shows demonstrating traditional training methods, such as those used for logging. He was enticed to leave the camp and head to Japan in the hope that it would be a better job. 'It sounded like a good idea, but we were treated like slaves,' he explained. Most of the work was similar to what Thong Dii had been doing: training elephants for shows at the zoo, including for dancing, hoola hooping and soccer. Lord also worked in a number of roles for TV and film, where besides elephants he mainly worked with dogs; tigers and lions were Thong Dii's specialty.

The work at the zoo was exhausting. Besides training animals, Thong Dii and Lord performed many menial tasks such as cleaning cages and building enclosures and other infrastructure. They had poor accommodation and felt like they would freeze to death every winter when the snow blanketed the landscape in an eerie whiteness. Despite the difficult conditions, Lord stayed in the position for five years, although Yuki was sent back to Thailand after two. 'Her visa expired,' Lord said. 'But I couldn't come home. I needed to make money so my kids could get an education.'

Thong Dii remained at the zoo for ten years. 'I wanted to leave earlier,' he explained, 'but I couldn't justify leaving and going back home to no job.' Boon Ma had similarly joined Thong Dii and Lord at the zoo but left after four years to work in a restaurant, where he made double the money and experienced much better working conditions. In the end, he also stayed in Japan for a decade, far away from his family and culture.

After leaving Japan, the men returned home to Thailand where they found work again in tourist camps, street begging or as labourers. It was 2005 and Sarot was working at a camp in Hua Hin, where he first learned about a new elephant welfare initiative in Ban Ta Klang called 'Take Me Home', which was to begin on 1 January 2006. Established by the government-run Surin Elephant Study Center, Take Me Home was intended to incentivise Guay mahouts to return to Ban Ta Klang by providing them with a stable monthly income to keep their elephants on-site. The initiative was primarily intended to reduce the number of mahouts and elephants begging on the streets of cities around the country; four years later, street begging would be banned outright. For many mahouts, coming home to Ban Ta Klang was about much more than the money. 'They wanted the Guay mahouts to come back and rejuvenate the elephant culture,' Sarot explained. 'This meant we could come home and stay with our families.' Sarot returned to Ban Ta Klang in October 2005 and, along with other mahouts, set up a small forest rehabilitation project within the village to prepare for the influx of elephants. Soon, Thong Dii also returned home, where he joined Take Me Home with Fah Sai, taking on her care from his brother. Thong Dii was excited about the initiative.

'There had never been anything like it. It was a great opportunity for Guay men to come home and not have to go anywhere else to make a living.'

Sarot recalled what the Surin Elephant Study Center was like during the early stages. 'There were over two hundred elephants, but the centre was still being built, so it didn't look like much. It was a big empty space of dirt and a few trees, but they'd kept the Pakham Spirit House and were building houses for mahouts and shelters for elephants. Soon, many more mahouts were coming home. It felt more like the old days.' While the centre took a few years to be completed, the available construction work meant mahouts had an additional way to make money and stay with their elephants at the same time. But the initiative did not take off as well as the government had hoped. The money did not compare to what could be made in camps, and the eternal problem of elephant food remained. In the absence of natural food, the mahouts needed to grow or buy sugarcane and elephant grass, which was very costly. As a result, many of the mahouts who had come home headed back to camps with their elephants.

Staying in Ban Ta Klang became more profitable when the government developed the small-scale tourism venture within the village – including the circus and elephant rides – which offered additional income. This primarily occurred due to a government callout for free or cheap elephant food from the neighbouring villages and districts. As Sarot explained, 'People brought old banana trees, grass and rice stalks to the centre to give to the elephants for free. Then we'd offer elephant rides in return.'

The new form of elephant tourism in the village started to attract tourists, primarily Thais, who came to the village and contributed to the local economy. However, as Sarot noted, while these aspects of tourism were beneficial for the village, the new state of play was different to how the Guay had traditionally worked with elephants. 'When it comes to life, earning money is really important,' he said. 'We don't really have any knowledge about business, but we need to adapt to changes in capitalism involving elephants and find ways to support ourselves. We raised our elephants based on what we were taught by our ancestors, but things are different now. People whose livelihoods depend on elephants must find the best way to make money using what they have available.'

As well as the SESC, the Surin Project – which began in 2009 – offered new opportunities for Guay mahouts to make money while staying in Ban Ta Klang. As a pioneer of the project, Sarot was excited to work with the Save Elephant Foundation and the SESC to introduce volunteer tourism to the village. He and the other mahouts I interviewed all worked on the Surin Project at some stage, and each had experienced benefits from the initiative – primarily in the form of a greater income and the provision of elephant food. Lord noted that the elephants' welfare was much better as a result. 'Walking with them and observing them means much less stress for mahouts and elephants. It's more relaxing for the elephants and, because the tourists keep their distance, we don't need to control them so much. They get to do all their natural behaviours. You can tell they are happy because sometimes it's hard to get them out of the water, that kind of thing. They want to stay and play.'

Despite these benefits, the mahouts said they continued to worry about the health and welfare of their elephants. As much as they tried to ensure their elephants had time off their chains, walking through the forest or swimming and wallowing in the dams or rivers, they still had to manage and control their movements. As Thong Dii explained,

'In any situation where there are tourists around, you need to keep elephants under control. It's too dangerous otherwise.' Further, as Sarot explained, 'Environmental problems have the biggest impact on elephant welfare. The problems are a lack of space, good food and adequate living conditions. When elephant food is treated with pesticides it can become toxic, which hurts their stomachs. And the conditions here change their behaviour. It makes them more aggressive.' Sarot also explained that stereotypical behaviour was common, particularly among bulls, who were always difficult to control. 'You need to keep bulls separate. Young bulls fight with each other. They might also fight with older females or try to hurt younger ones. Bulls also know when you are scared and will try to control you. It's not easy to manage them in a place like this.'

Lord explained the importance of hanging onto the traditional ways of training elephants for the sake of their welfare. 'Mahouts who are too business focused might rush the training. You need to be patient with them. You don't want to injure them; it affects the relationship, and if they're hurt, you can't work with them. A young elephant should be at least three years old before you do any training, not one or two, like they do in some places.'

'The main problem is that tourists want to see baby elephants, or elephants painting, playing soccer – that kind of thing,' Thong Dii continued. 'So it's not just a problem with mahouts and training, it's up to tourists to change their behaviour, too.'

Along with worries about elephant welfare, Thong Dii, Sarot, Lord and Boon Ma spoke of their concerns about the future of Guay culture and elephant traditions, which they believed were in decline. As well as having a greater focus on money, the nature of traditional ceremonies also changed, becoming more of an attraction to people outside the village, including politicians who wanted to participate in the Guay's unique traditions for show. Lord also described changes to the village's Loi Krathong celebrations – the yearly festival across Thailand where lanterns are released into the sky and small rafts known as *krathongs* fashioned from banana leaves are sent down rivers carrying candles and incense as the villagers make wishes. 'In the past, the women of the village would spend almost a year weaving silk to make a dress to wear to Loi Krathong,' Lord told me. 'They put on makeup, wore combs and flowers in their hair, and made very intricate krathongs, but that doesn't happen anymore.'

The mahouts also explained how the sense of community had changed over the past few decades. 'We used to congregate a lot more and there was a lot more unity,' Sarot said. 'People would share ideas with one another and work together to solve any problem. It's different now – there's not much incentive to work together and share resources, so that aspect of our culture has changed a lot.'

'A lot of the daily cultural practices have also changed,' Lord continued. 'We would always listen to traditional music, but now it's just loudspeakers and pop music. We used to make food by hand – using a mortar and pestle to crush rice to make noodles; now people buy it ready made. And now everyone has a TV. When we were very young, there was only one TV in the village. It was black and white and operated via generator, and all the kids would congregate there to watch shows. Once electricity came here and technology was cheaper, everyone got their own colour TV, so there were fewer reasons to get together.'

More recently, there were notable changes in the village in the numbers of men interested in being mahouts. When Sarot, Thong Dii, Lord and Boon Ma were younger, almost all the men in Ban

Ta Klang would take on the role, but young men were moving away from mahoutship culture in a desire to pursue other opportunities. Many would leave the village to attend trade schools or universities, moving to cities like Surin, Bangkok and Chiang Mai. Many who grew up with elephants now viewed the family 'pet' as a burden and did not want to be saddled with the animal's care as they grew older and their parents passed away. All the mahouts I interviewed placed great importance on earning money to support their children's education in the hope that they could have a less difficult life than their parents and grandparents. This would evidently have consequences for the future of the Guay's elephants.

I talked to two teenage mahouts about their experiences working with elephants and their plans for the future, one who wanted to continue to work as a mahout and another who did not. Seventeen-year-old Teerachai Malignam and thirteen-year-old Chukiet Padpai both started working with elephants when they were young boys and, like the older mahouts, were taught by their fathers. 'I've always wanted to work with elephants,' Teerachai explained. 'I don't care much for school, so when I finish at the end of the year I am going to spend all my time with my elephant, Bua Ben. I think of him as my brother. Every day before and after school I feed him and take him either to a dam to play or I hose him down. Elephants love water, so this is important.' When Teerachai was younger, he would spend two months of school holiday every year learning elephant husbandry from his father at a high-end eco-resort called Anantara in Chiang Rai, which offers low-impact elephant experiences to tourists and a good income for mahouts (see Chapter 12).

'First, when I was very young, I'd just observe them,' Teerachai explained. 'I'd learn about their moods and behaviours and watch how the mahouts trained and rode their elephants. At first I was scared but once I learned how to ride, after my father helped me with my confidence, I learned how to give commands and how to work with elephants so that they don't become aggressive. Bua Ben, though he's a bull, is very gentle, so I'm lucky. I once worked with a dangerous bull and I didn't enjoy it. That bull hurt my father, so instead we got Bua Ben.'

I watched Teerachai with Bua Ben on many occasions and witnessed the love the teenager evidently had for his bull. Every day he could be spotted strolling with Bua Ben around the centre, the bull often having been doused amply in water from one of their daily baths or covered in a blanket of red dirt and mud from a swim in one of the dams. As we spoke, Teerachai stroked one of Bua Ben's tusks, showing me how perfectly formed they were. 'We think of Bua Ben as being like a movie star,' Teerachai told me. 'Other people think so, too, and bring their female elephants here to have his babies. He has about forty children.'

I asked Teerachai what life was like as a teenage mahout. 'My life is comfortable and easy. I'm doing what I love, so it isn't hard. I live with my family, so I don't need a house to rent or to buy food. I make a decent income from the government, so really I'd like life to continue like this.'

Teerachai then told me how other boys his age viewed mahout-ship. 'Not many kids want to be mahouts. A lot of people at school want to move away, to go to trade school or to university. They think that being a mahout is a dirty, tiring job. I don't think so; I think it's fun and important. And there are others like me, a few boys who want to be mahouts. They are the same as me, they go to school but in their free time they come here to look after the elephants. I hope that when the old mahouts retire there are enough young people who want to learn how to look after the elephants, and see what a good job it can be.'

Unlike Teerachai, young Chukiet Padpai did not want to be a mahout and looked forward to leaving Ban Ta Klang. His father had just taken the family elephant to Phuket, but he had spent several years working with elephants before then and had enjoyed it. 'My father taught me how to look after them by leaving me alone to watch them. We had a baby elephant named Noppagao, so I spent a lot of time watching him, or his mother, Kham Saen. Then I'd follow my father to go get grass and sugarcane and learned how to feed and wash Noppagao. I learned to ride Kham Saen, but I didn't feel that safe at first. My father would sometimes get up to sit behind me so I would feel more confident.'

Chukiet would help his father cut grass and sugarcane before and after school and would also help wash the elephant and clean up manure, but he worried this was taking time away from his school-work, for he had dreams of getting a further education. 'I want to leave Ban Ta Klang after I finish school so I can join the army and become a soldier. I want to get the highest education that I can and I'll be able to help my family by sending them some money.'

After many conversations with mahouts, I learned that both children and adults alike wanted the younger generation to leave their rural lifestyles for professional jobs. As Sarot explained, 'Most mahouts don't want their children to be mahouts. Better to educate the children, to send them to a university, so they have different, better opportunities.' This view echoes Richard Lair's finding that, 'among nearly 200 civil service mahouts, mostly sons of mahouts, ... not a single man wanted his own sons to follow in his footsteps and not a single son intended to do so.' As a result, the Guay people 'are the cultural equivalent of endangered species'.[165] Centuries of knowledge about elephant keeping may disappear as the Guay's traditional art of mahoutship declines. This also suggests that the Guay's elephants face a precarious future. With a life expectancy of around seventy to ninety years, many elephants will outlive their current mahouts. Most of the elephants on the Surin Project were under thirty years of age and their mahouts were on average over forty. Because of the limitations of releasing elephants into the wild or into sanctuaries, there is a dire need to find a long-term solution to manage and care for the captive population.

I had many discussions with Sarot about this problem and soon found that there was more than just the care of the current population at stake. The Guay still follow the old traditions of breeding their elephants, a practice that will only mean more elephants with fewer mahouts to care for them in the future. They believe it is important to breed elephants to ensure the longevity of the species, and Sarot was especially worried about the health of elephants impacting their reproductive capabilities. 'Elephants are not healthy like they were in the past. We're not sure that they will be strong or healthy enough to reproduce in the future, and we worry about them. I am not sure how long elephants will stay on this earth.'

I witnessed one birth while I was in Ban Ta Klang and saw how important the event was and how it brought the community together. Community involvement at these times could mean the difference between life and death for elephant calves. In February 2013, a calf was born in the village who almost drowned in amniotic fluid. She was resuscitated by her owner but faced an uncertain 48 hours in which her owner and other villagers tirelessly worked throughout the day and night to keep her breathing and on her feet. Her distressed mother trumpeted and roared almost non-stop over the two days and nights and was watched over by villagers. In coming together to assist with this difficult birth the villagers saved the calf, who when strong enough was able to feed on her mother's milk.

Elephant welfare advocates and conservationists in Thailand are concerned with the breeding practices of the Guay and other elephant tribes such as the Karen. These are not sustainable and appear to be a confluence of ancient practices and beliefs so ingrained that they are done without analysing future issues associated with increasing the captive population. If the culture of Guay mahoutship is on the decline, and the mahouts do not want their children to follow in their footsteps yet still want the elephants to reproduce to 'save' the species, there will be a new generation born into captivity without a clear plan for their long-term care. The difficult task of managing the captive elephant population in Ban Ta Klang will only become even more so.

What, then, is the solution to this problem? How can Guay practices be supported and their concerns considered when caring for the population means potentially further imperilling it? I agree with the argument against further breeding, yet at the same time also agree with that put forth by Fred Kurt, Khyne U Mar and Marion E. Garaï, that 'all captive Asian elephants are important for conservation, if one considers they account for 25–33% of the entire dwindling population of this species', including both within Asia and at zoos, conservation sites and sanctuaries in Western countries.[166] While there are places that are better prepared to breed elephants for conservation purposes than Ban Ta Klang, the village and its mahouts evidently could make an important contribution to conservation when focused on improving welfare, promoting reforestation and potentially encouraging young Guay to manage the existing population, though the latter may depend on mahoutship becoming a more profitable and 'noble' occupation. Indeed, as captive elephant management specialist Ingrid Suter contends, 'private elephant ownership is an untapped advantage for conservation', leading to possibilities where 'elephants can still live a safe and content existence alongside humans, bringing many benefits to the captive population as well as local communities'.[167] Ideally, there needs to be a balance between reducing the number of elephants born or living in captivity and the broader conservation of the species, though this will clearly be difficult to achieve.

The stories shared in the past three chapters demonstrate how mahouts consider elephants as 'kin who have agency' – family members affected by and affecting the socio-cultural, spiritual and ecological world of the Guay throughout history in a complex mutual coexistence.[168] The intimate knowledge Guay mahouts have of elephant management in an array of situations – from life before and after the forests, in tourist camps, and back again to a very changed village – mean they are uniquely placed to help guide the creation of new tourism ventures that are designed to uphold elephant interests. Guay mahouts might be brought into future discussions around captive elephant management by sharing their experiences of traditional mahoutship and their intimate understanding of the impact of deforestation.

My time in Ban Ta Klang showed me that the Surin Elephant Study Center and the Surin Project had the potential to revive the culture of Guay mahoutship. The SESC enabled families to stay together, which had the effect of renewing the village, and the small tourism industry that sprung up in Ban Ta Klang brought new revenue into the area, including from volunteer tourism, which has proved popular (there was rarely a shortage of volunteers on the project). By exerting their influence, the mahouts also guided the development of effective enrichment programs for the elephants that were also enjoyable for the volunteers. A degree of autonomy – combined with a decent income – could potentially improve the status of mahoutship, making it more lucrative and appealing. The strong involvement of mahouts also pointed to possibilities for the project to eventually be run independently by the Guay. Overall, the Surin Project was an excellent example of how, by involving local communities in decision-making processes, volunteer tourism can meet the interests of people reliant on tourism for their livelihood.[169] According to tourism theorists Stephen Wearing and Nancy McGehee, this 'ultimately provides a more positive platform for cross-cultural exchange between volunteer and host community' than more traditional forms of tourism.[170]

Welfare and conservation organisations across Thailand are already drawing on mahout knowledge to help manage captive elephants with the aim of supporting the traditional cultures of Indigenous peoples and caring for elephants in more optimal ways. One example is the Asian Captive Elephant Working Group, comprising elephant specialists, veterinarians, researchers, camp managers and conservationists who use scientific knowledge to address the current situation of elephants in tourism in ASEAN countries.[171] The group has a number of goals that will determine the future direction of captive Asian elephant management, including promoting positive elephant welfare practices; developing guidelines and support for camp managers and the public with a baseline for elephant care; encouraging good business practices within a variety of elephant management contexts; using accurately researched science; and promoting education and awareness among the public. Importantly, the group places a strong focus on respecting and maintaining traditions and cultures of mahoutship when developing effective and humane elephant management plans. Taken together, these goals demonstrate that tourism can be influenced by extensive research into elephant management practices alongside traditional mahoutship.

Another example is the Mahouts Elephant Foundation, which is working towards a Rescue, Rehabilitation and Rewilding (3R) model that relies on collaboration with Karen communities to manage elephants in traditional villages with surrounding areas of remaining forest. Like the Surin Project and Journey to Freedom, the aim of the model is to provide Karen mahouts with a financial and social incentive to bring their elephants home. They are able to 'return to more traditional roles as elephant and forest guardians' while still benefiting from tourism:

> The Karen mahouts patrol the forest and monitor elephant movement, reducing human-elephant conflicts. Karen mahouts develop ecotourism in their communities, guiding ecotourists into the forest habitat to observe the elephants unobtrusively. The 3R model brings the economic benefits back to those rural communities that coexist with elephants.[172]

Preliminary 3R model efforts have shown success, with elephants 'learn[ing] to navigate space and terrain, to forage for themselves on a host of native plant species, and to form natural social groupings

… stereotypic behaviors born of captivity and restricted space and activity begin to abate'. A similar model has been implemented by the Never Forget Elephant Foundation (NFEF) in northern Thailand, which also brought several captive elephants back home to traditional Karen villages where they are tended to by mahouts and their families as part of a sustainable solution that benefits both elephants and their natural environments. NFEF offers seven-day immersive experiences within the village, where tourists stay in traditional bamboo huts and observe elephants from afar. They follow elephants on foot through their natural surroundings and participate in community projects such as building structures and education programs for local children. They also learn about Karen culture, with their involvement supporting the local economy. As Nicolas Lainé succinctly explains, the aim is 'not just to rewild elephants in the forest … but to integrate their close human partners in this venture'.[173] By involving the holders of Indigenous knowledge within decisions that affect their lives and those of their elephants, this is an inclusive approach that has great potential to solve Thailand's 'elephant problem'.

* * *

Since my last visit in 2015, the Surin Project underwent several changes. The project's base, including infrastructure and housing for the volunteers as well as shelters for elephants, was relocated outside the Surin Elephant Study Center. Sarot was still the head mahout, and Ocha and several Thai coordinators managed the volunteers. Elephants and mahouts had come and gone, some returning to elephant camps in an effort to make more money, while others had come home from camps after leaving the project years ago. These

changes represent the natural ebb and flow of an animal conservation and welfare project working in a complex socio-cultural and
economic milieu, and the tricky balance between providing a more
'natural' environment for elephants and a livelihood for mahouts.
Despite these changes, there was plenty of evidence from recent volunteers and volunteer coordinators that the project was still achieving
its aims for some of Ban Ta Klang's elephants while also supporting
the local community.

Before the COVID-19 pandemic began, I believed that the Surin
Project might be able to support additional mahouts and elephants
while staying small and sustainable, and shifting to a wholly
community-run model. The project could have been replicated in
different locations around the village without increasing the number
of elephants roaming in one area. I discussed some other possibilities
for the future with Wills and Kirsty Sandlilands and my interpreter
Pum Boonwan, such as involving the Thai tourists who visit the SESC
in observational and walking activities in addition to or instead of
watching the circus or riding elephants. Volunteer tourism has not
yet become especially popular among Thai people, likely because of
the cost involved, which is far more affordable for foreigners than for
locals. But involving Thai day tourists – who visited Ban Ta Klang in
large numbers – would have been a way for the Surin Elephant Study
Center and the Surin Project to work collaboratively and provide
options for more mahouts to participate in enrichment activities
with their elephants. In a single morning or afternoon, these tourists
could also experience aspects of Guay community life, learn about
the culture and interact with elephants in lower-impact, welfare-
positive ways.

Chapter 10

BURM AND EMILY'S
ELEPHANT SANCTUARY

After leaving Ban Ta Klang in November 2014, I headed to Burm and Emily's Elephant Sanctuary (BEES), located in Mae Tan, a sub-village of Ban Thung Yao in the northern Mae Chaem region. A small, community-based sanctuary, BEES is nestled in a quiet valley between forested hills. Brilliant emerald-green grass and bamboo are thick on the ground in the sanctuary's fields, which provide ample grazing for elephants. A creek transects the property, meandering through the valley between granite boulders and fallen trees, burbling over mossy rocks, and leading anyone who follows it towards a gushing brown river deep enough to cover an elephant's entire body as they tumble and play in the water.

Mae Tan sits amidst a landscape that is part verdant and part arid, the result of land overuse. Areas have been cleared and appropriated for growing crops such as corn, leaving behind barren soil. Parts of the forest in the valley have also been cleared, the steep ground littered with fallen logs in a swathe of destruction. Yet BEES remains an oasis, a collection of huts, fields and forest in a serene world where visitors can experience what it is like to live with elephants. BEES boasts an interesting and informative volunteer program and charges a weekly sum that directly provides food for the elephants, an income for mahouts, funds for infrastructure development, and contributions to the village economy. Jobs undertaken by volunteers include cutting corn and sugarcane, cleaning the elephants' night yards, preparing fruit and vegetables for the elephants' consumption, and assisting with any building projects. Volunteers are involved in all daily activities with the elephants, which primarily include observation and walking with them through the valley and hills. They can also help out by caring for the numerous dogs and cats that have been rescued and live at the sanctuary.

The sanctuary's small size means that it can accommodate only a handful of volunteers every week, who become part of a close-knit group with plenty of opportunities to discuss elephants and the aims of the sanctuary with its founders, and to meet the mahouts and learn about what they do. With a relaxed schedule, volunteers also have time out in a tranquil environment between tasks where they can lie in hammocks and look over the green fields of the property. The two female elephants who lived at BEES at the time of my visit were Mae Jumpee (69 years old) and Mae Kham (54 years old), who were best friends. BEES founders Burm Rinkaew and Emily McWilliam provided the two aged elephants with retirement in a new home in which they did not have to work and could spend their days just being elephants.

After arriving at BEES in the early afternoon, having been picked up from my hotel in Chiang Mai by Burm and Emily that morning, my first encounters with the two elephants involved observing them as they grazed in the lush green fields. Along with Burm, Emily and one other volunteer, I sat low in the grass, observing the animals in as unobtrusive a way as possible. We watched them as they moved through the fields close by each other's side, with the freedom to wander around and make their own selection as to which grasses and bamboo were the most delicious, to scratch their bellies against branches and rough grass, to cover themselves in mud, and to communicate with one another acoustically and physically, rumbling and squeaking, rubbing up against and caressing each other.

One of the most profound parts of my experience at BEES was going on hours-long walks through the valley and forest with the elephants, which allow the elephants to explore their natural surroundings and for volunteers to observe their fascinating behaviours. On these walks, elephants could make many of the decisions about where they wanted to go and what they wanted to do. While gently guided by their mahouts, the elephants would go at their own pace, and we would follow. If they wanted to amble slowly, to take their time playing in the creek and the mud, they could. If they wanted to climb the steep sides of the valley and find the perfect selection of grass to munch on, they could. It was fascinating to see the choices they made given their relative freedom. Elephants are strangely adept climbers, and I was surprised to see them easily scale the hills around us, putting giant foot after giant foot as they ascended precarious inclines. They could stand there quite easily, their huge bodies somehow defying gravity. From those positions, high on the hills, they could contently eat and ignore us, because it was far harder for us to tackle those slopes.

Eventually, once the elephants descended to the creek bed, we could walk onwards towards the river. They would pick up the pace, knowing what was ahead. The power of the river was awe-inspiring. The strong current of brown-green water flowed in torrents through a thickly vegetated riparian environment. Standing barefoot on a shore of white sand and smooth pebbles, we watched the elephants wade into the water, revelling in the feel of the current against their bodies. They tumbled and played, diving headfirst down into the water, rolling around on the riverbed before rising up again, streams pouring from their backs, squeaking with joy. As I watched them, I thought of the conditions that most of Thailand's captive elephants live in, where such enjoyment and freedom was rarely possible. Here, at BEES, I could see what freedom for elephants really meant.

Over the next two weeks I would learn a lot about the sanctuary, its founders, its elephants and mahouts, and conducted a series of lengthy interviews with Emily. Herein, I recount everything I learned from her about the decision she and Burm made to set up the sanctuary, its aims and achievements, and their plans for the future. I will let Emily tell the story in her own words.

* * *

Burm is from Mae Tan, and I'm originally from the northern beaches of Sydney in Australia. We met at ENP in 2009 where Burm worked as a volunteer coordinator and my mum and I were volunteering. We became friends and kept in contact, and over the years, and my successive visits to Thailand, our friendship became a relationship. I had become extremely passionate about elephants and knew I wanted to help them in any way I could, and I wanted to do more than simply volunteer. Burm and I discussed the idea of starting our own sanctuary here in Mae Tan on Burm's family's land, and a plan slowly came together.

One of the first things I wanted to do in life was to work

with animals. My mum was the one who suggested going to ENP – she found it online and discovered that it was the main attraction in Thailand that was making a difference for animals. When we got to ENP we quickly learned that there was a pretty serious situation in Thailand in regard to the captive elephants, and I was inspired to help them. I'd had some experience volunteering with animals in Australia and found there were some similarities and some differences between my former experiences and what I got to do at ENP.

The ENP volunteer program was great. The routine worked well – cleaning elephant shelters, washing fruit and vegetables, and working on fences, those sorts of things. The work was not too hard, not too easy. I took a lot from it, both about what elephants need, but also about how much work is involved in looking after them. Feeding them fruit and vegetables shows you just how much they eat in a very small period. Cutting grass and corn shows you the strength of the mahouts and what they can actually do, and how it's a full-time job for them. You also see all these elephants who have been saved from a life of suffering, and what a big change it's made to their behaviour and their happiness.

From that experience I became determined to create something new to help elephants. We wanted to find a way to retire elephants to our property without buying them and to keep the owners involved in their elephants' lives. We wanted to give them an option to work with us and still earn money, but in a way that the elephants didn't have to work. Our plan was to make sure that elephants could enjoy a natural environment as much as possible, with the consideration that they still have to be secured during the night. The way that we've done this is through lease agreements. We've approached owners, offering to pay for them to keep their elephants here instead of taking them to camps. They sign contracts with us, which basically mean that they agree to keep their elephants here for one or two years. The way we afford to do this is through our volunteer program. All that money goes towards looking after the elephants, paying the mahouts, and any new infrastructure. It also supports the village; we believe it's very important to be not just accepted here but an integral part of the place, so we buy all our food – for both humans and elephants – locally, and we also make regular contributions to the village bank. We're not trying to make money out of it, we're just really trying to make a positive impact, to blend in, and help the community of both elephants and people as best we can.

Mae Kham was the first elephant to retire at BEES. It was the first time we successfully encouraged an owner to lease their elephant to us. It took nearly eight months to actually get people interested in what we were doing. During that time, there was a lot of going back and forth to tourist camps and various villages, and we learned a lot, looking at all of these places in different areas. In April 2012, Mae Kham's owner was very interested in moving her here after he found out about us. We ran into him in his village on our elephant research expeditions. He took us out to meet Mae Kham, and it took only a couple of weeks for him to call us and say that he wanted to retire her. Mae Kham lived in his village in a small area of forest near his house. The chain was of a reasonable length, but she was not being walked that often and she didn't have any other elephants around to interact with. She was in a camp for nearly two years and before that she worked in logging. She didn't do well in the trekking camp because she kept shaking tourists off her back, so she was considered dangerous. Her owner couldn't work her for that reason so he decided it would be better to bring her home to his village.

On 30 May 2012, after our negotiations with her owner were successful, we walked with Mae Kham to BEES from her village. It's about a 65-kilometre walk, and it was quite an incredible journey. We thought it was going to take three days, but she ended up doing it in two. She ran the whole way here. Somehow she knew she was walking to freedom. People from all the villages we passed through came out to see her, striding up and down the hilly roads with a determined expression on her face. It was something not many people around here had seen before, so it was very exciting.

As soon as she arrived, she just started eating. It was like she was seeing green grass for the first time. She could roam around and eat what she wanted and go down to the stream to play in the water and mud. Even though we had to chain her at night, she was free during the day, and it made a big difference to her personality. I guess people had thought of her as badly behaved, but she just needed a change in her circumstances. We sat down excitedly with her owner, who signed a one-year contract. Since then, he has always been happy to renew it. Just last month he signed a two-year contract again. He doesn't want Mae Kham to go back to work and he is happy to have her here, but he does want her to return home sometime in the next two years so she can take part in a spiritual ceremony, which is something we respect.

Elephants are a part of the Karen's spiritual traditions, and the ceremony isn't going to harm her, so we don't see any problem in him taking her home for a ceremony where she will be given a huge feast. I think it's fine to do that if it means at the end of the day she'll be coming back here, to a natural home where she can live freely and interact with her own kind. It's the same for all Karen hill tribe elephants as well – they are usually taken home once a year for a ceremony to bless the elephant and the village, so it brings good luck to them as well.

Two and a half months after Mae Kham's arrival, we were in negotiations to lease Mae Jumpee. She had also originally worked in logging before becoming a trekking elephant. She did well in the camps as she has quite a small build, easy for tourists to ride, and she was very well behaved. For the last three years of her life before she came to us, she lived in the bareback trekking camp in Thai Elephant Home, which is in Mae Taeng. While she had been there for three years, she had only worked for them for a year and a half. She couldn't carry tourists anymore – she was getting old and too weak and tired and was too slow out on the walks.

The owner of the camp built a large corral so that she could roam around freely, and he told her owner that he thought it was time to retire her. The camp owner – who had learned about our work – told him about us and what we do here. The owner came down to see the place and saw how happy Mae Kham was, and decided to move Mae Jumpee here. She arrived on 15 August 2012. Like Mae Kham's owner, Mae Jumpee's owner is happy for her to be here but would like for her to go home for a ceremony now and then as well.

It's interesting what freedom does for captive elephants. When they first arrived they were both inquisitive, but also standoffish and afraid to try new things. Their world had been very limited and they hadn't necessarily had good experiences with humans. Now, they've changed a lot. They can pretty much do whatever they want and are very happy roaming around, eating and exploring every day. They have their heads held high. They are proud to be elephants. They still live in a human world but being here has made a huge change in their lives.

We were quite concerned about how Mae Kham would react when Mae Jumpee arrived. Mae Jumpee had had a lot of interactions with other elephants in the camp, so she was socialised and comfortable with others. But she was also more than happy to be by herself. We released her into the grass fields the day after she arrived, after she'd had a night's rest, and she quite happily grazed. She had no interest in communicating with Mae Kham. She was just enjoying the fact that she could do whatever she wanted. But we needed to introduce them and have them get to know each other. This was fairly nerve-wracking for us.

Burm asked Mae Kham to follow him down to the grass fields. He hung onto the small rope around her neck, guiding her to the fields then letting her go. He told her, 'Look around, smell, do whatever you want, everything is fine, don't be afraid!' When Mae Kham came across Mae Jumpee's manure, she freaked out. Remember, she hadn't had any interaction with other elephants for years. She trumpeted, screamed, ran away, and it was really difficult to get her back.

It took over two hours to settle Mae Kham down and try to introduce her to Mae Jumpee again. Meanwhile, Mae Jumpee was still happily eating, not caring that much about what this emotional elephant was doing. We tried again – Burm led Mae Kham down to the fields, and Mae Kham once again smelled Mae Jumpee's manure. She stepped back, and then took two steps forward, very unsure. We were in front of her, calling to her, saying, 'Come on Mae Kham, it's okay, come down.' We got her to a point where Mae Jumpee was in her view and then we hid in the grass watching them. It was very stressful. We definitely worried that something terrible could happen, that they wouldn't get along and would fight.

Mae Kham slowly made her way down to Mae Jumpee, who was at that moment munching on Burm's father's bamboo, which he'd planted three years before and was lovely and thick. She was completely destroying it but that was fine – she was very content. Mae Kham made her way down there to the bamboo and cautiously walked over to Mae Jumpee. Elephants communicate a lot with touch and smell, and manure is an important part of that. So often when they meet for the first time, elephants will touch each other's anuses with their trunk to learn about the other elephant. The moment she touched Mae Jumpee's anus, Mae Kham just went crazy. Her vocalisations were so loud they shook the ground. It was just incredible. It felt and sounded like a truck rally was going on in the grass fields! But while Mae Kham was out of her mind with excitement and apprehension, Mae Jumpee was cool and calm, wondering what all the fuss was about. They then both started sniffing each other, rubbing their bodies against each other, touching and talking. Ever since that day they've been inseparable. Even if they get separated just a little bit – if Mae Kham can't see Mae Jumpee because she is behind some trees, for instance – Mae Kham sounds a very deep rumble, and when she gets a response, she just goes straight to her.

Mae Kham struggled recently when Mae Jumpee had to go to the elephant hospital in Lampang, two hours from here. Mae Jumpee had an obstruction in her gut and they needed to remove it manually. That was the first time they were separated since they met, and it was terribly hard for Mae Kham. She really needs constant interaction, especially as she was denied it for so long. Elephants are known for their tight social structure, so to have gone from no interaction to making such a strong friendship, then not having her friend for the six days she was in hospital would have been terrible for her. But to see them back together again, it was like nothing had changed.

I like to describe their relationship as a granddaughter with her little nanny, because Mae Jumpee is slightly smaller in shape and form than Mae Kham, and because of their age difference. It's been interesting to see how their relationship has developed. We always thought that Mae Jumpee would automatically be the matriarch, but generally Mae Kham is in control, unless there is some sort of danger or some sense that something could possibly be wrong, and then she defers to Mae Jumpee. Mae Kham has great respect for Mae Jumpee, but if there are treats or snacks involved, Mae Kham happily pushes Mae Jumpee aside. She'll be the first to receive them and she doesn't like to share. Mae Jumpee is very gentle and she doesn't like to fight, so she just hangs back and lets Mae Kham eat and takes what she can get. Once there is nothing left, Mae Kham goes back to being Mae Jumpee's friend rather than her competitor, and everything returns to normal.

They've adapted very well to being elephants, and to working out their place in the world where they're not being made to do things for humans all the time. They've changed both individually and together, building their relationship, and I think that's what's been so powerful to observe. Their own individual personalities were so different before they met each other because of their circumstances. That's particularly the case for Mae Kham, who was seen as this dangerous elephant.

When we first met Mae Kham, she was sad, her head hung low, the end of her trunk just lay on the ground, not moving. She was a depressed-looking elephant. But now she's got her head held high, she's very boisterous and cheeky, she loves to trumpet from the rooftops that she is the boss, and she's very sassy. She really loves to proclaim loudly: 'I'm right, you're wrong, I can do what I want!' When she wants to listen she will, and when she doesn't, she doesn't. We're just happy that it's up to her to make decisions about her life as much as she can.

Sometimes, when Mae Kham is feeling full of herself, Mae Jumpee will put her in her place. Mae Jumpee has also changed because, although living in the corral at Thai Elephant Home was okay, she still had never experienced freedom on a greater level. Ever since she's been living here, she's also become more confident. She's always been very shy, but she's become very different now that she can make her own decisions. Now her freedom means access to different types of grasses and other food, the space to breathe and to take in her environment and make it hers. Ultimately, they've both really stepped into the role of doing what they want.

Mae Kham and Mae Jumpee definitely have a particular type of relationship and we love watching it evolve. They are very entertaining to watch, and we always think, 'Why would you want to ride them when you can sit here and watch them all day?' That's really what our volunteer program is about – the focus is on observing and learning about elephant behaviour rather than riding them. I think really that most people want animals to be happy and treated well, they just don't know any other way. So it's great that there are more places now that are providing alternatives, and we're very proud to be making an important contribution in that sense.

Something that was very important to us was hiring responsible mahouts who would take really good care of the elephants. The lease contract we have with the owners doesn't involve the owners themselves, who aren't necessarily mahouts, so we needed to find mahouts from elsewhere. It's been a long process because it's hard to find mahouts who are willing to try new ways of working with elephants not in a camp, because it's very different working with them out in nature. I think they think it will be more dangerous, because they've worked with them one way their whole lives and making a change seems scary. That went on for a year, and we started to think that we would never be able to find anyone suitable. But I am very, very happy about where we are today because we now have two excellent mahouts – Aner and Pong.

Pong was here first, before Aner. Mae Jumpee had been here for about three months when we first met him. We were never too worried about finding a mahout for Mae Jumpee because she's a very gentle, laid-back, easygoing elephant. She's happy to do what you ask of her, she's happy to be out there grazing in the grass fields, and if you want her to have a bath, or give her treatments, she's usually very good. And because Mae Jumpee and Mae Kham go everywhere together, we thought it could even work to just get one mahout in to take care of both of them.

Ideally we thought two people would be better, but it was very difficult to find two at the same time that weren't always at loggerheads with one another, always arguing about who knows what and who knows best. But at the end of the day, there were never going to be that many mahouts who had the experience we wanted because there aren't many places in Thailand that are like this, that offer this kind of environment for both mahouts and elephants to live in. So there was no way that mahouts from around here would necessarily know how to work in a sanctuary environment.

We were very lucky to find Pong – or really, for him to find us. About three months after Mae Jumpee arrived, Pong had returned home to Mae Tan after some time away in Chiang Mai, where he was helping his mother with her farm. He saw what we were doing and was so interested in the elephants that he decided to set up a tent in one of the volunteer houses, where he stayed for about three weeks. He intended to go back to Chiang Mai where he wanted to work as a carpenter, but he had trouble finding work that was properly paid and that actually respected him for who he was.

Pong is a bit different. He's not the same as everybody else. He might not pick things up that 'normal' people do, but he excels in areas that 'normal' people might not. He's very visual. You can't ask him to write a mathematical equation and solve it, but if you put a Rubik's cube in front of him, he can complete it in five minutes. He just excels in different areas. He's very quiet and he's been treated badly by a lot of people because he is a little bit different. Coming here, setting up his tent, and entering this environment was life changing for him. It gave him purpose. He wasn't scared of the elephants at all; they're massive creatures and can be intimidating, but he was out in the fields with them every day, just enjoying their company.

One day he asked if he could come with us on one of our walks to the river, and we were very happy for him to come along. We realised quickly that he had a special connection with Mae Jumpee. There was something about the way they interacted with each other that was unique. He was so gentle with her and she respected him for that. She gave him security and happiness and warmth. He had never had those things before. He was perfect for her. We'd tried for so long to find someone suitable and he just fell into our hands. It was definitely fate. He's not really a mahout because he's never had that training. He's more just somebody who takes care of Mae Jumpee. You might consider a mahout to be the 'boss', but Pong is just Mae Jumpee's friend. He's not forceful. He's just a kind boy who needed something in his life, and Mae Jumpee is his something.

Aner came to us in February 2013. Mae Kham's owner brought him here; they come from the same village. At first I felt intimidated by him, as he was very loud and obnoxious, and I thought, *He's just going to be like everyone else.* But he's changed so much. He's Burmese and he's had a terrible life. He crossed the Burmese border when he was thirteen. He saw his family murdered and was forced to become a child soldier. He and his friend escaped and crossed the border, where they fell into the hands of a government official, who fortunately took them in and got them registered. So he's been very lucky in that sense, but he's had so many bad things happen to him.

When I think about what Aner went through, and what lots of people go through, I think about how we must not rush to judge people. We've definitely seen people treat themselves and others badly, including elephants, but so much of this behaviour comes from their past lives and their experiences. If they're angry and upset, they bring that to work. That's what you see a lot in tourist camps – men who for whatever reason have had a terrible life and take it out on their elephants. Of course, we didn't want anything like that to happen here. Aner understood what we were trying to do here and how elephants needed to be treated. But it was extremely different to anything he'd ever done before and it took him a long while to settle in. It took about three months until he really became focused on the job. Now he's really taken on the role, and we see him as the ideal mahout.

We know how fortunate our elephants are to live in the forest. We know that it won't be possible to release all the captive elephants into the wild. That would require millions of dollars, not just to put the land aside, but to employ rangers to protect the forests and be prepared to take on the poachers. Even if it were to happen, there isn't enough forest to contain all the captive elephants in Thailand. We very much believe that alternative solutions to tourist camps are needed for the future and that the bigger picture means using sustainable, community-based forms of tourism.

BEES is a small sanctuary, but things are working well in that we have interest from tourists and locals, and we can work with both groups to develop ourselves. It's really important to involve the local community and we're very open to them coming in and meeting the elephants, or talking to us about what we do, and focusing on protecting the environment. Sometimes the local kids will come to feed the elephants, and we'll get to teach them about elephants and about the forest. We let people come and visit when they want. We also allow people onto the property to go fishing, so we haven't taken their access to the river away. Sometimes we go for walks with people in the community to collect rubbish that accumulates along the river in the rainy season. Last year we organised for three hundred trees from the Forestry Department to be brought here in big trucks so we could have an education day planting trees on the protected temple land up in the village.

We've found that people really want to be involved. There are always talks and discussions and everyone in the village is very interested in what we do. They are starting to come in and ask us for help with their animals. We provide free rabies vaccinations for their cats and dogs if they need them, and antibiotics. That's something else that comes out of the weekly cost of the volunteer project. We also take a hundred baht from the weekly cost and put it into the village bank. We also want to directly involve the community in the volunteer program through a homestay program, which is slowly picking up. This means that the volunteers can stay in the village in the houses of local people, where they can eat with them and learn about their culture. The owners of the homestays earn a wage every night that someone stays in their house, and another hundred baht from each volunteer staying in a homestay goes into the village bank.

The village bank provides money that can be used in an emergency; say if a fire comes through that knocks out the water pipes, we can get the pipes replaced with the money we've donated. The villagers want to build a temple one day, up on the protected land where we've been planting trees with their help. Now, we'd really like to work with the villagers to raise the funds to build the temple. At the moment, the closest temple is two and a half hours walk away, and often there aren't enough trucks to take everyone there, and sometimes some of the elderly folk end up walking the whole way. It would be so good for there to be a community temple that everyone can be a part of. We feel that if we can help them with the temple then we can show them that we respect their local cultures and religion, and that we want to be a part of the community. The temple will become the hub of the village, the place where we can all gather.

It's really important that we respect the village and the

people who live in it. This means letting them know if we are going to do anything that affects them. When we walked Mae Kham through here, we alerted the villagers, as it could potentially have been dangerous to have her racing through. They were waiting for her with bananas and sugarcane in baskets by the side of the road. We didn't expect them to do that. We just told them that we were coming through at this particular time, so just be careful. But they were really excited about her coming and wanted to be part of it. It was something unique and special for them.

Involving the community has had benefits for everyone. The community has only ever been positive about us being here, and we've done our best to become part of the village and to be a force for good. We've got a long way to go in terms of involving the community more, and we need the money to do it. But we have a lot of ideas about what we want to do to help them, it's just going to take a bit of time.

For Burm and me, the future of elephant tourism involves developing sustainable programs and projects that involve communities and mahouts. It's a shame that elephants are still being used for tourism but there's really no alternative. I mean, even here, we only survive because of tourists. Just having elephants is tourism. But you can be involved in tourism and put the needs of the elephants first, treating them with care and simulating a natural environment as much as possible.

We want to continue to grow and to bring more elephants here, but we want to remain sustainable and small because things work very well here on a smaller scale, and it means we don't have to worry about overusing the land. I wish we could take in many more elephants but we can only manage a handful. That's a problem everywhere in the country. There just isn't the space. We're not saving the world by any means, but we'll do as much as we can to help as many elephants as we can, while also supporting our mahouts and the local villagers. That's the best way we can make a difference here, just doing what we can as a small sanctuary to be part of a bigger movement.

* * *

Some things have changed since my visit to BEES. Sadly, in February 2017, Mae Jumpee's owners decided to move her from BEES to a tourist camp to keep her daughter company. While she would not be working in the camp, the conditions she would be living in would be very different to those in which she spent many years in happy retirement. Rather than living amidst the tranquil forests, she would be back in a busy location, surrounded by crowds. The loss of Mae Jumpee led Burm and Emily to consider whether it would be better to buy elephants rather than lease or rent them from their owners. As Emily explained, on the one hand, buying an elephant could cause issues if owners decide to replace that elephant with another and send her to work in a tourist camp, therefore starting the cycle again. On the other hand, as the case of Mae Jumpee shows, renting an elephant may mean that the owners take the animal back after BEES has provided long-term rest and health care. Further, after integrating with the small herd at BEES, the elephant is then removed and loses her social bonds as well as all her opportunities to roam and forage. While buying is a costly enterprise, so is renting an elephant, at around 20,000–30,000 baht (approx. US$700–1,000) a month.

Distraught at the loss of her companion, Mae Kham has been lucky to find a new best friend in a new addition to the sanctuary – Mae Dok, an older elephant who had been part of a Karen family for almost sixty years. Mae Dok once worked in logging; after the ban, she worked in tourism for decades before her owner, an elderly lady named Mee, moved her home to live by her property in northern Mae Hong Son. Mee was very attached to Mae Dok and did not want to retire her, but her children recognised the elephant's need for freedom and socialisation and decided to send Mae Dok to BEES in March 2019 after Mee passed away at the age of 108. Today, Mae Dok lives in happy retirement among the green fields, after connecting almost instantly with Mae Kham. The two are now inseparable. Since my visit, BEES had also taken in three other elderly female elephants – Boon Yuen, Mae Mor and Fluffy, each who died at an old age after being cared for lovingly by everyone involved in the sanctuary.

BEES is also home to Thong Dee, and elderly elephant on her last set of teeth; elephants go through six sets in a lifetime. Her devoted mahout Or Kham shreds her feed, peels bananas, feeds her figs by hand and cuts banana trees into manageable pieces, as well as guiding her to the best foraging sites around the sanctuary. Thong Dee was best friends with Boon Yuen. Since her death, Thong Dee has not really connected with Mae Kham or Mae Dok; however, she and Or Kham are strongly attached, and their relationship and Thong Dee's retirement will allow the elephant to live out her remaining years respected, loved and cared for.

BEES has also shifted to a strictly hands-off policy after originally offering tourists opportunities to wash and feed elephants. This has had the effect of providing their elephants with a more natural experience of their habitat, with tourists observing from a distance. By offering a fully observational program, BEES has precipitated a further shift in Thailand's elephant tourism industry, now reflected in broader changes taking place in other elephant sanctuaries across the country.

Burm and Emily have also secured new land in Mae Tan that they have protected from further deforestation, which now provides more ample space for Mae Kham, Mae Dok and Thong Dee to roam, forage and socialise. BEES has also built an observation tower and has worked towards developing fenced enclosures for elephants to be corralled in, eliminating the need for chains or other restraints. Their work is a shining example of how elephant tourism can be re-oriented to respect elephants, elephant people and the local culture. By encouraging locals to help in the running of the sanctuary, supporting the villagers themselves, and working collaboratively with Karen families who own elephants, Burm and Emily are forging a path of elephant tourism that retains the cultural integrity of the village while also liberating elephants. BEES operates as a sustainable, ethical example of elephant tourism in Thailand that is supported by volunteer funding and labour and allows elephants to experience life in near-natural surroundings. It approximates what Kurt, Mar and Garaï suggest should be 'a preferred solution for maintaining elephants'. In their view, an ethical future for elephants in captivity would be best achieved through the creation of the following types of spaces:

Large areas of at least a quarter of a kilometer could be fenced and furnished with adequate sources of water and shady places to become a home for orphaned, surplus, dangerous, or otherwise problematic elephants. Elephants kept in such elephant parks have to be given supplementary foods and regularly checked by veterinarians. Apart from this, contacts between men and these elephants should be reduced to a minimum.[174]

As those authors explain, such a model has been successful in elephant management in South Africa, and 'it would be worthwhile for Asia-based elephant managers to learn about this from South African experts'. Indeed, it appears that the methods of management practised by Burm and Emily – from allowing ample time for roaming, foraging, socialising and playing throughout the day, to building enclosures and moving towards observation-only tourism – already make them experts in caring for captive elephants. The work of BEES also parallels elements of the Rescue, Rehabilitation and Rewilding model presented by the Mahouts Elephant Foundation, whereby elephants may be guarded by their mahouts and observed at a distance by tourists, but are otherwise able to experience agency and autonomy in the forest. In particular, by shifting towards observation-only tourism, BEES has forged a new path with significant benefits for elephants. As part of a broader movement towards more ethical tourism, BEES demonstrates how sanctuary operators, tourists and locals can work together to improve elephant lives.

Chapter 11

THE SURIN ROUND-UP AND BAN KRABUEANG YAI

I n 2015 I attended the Surin Elephant Round-Up – the famous festival that the Guay mahouts had told me about during our interviews. Held every November, the round-up brings several hundred elephants from around Thailand to Si Narong Stadium in Surin city for a three-day event. It epitomises Thailand's contemporary elephant culture, where elephants are tourist attractions and their historical uses have been appropriated into performances and parades. I planned a visit with my latest interpreter and research assistant Nong Wongvanich, who had organised a multitude of interviews with fascinating people in various locations. In Surin, Nong and I stayed in a small guesthouse not far from the city centre on a narrow road that buzzed with motorbikes, bicycles and numerous tourists. The round-up, to which the Guay had brought their elephants for decades, was one of the most lucrative events in the calendar for mahouts around the country.

On the first day of the festival, Nong and I attended the annual Elephant Feast, held along the streets leading to Si Narong Stadium, two-lane thoroughfares of shops, street stalls and houses. Several city blocks were lined with a stretch of tables laden with mountains of fruit and vegetables. These delicacies included bundles of bananas, armfuls of pineapples, piles of sugarcane, and baskets overflow-ing with watermelons, pumpkins, cucumbers, potatoes and yams. Behind the tables stood an excited assemblage of tourists and locals awaiting the spectacle, many from local schools, shops and other or-ganisations who had contributed to the feast.

Soon after ten in the morning, the elephant parade began. Dozens of elephants, many dressed in colourful attire including headdress-es, coloured robes, garlands of flowers, and decorated howdahs and blankets, ambled down the road accompanied by mahouts, some astride the elephants, others walking beside them. Many mahouts were traditionally attired in *chut thai* (formal dress) comprising *chong kraben* (wrap-around cloth pants) and a *ratcha pateen* (a Nehru-style shirt or jacket), as well as colourful head wraps, some made from locally sourced silk. Ambling alongside the tables, the elephants snatched fruit and vegetables with their trunks, crunching and munching on the delicious treats before continuing their way down the road, much to the delight of onlookers.

Nong and I watched the procession from behind the tables in relative safety, for there were quite a number of bulls and we were happy to keep our distance. Calm as they were – despite being near each other – I was vividly aware of just how quickly bulls could charge. As I marvelled at the bulls' decorum, I also stared in bemuse-ment at tourists contentedly walking among the elephants; between two bulls, patting and pulling at trunks, stroking tusks and testing the pointy bits, jumping into the middle of the road to take photos. They appeared blissfully unaware of the potential danger. The Guay mahouts have told me that almost every year, someone is seriously injured or dies at the round-up. Some mahouts refuse to attend, stressing how dangerous it is to have so many bulls in the one place, especially as many of the animals are not properly socialised and find interactions with others stressful. Fortunately, no one was injured at the feast, but not for want of trying.

At midday, Nong and I stood in a patch of shade in the bleachers of Si Narong Stadium, watching a reenactment of the Burmese-Siamese wars of 1547–49. Mahouts wielding swords, bows and arrows, and long golden spears rode highly decorated elephants in displays of the elephants' prowess and skill and traditional battle manoeuvres. The heat was oppressive, and as I sucked down my third coconut water of the day in an attempt to ward off dizziness, I wondered how the elephants were faring in the stadium all day, performing for us. The battle was soon over and a new troupe of elephants took their place – two teams of five for a soccer game, one in red and the other in yellow. We watched the lumbering pace of the game for a while, the elephants directed by their mahouts to chase the ball this way and that, aiming to boot it through one of the goals on either side of the stadium.

Needing respite from the heat and noise of excited spectators, Nong and I made our way around the outskirts of the stadium, where elephants and mahouts rested in the shade. While many elephants looked in fair health, others had ribs showing through their hides. Some had head wounds encrusted with blood and purple antiseptic spray, the product of being hit with hooks. Others were streaked in days-old manure and urine. One female elephant had a badly injured, possibly broken leg; I found out later that negotiations were being made between animal welfare advocates and the elephant's owner to purchase and rescue her.

We were accosted by several mahouts who demanded money in return for photos with their elephants or for bunches of sugarcane.

I recalled what my friends in Ban Ta Klang had told me about less experienced mahouts who cared more about money than elephant welfare. My direct interactions with mahouts so far had largely been positive, and it would have been easy to romanticise mahoutship when viewed through this lens. However, these negative experiences – along with the instances of neglect and cruelty I'd seen in Ban Ta Klang – reminded me that the quality of mahoutship ranged across a spectrum and that not all mahouts strived for the same welfare outcomes. To me, the pushiness of those mahouts worked against their interests. Annoyed by the confrontation, I gave them a wide berth, and observed other tourists doing the same.

We came across an old friend – the enormous, powerful, half-white Thong Bai, whose tusks almost scrape the ground. Thong Bai had been painted white as the festival's star and showpiece and festooned with gold and red finery, a long drape of cloth over his back and decorative ribbons adorning his tusks. Nong chatted to his mahout, who was similarly attired in red and gold, and asked him why Thong Bai was so well behaved despite all going on around him. The mahout had asked the spirits for their blessing to attend the festival; they had offered it, meaning he could attend in the knowledge nothing would go wrong. Having already met Thong Bai and heard about his unlucky mahouts, I appreciated how much spiritual approval could mean. Luckily for Thong Bai's mahout, the blessing appeared to have worked and Thong Bai behaved decorously for the remainder of the festival, stoically enduring hordes of tourists and endless photography.

That evening, Nong and I met Lek at Thong Tarin, an ageing grandiose hotel near the centre of town where she and her team of vets and media assistants were staying. We chatted in the marble-walled lobby, sitting on brown velveteen Victorian armchairs uncomfortably close to two enormous tusks pointing upward from the floor, their length rivalling those of Thong Bai's. Fortunately, these were not real ivory. Lek had spent the day monitoring the welfare of elephants, and had time to chat for a few minutes, so I made the most of it, talking with her about her experiences in Surin. She told me she rescued one or two elephants a year, selecting them based on the seriousness of their welfare issues. Elephants with injuries, those with poor health, and those that were aged were all candidates for rescue. After negotiating with an elephant's owner, which could take hours to days and involve attending to specific cultural sensitivities, she would buy the elephant and transport it to Elephant Nature Park by truck. Such was the case with Mae Bua Loy, the female elephant I had seen released into ENP's welcoming herd in 2008.

The next day, Nong and I took to the streets of Surin to find mahouts to interview. Now informed about the world of Guay mahoutship, I was interested in how other Indigenous groups with cultural and spiritual relationships with elephants engaged in tourism practices. I was also interested to understand the mahouts' perspectives on the festival given that the Guay mahouts had told me that they no longer took part. As Sarot had explained, 'The festival used to be really fun. Everyone wanted to come and take part, and people would come from many different provinces. It was a good excuse to come home if you'd been working elsewhere.'

Lord had told me what the experience had been like when they were younger. 'We'd walk to Surin with children from every village we passed through following us the whole way. They were really excited to see the elephants. The walk would take a few days, and we'd stop along the way to hunt or fish. Then we came to the city, where we stayed in army barracks with the elephants on-site. The next week would be really busy – organising elephants for processions and shows.'

Thong Dii had explained why they no longer took part in the festival. 'It's too dangerous now. Too many tourists, too many elephants. It's exhausting for them and us, and the money isn't really worth the effort.' The mahouts had told me that there were generally fewer older mahouts participating in the festival, with younger men more likely to attend. 'They might have more energy or need more money,' Sarot had said.

After walking around the back end of Si Narong Stadium, Nong and I soon met Supol, a 35-year-old Lao Isan mahout who was selling sugarcane to tourists to feed his four-year-old female elephant Nuando. Supol was from the village Ban Krabueang Yai in Chumphon Buri district, east of Surin city, and had been around elephants since he was born. Similar to the Guay, he had learned mahoutship from his male relatives, primarily from his brother, with his family having kept elephants since his grandparents' generation. The Lao Isan are also an elephant people and may not be just Lao but rather a mix of ethnic Lao and ethnic Guay.[175] Indeed, as I found, there were many similarities between the stories of the Guay and those of the Lao Isan mahouts. Supol also described Nuando in familial terms, as 'my own daughter'. He explained that he had bought Nuando as a calf and had brought her to the festival for three years, where he made money for elephant food and his own income. As he explained: 'Normally, working with Nuando makes me six to seven hundred baht each day, but at the festival I make one to two thousand baht daily. Nuando eats around two hundred kilograms of food per day. I mainly buy her sugarcane and grass, spending thousands of baht per day [on good food] because eating too many bananas and cucumbers can give her diarrhoea.'

He also explained that his usual work involved taking Nuando to offer rides or beg for food in Surin, Buriram or nearby Sagaew. Working as part of a team, he explained that they split the income between them, but that 'the most important team member is Nuando.' As two more Lao Isan mahouts came over to offer sugarcane for forty baht, I bought some more for their elephants and chatted with them about their experiences attending the round-up. One usually offered rides or begged with his elephant locally, while the other worked in a tourist camp but came to the round-up every year to make money.

While on a break from interviews, I spoke to two American tourists who were interested to know why a Westerner was sitting in a gutter writing notes surrounded by elephants. Their names were Jim and Barb and they had come to Thailand specifically for the round-up. They had dreamed of seeing the festival since watching YouTube videos of the reenactments and had loved seeing them firsthand. They were staying in a hotel quite close to Si Narong Stadium and had spent most of the past two days wandering around the festival looking at elephants. They had enjoyed the Elephant Feast immensely, walking among the elephants along the length of the procession, and assured me that they had kept their distance but taken lots of photos. When I told them about my research, Jim and Barb looked at each other in consternation. 'We saw some elephants behind the stadium that didn't look too good,' Barb told me. 'And we've been hassled all day, but I feel bad for the elephants and guilty for some reason, so we've bought so much sugarcane.'

'It's really been great,' Jim noted, 'but I'm not sure if it's exactly what we expected. It's been cool to see all the elephants and some of the reenactments have been just spectacular, but it's been very hot and we're kind of exhausted. I think it would be nice to see them in a bit of a lower key situation, somewhere where they're not working so hard.' I mentioned to Jim and Barb that there was a number of places where they could see elephants in Thailand doing just that and wrote down a few recommendations. After the festival they would be heading up to Chiang Mai for a few days and said they might check out Elephant Nature Park or one of the smaller projects offered by the Save Elephant Foundation. As they wandered off, heading back to their hotel for a break, I wondered if the proliferation of alternatives to traditional forms of elephant tourism like the round-up would mean that more and more Western tourists went elsewhere. I also wondered whether the thousands of Thai tourists who attended the round-up every year might be similarly encouraged to visit different elephant tourism sites. As previously mentioned, volunteer tourism has not taken off in any significant way among Thais. The majority of Thai tourists I had seen on my journey had been those watching the circuses or going for rides in Ban Ta Klang. These people were fairly local to the village, usually from neighbouring provinces.

My observations in Surin showed me that the number of Thai tourists far outnumbered Westerners, yet I had never investigated the experiences of non-Indigenous Thai people participating in elephant tourism. I realised I had a small opportunity to do so after returning to the guesthouse that evening. There were around ten Thais staying in neighbouring rooms; this included two friends named Tip and Som who were visiting from Ubon Ratchathani, a city east of Surin. In conversations that were a mix of Thai and English, we discussed their reasons for visiting the round-up, which primarily related to the cultural significance of the event. Tip explained that she had been to the round-up multiple times since she was a child. 'In Thailand, elephants have a lot of importance, and my parents always taught me that it was good to be around them,' she explained. 'I like to come here still because it's one place where you can see elephants and many other things that teach you about Thai culture.'

Som shared his own view of the festival. 'I like watching the elephants, but I also like the experience of being here. It has an exciting feeling to it, with so many people from so many places. You get to see a lot of historical and cultural things and it's a celebration of Thai people's love for elephants.' Tip and Som were interested in my research and shared what they knew about the newer forms of elephant tourism, such as sanctuaries. 'I do know that there are new places to see elephants now, like in Chiang Mai,' Tip explained. 'I haven't been to any; I'm interested to go, but I wouldn't usually go to Chiang Mai for a holiday. If I want to go somewhere, I'd go to Bangkok, or maybe Koh Samet [a small island in the Gulf of Thailand] if I wanted to go to the beach.'

Som concurred. 'It's unlikely I would volunteer at an elephant sanctuary if I wanted a holiday. Maybe if I was in Chiang Mai, I'd go for the day. I haven't really thought about it.'

* * *

On the final day of the festival I spoke to several more Lao Isan mahouts about deforestation and whether it was an issue in Chumpon Buri district, where the men had grown up and still lived. Each had agreed that the loss of the forests had had negative consequences for Lao Isan people and their elephants. Nong and I were invited to visit the men's village. Like Nuando's mahout Supol, they lived in

Ban Krabueang Yai, so we made arrangements to head there after we finished the mahout interviews in Ban Ta Klang.

Some 25 kilometres northwest of Ban Ta Klang, Ban Krabueang Yai is another village where people live with their elephants in a traditional setting. Sarot knew several Lao Isan mahouts well, including the head of the village. Along with the invite from the mahouts in Surin, he called to confirm that they were happy to take in a couple of visitors armed with questions. As Nong and I packed up a borrowed motorbike to head off for the day, Sarot mentioned in passing that the Lao Isan mahouts 'would never bring their elephants to Ban Ta Klang'. I wondered what Ban Krabueang Yai offered that differed from the Elephant Village. Having met several Khmer mahouts in Ban Ta Klang who were originally from Cambodia and having had some interactions with the Karen of Mae Chaem, I was aware of some of the differences between Thailand's various elephant people, but equally understood that they all shared a key similarity – an ancient heritage of cultural and spiritual traditions connected to elephants.

The ride to Ban Krabueang Yai took us across the river and straight up the highway, heading away from Surin city. We whizzed alongside buses and trucks, passing shops, mechanics, open-air restaurants, and large lots selling statues of Buddhas and spirit houses – the usual highway-side landscape of much of northeast Thailand. Soon we turned off a side road and the landscape started to change. An unsealed road took us between several small houses built in the traditional way, with the usual mix of dogs of various pedigrees following along beside the bike, interested in the interlopers. Soon we stopped at a small grocery store, where Sarot had organised for us to meet one of the older mahouts from the village. After a short chat, Nong told me that we were welcome to talk to several of the local mahouts, including the village's kruba – 92-year-old Ta'Tao. His house was a large brick and tile construction with a colourful spirit house in the front yard, complete with its various offerings.

Ta'Tao sat on the porch in an armchair, his young granddaughter at his side. She explained that she would help in translating the questions to her grandfather, who was hearing impaired. With few questions for guidance, Ta'Tao shared his life experiences at length, beginning with his own stories about capturing elephants before the border with Cambodia closed.

'I was involved in about three or four elephant hunts,' he said. 'Each time it took about two months, and we would need to perform a ritual asking the spirits for protection before catching elephants. I went with a dozen other mahouts, across the border with Cambodia and Laos. I captured five elephants myself, but I didn't keep them. They were all sold years ago, with the last before my granddaughter was born.'

Ta'Tao had first caught an elephant at the age of sixteen, when he was already married. It was essential that his wife stayed at home during the hunt or he would be in grave danger. It would take about a month to train an elephant, and he learned from his father, who had also captured elephants. Ta'Tao described the conditions of the hunts. 'It was rough going out – living in the forest, without changing clothes,' he explained, showing further parallels with the Guay's experiences. 'I had to follow the headmaster in every step. Meals had to be served to the headmaster first. He got to sleep first, eat first, and made all the decisions. Whatever you did, you needed to ask the headmaster first.'

While all the other krubas in Ban Krabueang Yai had died, it was clear that Ta'Tao was keeping the tradition alive through storytelling.

His granddaughter explained that he told her a lot about his elephant hunting experiences, and that she understood the significance of the Pakham Spirit House. She invited us to go and see it; it was not too far from her grandfather's house. As we walked down the dirt road, Ta'Tao's granddaughter explained that the area had once been covered in dense forest, with each house quite far from the next, but that over the past decade new houses – like her grandfather's – had been built between the huts. This had the effect of creating a village that was half traditional wooden houses and half constructed from modern brick and tile. As we reached the Pakham Spirit House I noted the similarities between it and the one at the SESC, it also being an ancient wooden structure containing a coil of Pakham rope and offerings for the spirits.

We were met by Wichien, one of the younger mahouts in the village who had been employed more recently to capture elephants in Burma, where they were still used in legal logging. 'I didn't originally go to Burma to capture elephants,' he explained. 'I went to make *lek lai* [metal amulets], but then I stayed with Karen people and captured elephants with them. They also have the Pakham Spirit House, but they speak Karen and Burmese to comply with the local spirits' languages.' Wichien then explained how Ban Krabueang Yai and Chumpon Buri had changed over the years, with further parallels with Ban Ta Klang. 'Not long ago there was a forest here called *Pa Lieng Chang* [captive elephant forest, where they kept captured and trained elephants] along the Mun River, but ten years ago we lost the forest when it was sold to a businessman who planted eucalyptus, killing the other trees and causing drought.'

Wichien then described how the Lao Isan people in the village tended to their elephants, usually taking them to foraging spots around the village or areas of shade where they could eat sugarcane and grass purchased by the mahouts, while chained up or closely supervised. They would stay there until around five or six in the evening, then would be brought back to the mahouts' houses where they stayed chained up under shelters at night. Wichien also shared information about how the Lao Isan cared for elephants when they were sick. 'We use herbal and local medicines, such as a whole red ant colony, which is boiled with Burma Paduak bark and helps with bruises and infected wounds,' he explained. 'However, that is not really an original recipe. The recipe for an authentic medicine for elephants comes from Sri Satchanalai, Sukhothai. It is local wisdom passed on from generation to generation and isn't recorded in any book.' Wichien explained that the recipe consisted of braised duck, kaffir lime leaves and Chinese herbs, and that it was also very good for people. According to Wichien, elephants given this treatment recovered from sickness very quickly. He attributed the longevity of Ban Krabueang Yai's elephants to such care. 'We had a very old elephant,' he explained. 'He passed away from senility at over a hundred years old and was very tall – 3.21 metres high – even taller than Thong Bai.' Wichien then explained that he had sold the bones of the dead elephant to rich people in Nakhonpathom, and that the buyers had wanted to buy the elephant when he was alive, but the owner would not sell him.

We then discussed whether funding was provided from the government to support mahouts and elephants – similar to the Zoological Parks Organization in Ban Ta Klang. Wichien explained that there had been difficulties negotiating with local government agencies about financial support, and that he hoped the newly developed tourism venture known as Elephant World in Ban Ta Klang might provide employment for some of the men. At the time of my last visit, Elephant World was still in development; some of the land within the Surin Elephant Study Center and fairly barren areas surrounding it had been repurposed with the aim of building a replica village amidst a series of human-made streams and reforested land. This was intended to attract more tourists to Ban Ta Klang to see elephants and learn about mahout culture. Wichien also mentioned Lek, who he said thought of him as a little brother. He was effusive with praise for all she had done for elephants and their people. 'She was born poor, from a tribe with elephants, so she understands what it is like,' Wichien explained. 'Once she was at a stage in her life where she could help others, she did it. Not only to help elephants, but all other kinds of animals, such as dogs, cats, monkeys and so on.'

We then turned to the subject of the future of elephants in Surin more broadly. 'I want to try new things, to make more money,' Wichien said. 'I started a business selling drinking water, which I want to pass on to my children. I have a daughter and a son, and both are scared of elephants. They have no interest in working with them. They're studying at two different vocational colleges and will graduate in a year. I don't want my kids to work with elephants; if kids get too involved they usually drop out of school. So I just shut down that part of their brains. If they spend too much time with the elephants, I worry they will have no future.' Wichien said he felt sad that he could not pass his knowledge of elephants down to his children, but that he had students to inherit it. 'I have two students studying with me at the moment. Not many people dare to take on this dangerous occupation, but there are still some who are interested.'

Wichien suggested that we visit a young mahout nearby who intended to stay in the elephant business and to pass his knowledge on to his children, so we got back on the bike and drove a little further through the village, following Wichien up ahead on his moped. We stopped at a spot by the river's edge. Cranes perched on precarious legs in the clear shallows, fishing among the reeds against a backdrop of riparian green and a calm sky dotted here and there with the odd cumulus cloud. In the distance came the low thrum of traffic, the highway nearby yet out of view. After the madness of the round-up and the everyday bedlam of trucks and tour buses, the circus and the odd night of full blast karaoke in Ban Ta Klang, the serenity washed over me like a salve. Across the other side of the small dirt road sat several houses not unlike those in Ban Ta Klang – wooden structures on stilts with open areas for sitting underneath or space for chickens and roosters. Wichien beckoned us to follow him on foot, so we sidled through a narrow gap between two of the houses until we came face to face with a small bull elephant standing under a lean-to at the side of one of the houses, sheltered from the sun by a large stretch of thick shade cloth and the surrounding wooden walls. Like many household elephants, he was chained by one foot to a cement post sunk in the ground. By his side was a young mahout who introduced himself as Boon Li and his elephant as Somwang.

Boon Li stroked Somwang's trunk as Nong explained the purpose of our visit. I asked Boon Li how long he had had Somwang and what he was like to work with. 'I have had Somwang for two years,' he explained. 'Before that, I had an older elephant, and learned on one that was fully grown. I learned from my paternal grandfather, and it was scary at first. Somwang is a very tame elephant; he learns very fast. It only took five or six days for me and Somwang to get along, for him to start following me places. It's not usual for that to happen – to have a connection with an elephant like that.' Boon Li also explained that while Somwang was too young to undertake proper training, that he had started teaching the young bull some tricks while they had been living together, side by side in house and shelter.

Boon Li explained that he had bought Somwang and his mother Somjai from the Maesot district in Tak province from Karen people, at a cost of 1.4 million baht (around US$50,000). This was quite cheap but no one else wanted to buy them because they were not well since their previous owner had overworked Somjai in the illegal logging industry. 'I hesitated to buy them, but I felt bad for them and wanted to take care of them,' Boon Li explained. 'The mother was very skinny, but after four or five months of feeding her, she looked much better. At first Somjai didn't have much milk and he was also very skinny. I boiled some rice and fed him with it. I was afraid the pair would die.' He also gave young Somwang food meant for cows mixed with water, as well as formula milk to keep him alive.

Boon Li had worried that Somwang would die after suffering without enough food or water for a long time, despite the lushness of the Maesot region. 'They didn't feed them enough water, only a handful of grass. Those people just didn't care. Somjai took less than a day to eat a whole truckload of grass once they came to live with me. Unlike his mother, Somwang wasn't an eater, but his appetite grew and he is healthy now. When Somjai gained weight, someone asked to buy her and she is now at a camp in Pattaya. I've seen pictures of her life in Pattaya and how nice she looks. I regret selling her as she looks really great.'

I asked Boon Li if he took Somwang to many events, thinking of the Lao Isan mahouts I had met in Surin. He had not been to the round-up recently, but usually attended ceremonies during the dry season to make money. 'I'm leaving here early tomorrow morning to go to a religious ceremony to raise money for a temple as well as an ordination ceremony, Boon Li said. 'I'm going with a team of ten mahouts and five elephants on three trucks. One is just a calf; he's not really booked for the ceremony, but he will tag along with a big female elephant.' The team would be paid 8,000 baht (US$240) and the organiser was one of his relatives who hired the team every year and received a special price as a result.

During the rainy season when there were fewer or no ceremonies, Boon Li still had enough food for Somwang. 'I grow my own elephant food, but sometimes I buy it,' he explained. 'When visitors come to the village and see how cute Somwang is, they give us food for free.' Boon Li also said that he had no interest in travelling further to make money from his elephants, and that he was not interested in going to work at a tourist camp like some of the mahouts from Ban Krabueang Yai, or a site like the SESC or Elephant World. 'It's not enough money,' he said, 'and it's too far from home.' He also noted that he would not ever travel further than Tak province, about 650 kilometres from Surin. 'When I bought [Somjai and Somwang] and they travelled here, they were so exhausted.'

With the familial nature of many mahout-elephant relationships in mind, I asked Boon Li about Somwang's place in his family. 'Somwang is my *loog taewada*,' he said, a phrase meaning 'the precious child that parents give anything he wants'. 'I have always loved elephants,' he continued. 'It would be hard to live a life without them.' I asked what Boon Li wanted for Somwang's future, considering the young age of the elephant. He told me that he had two children, aged fourteen and eight. 'They come home from school and play with Somwang every day. Looking after Somwang is absolutely something I will pass down to my kids.' It was interesting to note the differences between

Wichien and Boon Li's viewpoint on their children's future in terms of the continuation of mahoutship culture, giving me further hope that, like Teerachai and his friends in Ban Ta Klang, there would be a new generation of mahouts ready to care for the population after their fathers retired.

It was time for Boon Li to collect food for Somwang's dinner. Nong and I walked back out onto the quiet dirt road, and I watched as a crane rose from the river with a wriggling fish in its mouth, dripping clear water as it winged away. My gaze alighted on two elephants in the distance, gamboling in the water while their mahouts watched from the shore. I had rarely seen such an image outside the sanctuaries I had visited and Journey to Freedom. This was the closest expression to elephant liberation I'd encountered in Surin and I wished – not for the first time – that this was a more common scenario.

As Boon Li grabbed his machete and moped, I asked him what Somwang's name meant. 'Somwang means "to be successful and meet goals you set, or get something you expect, want or hope for",' he said. 'My relatives gave him the name because I wanted an elephant and I got what I wanted. Somwang and I were both lucky to find each other, as if we were meant to be.' Boon Li waved farewell as he mounted his bike and drove away. Returning the gesture and looking out again at the two elephants in the river, green trees beyond them, I realised I had the answer to my question about why the Ban Krabueang Yai mahouts might not want to go to Ban Ta Klang with their elephants. With their calm surroundings and greater opportunities for elephant enrichment, some of the Lao Isan people of this particular village appeared to have developed an elephant economy that worked to their benefit and was better for their elephants' welfare. It was clear that the more traditional forms of elephant tourism – from the Surin

Round-Up to participating in religious ceremonies – still provided mahouts like Boon Li with enough of an income that they did not have to leave home. While a small village, I wondered if Ban Krabueang Yai could be a place where future generations might care for captive elephants in a community setting. As we drove back to Ban Ta Klang, I reflected on the fortuitous nature of my journey, which at every turn provided me with insight after insight into the complex relationships between elephants and their people. There was one final place to visit before I headed back to Sydney, different to anywhere I had been before.

Chapter 12

ANANTARA AND THE GOLDEN TRIANGLE ASIAN ELEPHANT FOUNDATION

After leaving Ban Krabueang Yai, Nong and I brainstormed ideas for one final research trip. There were so many more projects around the country that were helping elephants – a heartening situation considering how things had been when I began my research so many years ago. I had never been further north than Mae Chaem and had always wanted to visit Chiang Rai. I was also interested in the work of the Golden Triangle Asian Elephant Foundation (GTAEF), an organisation operating throughout Thailand, Laos, Cambodia, Vietnam and Burma to help elephants in a variety of situations – from captives in camps in Thailand to wild elephants in Cambodia, where GTAEF has funded a wildlife corridor in partnership with charity Wildlife Alliance. Funded by parent company Minor International and its chief executive Dilip Rajakarier, GTAEF is primarily supported by the work of two high-end eco-resorts – Anantara Golden Triangle Elephant Camp and Resort and Four Seasons Tented Camp Golden Triangle – located in the lush landscape of the Mekong River where Thailand meets Burma and Laos.

I had thought about Anantara many times during the past few weeks, mainly due to my conversations with Lord Insamran of Ban

Ta Klang, who had worked at Anantara Golden Triangle Elephant Camp for many years and was still considered head mahout. Lord had first started working at the resort after John Roberts, Anantara's Director of Elephants and the Director of the GTAEF, found him begging on the streets of Bangkok with his elephant and offered him a job. Lord had explained how working for Anantara had changed his life, providing him with an income that had given him and his family a lot of opportunities and freedom. His son had followed in his footsteps, with both working with one of their family's elephants at the resort. Lord had also described Anantara's interesting set-up: of thirty elephants, eight were used in a small-scale tourism venture that primarily involved bareback riding and a mahout training course for tourists, while twenty-two others were involved in the GTAEF's research program, whereby veterinarians, biologists and conservationists could visit to conduct social and behavioural research. Lord helped guide both the tourism and research aspects, working with tourists wanting to learn mahoutship skills in an organised weekly or monthly program, and helping researchers work with the elephants, for example by giving the animals commands so that biologists could study areas such as foot health and reproduction. He also worked as a 'mahout ambassador', responsible for finding other mahouts and elephants to employ.

Overall, Lord's extensive experience working with elephants had led to a new life in the Golden Triangle, and while he visited Ban Ta Klang as much as possible, the situation at Anantara was a far cry from that of his home village. 'It's very different there,' Lord had noted. 'Up there it's very green, with lots of elephant food and space to roam.' His descriptions had piqued my interest. Like Burm and Emily's Elephant Sanctuary, Anantara sounded like another place where a more ethical form of tourism was offering new opportunities for mahouts and elephants in a more natural environment. So I suggested to Nong, 'How about we head up to the Golden Triangle?'

An email to John Roberts was met with enthusiasm for our visit and an offer of affordable accommodation on-site. After a roundabout trip via Lampang and Chiang Mai, we boarded a bus that would take us to Chiang Rai. This was a three-hour journey to the northernmost part of the country. The bus was smaller than I expected and fully packed, the roof mere centimetres from my head, but somehow I slept through to our arrival at the small Chiang Rai bus station. After a quick bowl of noodles, we grabbed a ride to Anantara, where I almost fell out of the tuktuk in amazement as the driver navigated through the front gates and up a long driveway, past walls painted with friezes in traditional Thai style before stopping at a wide, towering building of carved wood and stone painted terracotta red. As we walked into the grand lobby I looked down at my dusty boots, dirty shorts, and scratched and bruised Surin legs, and hefted my stained backpack higher on my shoulders. Hotel guests more appropriately attired in neat, stylish summer casuals sat at tables on an expansive verandah at the other side of the lobby, overlooking luscious green fields that spread to the horizon.

Nong checked us in and we were led to two rooms that were ours for the night. As we opened the door to each, we looked at each other in amazement. What we had thought would be two very reasonably priced rooms on-site turned out to be gorgeously decorated, expansive, *expensive* guest suites. With nothing to do until later than evening – a dinner planned with John and some of his GTAEF colleagues – I turned to Nong and said, 'See you at five!'

'First thing I'm doing is having a bath!' he giggled as he disappeared into the room and closed the door behind him.

After ditching my backpack on the polished wooden floor, I looked in amazement at my digs for the evening: a king-sized bed with immaculate bedding, two towels folded into the shape of elephants atop, and a huge bathroom – complete with spa bath – open to the room and the view beyond. I flung open the doors to the balcony and stepped out onto a covered wooden deck looking out over an abundance of colourful native plants – a mix of vines, flowers and ferns that smelled fresh and cool. The vista beyond was the same I had seen from the lobby; here I could sit and look out upon a spectacular landscape of fields, forest and creeks, listening to the birds and the soft sounds of the wind through the long grass. In the distance I could see several elephants grazing; by their side were a pair of mahouts chatting in the shade.

That evening, after a long soak in the bath and a few hours of note taking on the balcony, I headed out to dinner at a local noodle shop with John Roberts and his colleagues. After hearing about GTAEF's exciting work with elephants and mahouts, I organised an early morning interview with John to discuss further. We sat at a table on one of the balconies looking out over the fields, the morning air crisp and fresh, and began our conversation. John explained that the hotel which had preceded Anantara had no elephants on-site, but a huge amount of grassland with the potential to support a number of elephants. Initially, when Anantara was developed in 2003, four elephants were leased from the Thai Elephant Conservation Center, but by 2006 street-begging elephants and mahouts, and injured elephants rescued at the Surin Round-Up were brought to the hotel grounds to begin new lives, with funding provided by the owner of the hotel and its guests. John then set up GTAEF for the purpose of caring for elephants in Thailand across the Golden Triangle, having previously worked in elephant conservation in Chitwan National Park, Nepal.

Passionate about supporting positive mahout-elephant relationships, John developed a program that reconnected mahouts to their traditional culture by offering them roles more akin to mahoutship of the past, living and working alongside elephants amidst forests and fields rather than city streets or tourist camps. In a sense, this constituted the 'rescue' of mahouts and their families, as well as their elephants. The GTAEF operated a 'Train the Trainer' course, offering elephant training sessions for mahouts that encouraged more gentle methods, such as positive reinforcement and target training. The GTAEF also provided an income for the mahouts' wives, who are trained in sericulture (silk farming) and sometimes also care for the elephants. With whole families living on-site, Anantara offered plenty of opportunities for the mahouts' children to become involved in aspects of mahoutship, keeping the culture alive through the generations.

'Our hope here has been to provide a model for responsible tourism that keeps the mahouts and their elephants off the streets and ideally away from tourist camps,' John explained. 'We want elephants to be in a better place; we can't stop mahouts from leaving if they want to try something else, but we try to provide conditions which keep them here. The most important thing we do is to ensure that elephant welfare is at the highest standard possible, both by encouraging sustainable forms of tourism and offering research programs that are scientific and involve a range of people with appropriate knowledge.'

This scientific perspective is central to the work of the GTAEF, which utilises studies of elephant behaviour to establish and fulfil the animals' needs, such as by utilising peer reviewed research on roaming and herd behaviours. By working in cooperation with conservation organisation Think Elephants International, the GTAEF aims to understand the ideal conditions for elephants in captivity while also creating tourism standards and guidelines. As John explained, this scientific approach can be used to develop sustainable forms of elephant tourism that successfully balance welfare and conservation concerns with the deeply entrenched traditions of elephant people. Considering the diversity of situations in which elephants are kept in Thailand, this universally scientific approach makes a highly beneficial contribution to ethical captive elephant management in different contexts.

After breakfast, Nong and I headed out to Anantara's elephant camp – a small, tranquil place surrounded by trees, where Karen and Guay mahouts lived alongside their elephants. John had arranged for us to speak with one of the mahouts, a 27-year-old Karen man named Preecha, who was from a village called Mae Na Jon in the Mae Chaem region, not far from BEES in Mae Tan or Journey to Freedom's Mae Satop. Preecha had worked for Anantara for five years with his 47-year-old female elephant. Previously, he was employed by a tourist camp in Chiang Mai for four years after spending several years moving from camp to camp in an attempt to find better conditions. As he explained, 'Anantara is far better than any other camp in terms of wellbeing and welfare for me and my elephant. Many other camps are getting better in terms of welfare too; it is becoming very competitive between camps to be better because tourists want to see healthy elephants.'

Preecha explained that Mae Na Jon no longer had many elephants and was losing its elephant culture as many young men moved away from the village to seek an education. 'There are only three or four elephants left at home,' he said. 'Lots of people have moved away to study, so it is mainly just old people left. Keeping elephants is what my family has been doing since my great-grandfather's generation. It hasn't always supported us enough financially, but the knowledge and skills have been in my family for a very long time. I don't want to throw it away.'

Preecha reflected on his relationship with his elephant within the context of working for Anantara. 'She was passed down to me from my grandfather and has been a really great girl. She makes life very easy for me. I mix more traditional training with new, more positive training, like using bananas to train her to do tricks, not by hitting her with a hook.' He also explained what it was like coordinating bareback riding tours. 'All of the elephants here are very safe for humans to ride on. At camps, on a very rare occasion – like once in ten years – an accident might happen where a tourist falls off an elephant's back, but it has never happened here. And no elephant has ever purposely hurt a human, in my experience.'

We also discussed how the GTAEF had helped mahouts and elephants at Anantara. 'There are more people coming to see the elephants, and more donations to help them. Elephants receive any treatments they need, completely free. There are two vets, and in severe cases, elephants are taken to the elephant hospital in Lampang. And mahouts are supported well here. The busiest period is from December and January, and even when there are no tourists we are still paid as we have long-term contracts.'

As the interview drew to a close, I noticed three Western tourists enter the village, preparing for a mid-morning elephant ride. They were dressed in simple cotton pants and shirts – the same style of

clothing worn by the mahouts – provided by Anantara as an alternative to dirtying their own clothes. Preecha explained that the tourists
were participating in Anantara's mahout training course, which
would teach them some of the skills of mahoutship over a week
or longer. I recalled what Lord had told me about his experiences
teaching tourists these skills, and how the training course differed
from other types of tourism in which he had been involved.

'Any kind of tourism is good where the money goes to elephants –
that's the most important thing to worry about,' Lord had explained.
'But I prefer the mahout training course style of tourism because I
can share my abilities with tourists, and the tourists can help me, too.
I also like learning about them. In normal elephant riding, there's
no connection between mahout and tourist.' He also explained how
he enjoyed the longer-term nature of the mahout/elephant/tourist
relationship. 'I had one tourist who came for a week but extended
his stay for a month because he loved it. We got to know each other
and he learned a lot. Some tourists come just for a day but still gain a
lot of knowledge they can tell others about. They can learn about the
mahout's life and a bit of our culture, rather than just taking a photo.
It's good that tourists can appreciate our skills and knowledge.'

During my visit, elephants at Anantara did not wear howdahs;
instead, tourists rode bareback, with just a piece of rope around the
elephants' necks to hold onto. Lord believed the elephants were much
happier to be ridden bareback, with just one tourist sitting across
their neck, the animal guided by the mahout walking alongside.
Today Anantara has moved away from offering riding at all. Now
tourists participate in observational tourism only – either watching
from a distance or walking with elephants.

As I watched the three tourists clamber aboard the elephants, helped up by the mahouts, Preecha asked Nong if he or I would also like to go for a ride.

'No, thank you,' said Nong.

I echoed his reply. 'I'm okay, thanks!'

One of the tourists, now some two metres above us, clutching the neck rope, uttered: 'Why not? It's amazing up here!'

I laughed nervously. Despite Preecha's confidence in the safety of the elephants, images of horses bucking and bolting on me – despite bridle, saddle and my own riding skills – flashed through my mind, along with a gurgling reminder in my stomach of my fear of heights, a phobia I apparently shared with Nong.

'I'll just walk behind you,' I said, wiping cold sweat from my forehead with the sleeve of my t-shirt. 'I can appreciate things from here.'

Nong nodded in quick agreement. 'Yes, we will walk. Thank you.'

So began a wonderful adventure into the fields and forest beyond Anantara, following mahouts, tourists and elephants as they strode down dirt paths shaded by foliage thick with bird song. Soft droplets of moisture trickled down from the tropical canopy, running coolly down my face and neck. The long grass stroked my legs as we weaved down into the valley, which stretched before us like a green mirage. This was a land made for elephants – where tourists were part of the scenery, but their impact was strictly managed.

As well as being supported by the GTAEF and Think Elephants International, these features of Anantara's captive elephant management practices were bolstered by extensive research conducted by veterinarians, conservation behaviourists and biologists from the Asian Captive Elephant Working Group, of which John Roberts is co-chair. The work of this group has been instrumental in advocating for evidence-based approaches to captive elephant management that aim to improve welfare while also respecting and reviving mahout culture. Anantara was clearly a manifestation of these aims, presenting a unique form of tourism that provided elephants with more opportunities to express natural behaviours in suitable surroundings.

The GTAEF and Minor International have also been supportive of mahouts and elephants in Ban Ta Klang through the development of a mobile elephant veterinary clinic, in conjunction with the Zoological Parks Organization, which also partially funds the Surin Project. They also raise money through novel fundraising ventures such as the annual Elephant Boat Race and River Festival, last held in Bangkok in March 2020, which supported Ban Ta Klang mahouts, their families and elephants through conservation workshops, and paid English teachers to provide schoolchildren with greater educational opportunities. In addition, the GTAEF supports programs that tackle human-elephant conflict, and also provides elephant hospitals with veterinary equipment, such as a purpose-built elephant ambulance now in use by the Thai Elephant Conservation Center.

In combination with on-the-ground advocacy and activism on the part of sanctuary and welfare project operators, the work of the GTAEF contributes to a holistic approach to elephant management that shows how the issues associated with captivity can be addressed from various perspectives. The long walk we took that morning, descending into the valley, was the perfect ending to yet another fieldwork trip that had taught me so much about Thailand's captive elephants. Amidst the greenery and sounds of undergrowth crackling under elephant feet, I reflected on how far I had come on my journey since observing the elephant at Doi Suthep some seven years ago, and the numerous positive changes to captive elephant lives – and those of their mahouts – I had learned about and witnessed. Soon, Nong and I would be leaving Anantara and getting the bus back to Chiang Mai, where I bade my research assistant farewell and caught a flight home to Australia. I would spend the next six years piecing this story together, analysing my interviews with mahouts, conservationists, welfare advocates and tourists, extensive field notes, thousands of photos and a wealth of literature on elephant behaviour, welfare, conservation and mahoutship. This book slowly started to take shape, yet the story I had been tracing for years would have an unforeseen twist.

Chapter 13

AN UNCERTAIN FUTURE

As Ingrid Suter argues, 'elephant-based tourism is an industry that is here to stay and should be viewed as a contributory tool for positive change rather than a hindrance to conservation or elephant welfare'.[176] This book has provided evidence of such contributions from sanctuaries and community-based projects involving volunteer tourism and organisations like the GTAEF, which have developed sustainable forms of elephant tourism that also benefit mahouts. Sanctuaries like Elephant Nature Park and Burm and Emily's Elephant Sanctuary have paved the way for substantial changes in Thailand by promoting elephant-friendly tourism and utilising land to develop near-natural environments. A number of other sanctuaries have been founded over the past two decades, including Boon Lott's Elephant Sanctuary in Sukhothai, two sanctuaries operating in Phuket (Phuket Elephant Sanctuary and Tree Tops Elephant Reserve), and Samui Sanctuary on the island of Koh Samui. There are also now more than thirty saddle-off projects available across Thailand that are supported by Asian Elephant Projects and the Save Elephant Foundation, which provide better conditions for elephants.

Along with the positive changes to tourist camps, these ventures bode well for the future of elephant tourism in Thailand. However, in

2020 – as this book was nearing completion – the entire industry was dealt a crushing blow that upset the momentum for positive change. This was the COVID-19 pandemic. In early 2020 I booked one final research trip to Thailand to examine some of the new elephant-friendly forms of tourism that had sprung up around the country since my previous visit in 2015. I hoped to visit the new sanctuaries in Phuket, where I had previously visited two small tourist camps as a means of observing elephant welfare issues. I was excited to learn that elephant welfare advocate Louise Rogerson – who I had met several times in Ban Ta Klang, Surin and Chiang Mai over the years – had founded Phuket Elephant Sanctuary and Tree Tops Elephant Reserve as observation-only sites. I was keen to see the sanctuaries in action as well as visiting Samui Elephant Sanctuary for the first time, returning to see how BEES and the Surin Project had evolved over the years, and visiting some of the saddle-off projects. COVID-19 forced me to cancel my plans, with the pandemic devastating the tourism industry. Among the millions of people instantly out of work were the country's mahouts, once again faced with the problem of feeding their elephants in the most significant upset to mahout-elephant relationships since the logging ban of 1989.

In mid-2020 I messaged Sarot Ngamsanga to see how the mahouts and elephants were faring in Ban Ta Klang. 'Things are not good!' was his reply. 'Too many elephants, not enough food. Elephants are starving.' Another three hundred or so elephants had returned to the Elephant Village after camps closed around the country. Ban Ta Klang's mahouts were struggling to manage them due to the lack of space and shortages in food and water, which were already serious issues at the best of times. Elephants were chained up sometimes for twenty-four hours a day as their mahouts took on extra jobs to make ends meet. The government had implemented a strategy also used when the Surin Elephant Study Center was first created, encouraging people from nearby villages to bring harvest refuse (banana trees, corn and rice stalks, etc.) to Ban Ta Klang to feed the elephants. This was unlikely to be enough to feed that number of elephants, who could not survive on refuse.

At the time of writing in March 2022, Guay mahouts are still waiting for the camps to reopen, for while it may be good to be home, the village does not have capacity to manage this influx without the presence of tourists. They now rely entirely on support from organisations such as the Save Elephant Foundation, the affiliated Gentle Giants non-profit, and the Golden Triangle Asian Elephant Foundation. The elephants and Karen mahouts of Journey to Freedom have also been struggling during this difficult time. In April 2020 a forest fire tore through Ban Mae Satop and surrounds, destroying crops and important, limited grazing areas for elephants. Combined with the loss of income during the pandemic, this catastrophe has further complicated life in this isolated region, and the Karen and their elephants are also now reliant on the support of organisations like the Save Elephant Foundation.

Different strategies are being used to assist elephants during the pandemic until international visitors can return to Thailand in any significant number. Lek Chailert has mainly been working to provide for the hundreds of elephants and mahouts who have left tourist camps to head home to their traditional villages – the only option since their income dried up. One concern was that mahouts and elephants might be forced back into illegal logging to make ends meet, causing further stress and harm for elephants. Lek's primary focus has been on providing for these elephants while also working with mahouts to improve their situation. After the camps closed, elephants were taken by foot back to the villages by Lek, the Save Elephant Foundation team and their mahouts, walking for days through a variety of terrains and weather, and staying overnight in the forest. There were few food and water sources along the way, and a calf named Lanna struggled to keep up, meaning the elephant caravan stopped many times to motivate her to keep walking. These arduous journeys were further complicated because locals living in remote areas were unwilling to allow the team to walk through their villages for fear of COVID-19. But once the elephants arrived home to their mahouts' villages, they were welcomed with a Karen ceremony, and new agricultural projects were set up to provide elephant food. Donations through the Save Elephant Foundation, primarily from overseas private donors and international non-profit organisations, are being used to support mahouts and elephants. Lek is also committed to furthering the mahouts' education about welfare and training as a means of ensuring better welfare.

In other places around Thailand, conservationists and advocates have similarly been working to protect elephants during the pandemic. Louise Rogerson of Tree Tops Elephant Reserve has been committed to ensuring that elephants in need are given food and care, especially those from tourist camps that have been shut for over a year. With recent arrivals to Tree Tops and tourist numbers still low, the reserve has benefited from donations and the involvement of people such as drum and bass legend Goldie, who designed a graffiti-style logo for t-shirts and hoodies as part of the Wild & Grey clothing collection. Burm and Emily at BEES are also relying on donations through this difficult time to support their elephants and mahouts, with funding also going towards building a new home for head mahout Aner and his family. The GTAEF has continued its important work, maintaining its existing herd while bringing in new elephants and mahouts with financial support from the Thai Elephant Alliance Association.

In mid-2021 I was hopeful that tourism would return once vaccination rollouts were completed and Thailand reopened its borders to greater numbers of tourists. Yet, in 2022, the Omicron variant is still wreaking havoc globally, once again complicating international travel and, with it, elephant tourism. However, new possibilities may hopefully arise in terms of community-based tourism after the pandemic. Indeed, the Save Elephant Foundation is continuing to develop programs that will likely stay in place post-pandemic. I spoke to Ry Emmerson, Save Elephant Foundation's Projects Director, who explained that while COVID-19 had provided many challenges, 'it also gives an opportunity to reset the norms for elephant tourism'. As he explained, 'Many camps and elephant owners are now willing to consider a new ethical model working under the support and direction of the Save Elephant Foundation.' One example is Chokchai Elephant Camp, located in Mae Taeng, which the Save Elephant Foundation helped to transform from a traditional elephant tourism model to one that is more ethical. In conjunction with elephant advocacy and fundraising organisation Trunks Up, Lek and her team worked with the camp's owner to remove chains and build relationships between the fifty-four elephants living at the camp, who were otherwise separated due to the isolating nature of elephant enclosures and chains. This led to the creation of a small herd that is now managed by a team of mahouts without using hooks, who also participate in education programs aimed at continually improving elephant welfare. Like the Save Elephant Foundation's Pamper a

Pachyderm project, Chokchai's transformation epitomises a sustainable shift in camp operation that will hopefully continue after the pandemic. Indeed, as the GTAEF's John Roberts has recently noted, 'many elephant tourism stakeholders [have] demonstrated that they were amenable to change [and] could be persuaded to continually improve their practices with evidence-based advice', such as through welfare standards developed pre-pandemic.[177]

Hopefully, more ethical elephant tourism will continue to become a viable alternative to traditional elephant tourism post-COVID-19. Positive changes to camps will continue to be especially important as it is more than likely that mahouts will be drawn back to them for economic reasons. Indeed, in the case of the Guay mahouts, it will be necessary for mahouts to return to camps to reduce the strain on resources in Ban Ta Klang. However, it is still too early to know whether the industry will return to its pre-2020 state, including whether camps intend to employ the same number of elephants and mahouts. Tourism operators across the spectrum will need to move forward step by step as the new terrain of post-pandemic tourism is revealed. The ethics of the industry in a recovery period will need to be examined more closely than ever, but I am hopeful that the situation will continue to improve after the pandemic.

* * *

My years of research showed me that ethical elephant tourism is made possible by networks of conservationists, welfare advocates, tourists and mahouts working together to improve elephant lives. Since my early days volunteering at Elephant Nature Park, I have witnessed firsthand the profound changes that have reoriented the industry towards a more ethical focus. These helped me to identify four models of more ethical elephant tourism that exist in Thailand.

Observational tourism

Across Thailand, sanctuaries like Elephant Nature Park, Burm and Emily's Elephant Sanctuary and sustainable eco-tourism sites like Anantara have developed successful forms of elephant tourism that rely solely on observational activities, such as watching elephants from a distance and walking with them rather than riding them. Observational tourism ideally involves elephants having access to large range areas and swimming or wallowing spots like dams or rivers, and ample time to socialise while being monitored by mahouts. As an increasingly popular alternative to traditional tourist camps, observation may eventually become one of the primary ways that tourists interact with elephants. Aspects of this model are also represented by Journey to Freedom and the Surin Project, with their focus on walking with elephants and watching them interact and forage. While sanctuaries may be able to facilitate observation activities across adequately sized tracts of land, space limitations in places like Ban Ta Klang restrict the possibilities of observational tourism, with only a small herd of elephants being able to walk through the village at any one time. In Ban Ta Klang – a small space with an especially large population of elephants – this is a necessary restriction to protect villagers and tourists alike as well as other elephants and animals. Further, managing bulls is also an issue and not just in Ban Ta Klang. Any observational tourism project in a small or built-up village will need to either be limited to female elephants or must have a strategy in place to ensure that bulls are controlled.

Community-based tourism

Both Journey to Freedom and BEES are excellent examples of how sustainable and ethical forms of tourism can be used in a community setting to benefit elephants and local people. Similarly, by utilising the experience and knowledge of mahouts alongside a scientific research program, Anantara has developed a community of elephant people, researchers and tourists that makes a substantial, positive contribution to elephant welfare and conservation. Observational tourism in community settings is one of the best ways forward for ethical elephant tourism, with the creation of alternative habitats within protected, rehabilitated forested areas offering possibilities for the partial rewilding of elephants under the management of conservation organisations and the involvement of communities of mahouts and their families.

As another form of community-based tourism, the Surin Project benefited both elephants and the local community while offering a mix of observational and low impact hands-on activities, such as washing and feeding. I have often reflected on the potential of setting up something close to the Rescue, Rehabilitation and Rewilding model in the Elephant Village. This could draw on the skills and knowledge of local Guay people to rehabilitate the land and partially 'rewild' captive elephants. Unfortunately, the aridisation of the landscape in Ban Ta Klang and space limitations mean that such an undertaking would be extremely difficult. Yet I believe that the Surin Project offers one of the best ways forward for elephant tourism set within a traditional elephant-keeping community with space constraints and significant environmental degradation.

Post-COVID-19, it may be possible to develop other community-based projects in Ban Ta Klang, to the benefit of the Guay and their elephants alike, as well as in other similar locales where elephant-keeping communities need new strategies for sustainable elephant tourism. While my research in Ban Ta Klang showed that the culture of Guay mahoutship is on the decline, I am hopeful that investments in community-based tourism and an increased focus on involving mahouts in decisions around captive elephant management will improve perceptions of mahoutship. This would potentially lead to the development of a new, empowered generation of mahouts who will care for captive elephants and their habitats into the future, while also reinvigorating their cultures. Further, my work on the Surin Project showed me that the immersion of tourists in local elephant cultures could be a source of positivity in mahouts' lives, with volunteers expressing their enjoyment about working with the mahouts, learning about their elephants, and watching them display their unique skills.

Fundraising tourism

All the projects I studied used fundraising to achieve their aims. By receiving donations and generating income from visitors to the resort, Anantara is able to support the work of the GTAEF, thereby improving the lives of elephants and our understanding of their health and behaviour, all while supporting mahouts. Fundraising tourism is also represented in the work of sanctuaries like ENP and BEES and community-based projects such as Journey to Freedom and the Surin Project, which generate funds not only through their volunteer programs but also through efforts on social media. Overall, social media is a powerful way for ethical elephant tourism projects to develop and grow, with an engaged audience being able to watch videos and experience the intimate daily lives of elephants through their screens. For example, the GTAEF has used daily livestreams with Anantara's elephants to successfully raise funds during the pandemic while also educating viewers and bringing joy during dark times.

By sharing stories about elephant welfare and conservation, these places and organisations are bringing the plight of captive elephants into the homes of people around the world. As well as raising funds, this outreach has the effect of creating a global movement towards more ethical elephant tourism, with people who engage with those social media campaigns possibly being inspired to visit Thailand to see elephants in more natural surroundings. Observational and community-based tourism projects can similarly benefit from fundraising approaches through social media. For example, the Surin Project – through the Save Elephant Foundation and not-for-profit Gentle Giants – receives 'sponsorships' for its elephants that are driven by outreach on social media such as Facebook and Instagram. This is especially important during the pandemic when the usual funds from tourists (both day visitors and longer term volunteers) have been lost. Presently, all elephant welfare and conservation projects across Thailand appear to be relying on donations and sponsorships from outside the country to some extent as well as the fundraising work of organisations such as the Never Forget Elephant Foundation, Mahouts Elephant Foundation, Save Elephant Foundation and the GTAEF.

Lower impact tourism

This model envisions changes to more traditional elephant camps that still offer rides and shows. The Thai Elephant Conservation Center in Lampang is a good example of this model in action, with welfare standards guiding tourist activities. With an elephant hospital on-site, a research program and ample room for elephants, the TECC is able to monitor elephants and their care while also offering tourists a chance to ride elephants and watch them perform. The keeping of elephants on long chains in forested areas is also a significant welfare improvement over the majority of traditional camps. Lower impact tourism was also the outcome of the Save Elephant Foundation's influence on camps, some of which switched from riding and shows towards observation and other lower impact forms of tourism, such as feeding and washing elephants.

In terms of an uptake in this type of tourism, it is clear that some camp owners have rethought their entire approach to elephant tourism; for example, after meeting Lek Chailert and visiting Elephant Nature Park, a former camp owner named Montri Todtane decided to set up Phuket Elephant Sanctuary on a site that was once part of his family's village. An organisation called Asian Captive Elephant Standards, led by numerous veterinarians and elephant behaviour specialists, is also paving the way for positive changes to camps through certification and quality assurance, offering another research-based approach to elephant welfare and conservation with positive implications for mahouts and elephants alike. While perhaps being the least 'ideal' of the four models, lower impact tourism nonetheless offers broad opportunities for change across Thailand that would potentially reorient more than 200 existing elephant camps towards a more sustainable focus. As long as camps provide an income for mahouts – and, as a result, food and care for elephants – they will be an integral part of elephant tourism in Thailand. As such, a shift towards lower impact activities within these camps may benefit captive elephants, though more research is still needed to assess the impact of these changes on elephant welfare and wellbeing.[178]

* * *

After many years, this book has finally drawn to a close, but my time working with captive elephants and their mahouts is not over. I look forward to returning to Thailand soon, not just to visit old friends and new projects, but also to help facilitate further changes to the tourism industry as it springs back to life. My journey taught me so much about the plight of captive elephants and the people working together to improve their lives. It also showed me that including Indigenous people in captive elephant management will positively reshape elephant tourism while also benefiting local communities. I hope that this book will contribute to conversations and debates about captive elephant management and the role mahouts can play in improving their elephants' lives, both now and into the future. Ultimately, support for more ethical elephant tourism relies not only on the work of elephant welfare advocates and conservationists across Thailand, but the behaviours of and decisions made by tourists, who will always determine the direction and focus of the industry. Just as the longstanding human fascination with elephants has endured across centuries, so will our actions continue to impact upon their lives. By working together to ameliorate the negative consequences of these actions, we might envision a more ethical future for our relationships with this species.

Acknowledgements

I have many individuals to thank for their contributions to my research, and the inspiration they provided on my journey. Firstly, to all the elephants who allowed me into their worlds and taught me so much about their lives in captivity, especially Fah Sai, Euang Luang, Sai Fah, Nun Ning, Nong Nun, Neua Tong, Nong Lek, Tang Mo, Warin and Wang Duen, who I loved observing and interacting with daily in Ban Ta Klang. I hope that this book contributes to a better future for your species.

Lek Chailert's incredible work was the genesis for this research. Those first moments at Elephant Nature Park truly changed my life – giving me purpose and drive to become an advocate for captive elephants.

The mahouts I met on my journey – including the Karen of Mae Chaem, Lao Isan of Ban Krabueang Yai and, of course, the Guay of Ban Ta Klang – welcomed me into their communities, inspiring me to learn about their cultures and think about how we might help solve Thailand's 'elephant problem' using Indigenous knowledge. Huge thanks go especially to Sarot Ngamsanga for guiding the mahout interviews with enthusiasm, as well as Ta'Ma Supnak, Ta'Nui Salagnam, Ta'In Saendee, Ta'Mew Salagnam, Ta'Peng Yeeram, Thong Dii Salagnam, Lord Insamran, Boon Ma Salagnam, Teerachai Malignam and Chukiet Padpai for all the fascinating conversations about the past, present and future of Ban Ta Klang.

I could not have conducted the interviews with mahouts without the assistance of my amazing interpreters. Thank you Jureerat 'Pum' Boonwan for being such a joyous addition to my little research team, and for directing interviews in such a fun and collaborative way. As well as interpreting, Ocha Buddee was a fantastic volunteer coordinator on the Surin Project, whose delicious meals kept me energised during my fieldwork. Nong Wongvanich was also an amazing research assistant and adventurer, ready to procure a motorbike and head wherever we needed to find mahouts willing to be asked many, many questions. Rest in peace my friend.

Huge thanks to Kirsty and Wills Sandilands for all the inspiring conversations we had about the Surin Project, and for your passion and dedication to Ban Ta Klang, its elephants and people. Alex Godfrey provided invaluable information about the Surin Project during my first visit, while Chanatpapha 'Apple' Salagnam shared the story of the impact of tourism and deforestation on her family's life in Ban Ta Klang. It was also amazing to work alongside the Surin Project's wonderful volunteers, who were so willing to share their experiences with me. Special mentions go to Nicola Waudby, Siobhan McAuley, Kirsty Wright, Alina Kopowski, Marina Klammer, Marie Strauss, Rebecca Figge and Emily Parr for being awesome housemates, friends and fellow poo-shovelers.

My wonderful stay at BEES was made all the more inspiring and informative by Emily McWilliam and Burm Rinkaew, who showed me just how sanctuary tourism focused on observational activities and community outreach can pave the way for a better future for elephants. Thank you both for your hospitality and all that you do for the elephants and other animals in your care.

John Roberts welcomed me to Anantara and shared fascinating

insights into captive elephant management. I loved experiencing the wonderful world that the resort has built for its elephants and mahouts and hope to visit again soon.

My often quite random meetings with Louise Rogerson in various places around Thailand always came at opportune times and gave me a real appreciation of work on the frontline of elephant advocacy in Southeast Asia. I look forward to visiting Tree Tops Elephant Reserve in the near future.

Thank you Chakkrapong 'Jack' Chaiyakarn for the interesting forays to various elephant camps in Mae Taeng, as well as acting as an interpreter at Journey to Freedom.

Richard Lair took the time to answer numerous questions about the history of logging and the Thai Elephant Conservation Center in Lampang, while TECC staff also shared their views about captive elephant management and mahout culture that helped me piece together various parts of the story.

In the academic world, my former Masters and PhD supervisor Dr Fiona Probyn-Rapsey's passion for animal studies helped me to see the value of doing research about 'everyday' human-animal relationships.

As well as being a great friend, Dr Dinesh Wadiwel was a fantastic resource for all things animal studies while also providing useful feedback on an early draft. Our conversations about the importance of including Indigenous perspectives really helped to cement the focus of this book.

Over the past decade, Dr Stella North and I have had numerous discussions about animals and academia over cups of tea and plates of crispy eggplant and Shantung Not Chicken that helped me stay motivated – and very full!

As well as translating interview material, Siwadee Akkaraphot's thorough translations of literature written in Thai provided me with many important details about the history of the Guay.

Darby Rolfe has been an awesome media assistant, taking on a lot of tasks that would otherwise have kept me from finishing the book.

Kelly Somers provided excellent editorial assistance, while the team at Fontaine Publishing did fantastic work pulling this book together.

To my family and friends. My parents Meli and Nick read many, many early drafts, and my father's support and enthusiasm as my research assistant in Ban Ta Klang helped me at a crucial turning point in both my fieldwork and life.

I know that Leonie, Steve and Senda will be excited to see this book finally arrive on their bookshelves after so many years, as will all my friends – you know who you are! Thanks for being so supportive and interested in my work.

Finally, to Anna for her unfailing love and support. Thank you for listening to me talk about this book for the past five years, reading drafts, and bearing with me through so many submissions, changes, moments of motivation and moments of exhaustion. You are amazing and I can't wait to share Thailand with you!

Ethical Elephant Tourism Projects and Supporters

Anantara Golden Triangle Elephant Camp and Resort: www.anantara.com/en/golden-triangle-chiang-rai

Asian Captive Elephant Standards: www.elephantstandards.com

Asian Captive Elephant Working Group: https://www.mandai.com/content/dam/wrs/documents/conservation/ACEWG_Statement_March2017.pdf

Asian Elephant Projects: www.asianelephantprojects.com

Asian Elephant Specialist Group: www.asesg.org

Boon Lott's Elephant Sanctuary: www.blesele.org

Burm and Emily's Elephant Sanctuary: https://bees-elesanctuary.org

Elephant Nature Park: www.elephantnaturepark.org

Gentle Giants: https://thegentlegiants.org

Golden Triangle Asian Elephant Foundation: www.helpingelephants.org/

Human Elephant Learning Programs (H-ELP): https://h-elp.org

Journey to Freedom: www.elephantnaturepark.org/enp/visit-volunteer/projects/volunteer-at-journey-to-freedom-47/view

Mahouts Elephant Foundation: www.mahouts.org

Never Forget Elephant Foundation: https://neverforgetelephantfoundation.org

Phuket Elephant Sanctuary: www.phuketelephantsanctuary.org/en

Saddle Off Projects: www.elephantnaturepark.org/enp/visit-volunteer

Samui Elephant Sanctuary: www.samuielephantsanctuary.org

Save Elephant Foundation: www.saveelephant.org

Southern Thailand Elephant Foundation:
https://southernthailandelephants.org

Thai Elephant Alliance Association: www.thaielephantalliance.org/en

The Surin Project: https://surinproject.org

Think Elephants International: http://thinkelephants.org

Tree Tops Elephant Reserve: www.treetopselephantreserve.com

Trunks Up: https://jointrunksup.org

Notes

Preface

1   Cavalieri, 2003, pp. 42–43.

2   Derrida, 2002, pp. 395–396.

3   Carter & Charles, 2013, p. 323; Bhattacharya & Slocombe, 2017, p. 3.

4   Poole & Moss, 2008; Varner, 2008.

5   Savvides, 2013.

6   Van Maanen, 2011, pp. xiii, 2.

7   Kirksey & Helmreich, 2010, p. 545.

8   See Gray, 2003; Huspek, 1994; Pratt, 1986.

9   Mahoney, 2007; van Dooren, 2019.

10   See Braverman, 2015.

11   Plotnik & De Waal, 2014b, p. 5071.

12   Steward, 2009, p. 224.

13   Bekoff, 2008, p. 24.

14   Locke, 2017.

Chapter 1

15   Lair, 1997.

16   Bansiddhi et al., 2018; Godfrey & Kongmuang, 2009, p. 13.

17   Asian Elephant Specialist Group, 2017; Baker & Winkler, 2020, p. 3; Pintavongs et al., 2014.

18   Godfrey & Kongmuang, 2009, p. 13.

19   Bansiddhi et al., 2020a, p. 165.

20   Lair, 1997.

21   2008 figures from Kontogeorgopoulos, 2009a, 2009b; 2017 figures from Bansiddhi et al., 2020b, p. 2.

22   Bansiddhi et al., 2018, p. 20.

23   Kontogeorgopoulos, 2009b, p. 430.

24   Clubb & Mason, 2002; Clubb et al., 2008; Hermes et al., 2004.

25   Veasey, 2006.

26   Bansiddhi et al., 2018, p. 16; Suter, 2020.

27   As well as Western tourists, as Long (2019) notes, Chinese tourists are
      increasingly visiting elephant tourism camps and therefore also driving
      the industry. This paralleled my own observations at camps in northern
      Thailand and discussions with mahouts, who noted an increased
      demand for elephant riding as a result of a new wave of tourists from
      China.

28   Bansiddhi et al., 2018, p. 9.

29   Schliesinger, 2010.

30   Cuasay, 2000, p. xx.

31   Lainé, 2020, p. 1.

32   Lair, 1997.

33   Bansiddhi et al., 2018, p. 16.

34   Schliesinger, 2010, p. 28.

35   Baker & Winkler, 2020; Delang, 2005; Lair, 1997.

36   See Poole & Moss, 2008; Wemmer & Christen, 2008, p. 5.

37   Barua, 2013.

38   Lorimer, 2007, p. 923.

39   See Smith et al., 2012; Walpole & Leader-Williams, 2002; Leader-Wil-
      liams & Dublin, 2000.

40   Verissimo et al., 2011.

41   Greenfield & Verissimo, 2019; Stiles, 2004.

42   Whatmore, 2002, p. 50.

43   This observation is based on my own interviews with tourists.

44   Gómez-Pompa & Kaus, 1992, pp. 271–272.

45   Duffy, 2014, p. 92.

46   Matharu, 2015.

47   Kontogeorgopoulos, 2009a, p. 6.

48   Laohachaiboon, 2010.

49   Roberts, 2017.

50   Mason & Rushen, 2008.

Chapter 2

51   Sukumar, 2003, p. 62.

52   Srichandrakumara, 1929, p. 66.

53   Wannitikul, 2005, p. 103.

54   Cropper et al., 1999; Delang, 2005.

55   Bansiddhi et al., 2018, p. 2.

56   Sukumar, 2006.

57   Lair, 1997.

58   Lakanavichian, 2001, p. 170.

59   Bartsch, 2000, p. 197; Lohanan, 2002, p. 232, Tipprasert, 2002, p. 157.

60   Lakanavichian, 2001, p. 173.

61   Lohanan, 2002, p. 232.

62   Rittichainuwat et al., 2021, p. 52.

63   Lohanan, 2002, p. 233.

64   Bansiddhi et al., 2018, p. 2; Rittichainuwat et al., 2021, p. 53; Konto-
      georgopoulos, 2009a, 2009b.

65   Rittichainuwat et al., 2021.

66   Phuangkum, Lair & Angkawanith, 2005, p. v.

67   Bansiddhi et. al., 2020b, p. 165.

68   See for example Sobocinska, 2014.

69   Bansiddhi et al., 2018; Kontogeorgopoulos, 2009a, 2009b.

70   Bansiddhi et al. 2018 p. 3.

71   Kim, 2015, p. 233.

72   Srichandrakumara, 1929, p. 66.

73   Chaipraditkul, 2011, p. 1.

74   For my master's thesis I examined the rise of a training technique used
      in dressage known as 'rollkur' that has serious implications for equine
      welfare. For further information see Heuschmann, 2007.

75   Laohachaiboon, 2010.

76 Lair, 1997.

77 Kontogeorgopoulos, 2009a, pp. 7, 3.

78 Wearing, 2001; Wearing & McGehee, 2013.

79 Smith & Duffy, 2003.

80 McIntosh & Zahra, 2007; Wearing & McGehee, 2013.

81 Duffy, 2002; Horton, 2011.

Chapter 3

82 Bekoff, 2008, p. 15.

83 Taylor, 1993.

84 Veasey, 2006.

85 Fennell, 2012, p. 199.

86 Haraway, 2008, p. 21.

87 Serpell, 2019, p. 57.

88 Van Patter & Blattner, 2020, p. 173.

89 H-ELP Foundation, 2021.

90 Laule & Desmond, 1998, p. 302.

91 Moscarello & Hartley, 2017.

92 Sukumar, 2003, p. 135.

93 Abrell, 2017.

94 Doyle, 2014, p. 47.

95 Abrell, 2017, p. 3.

96 See Suter, 2020.

97 Seidensticker, 2008, p. xii.

98 Roberts, 2017.

99 Baker & Winkler, 2020, p. 4.

100 Thitaram et al., 2015, p. 53.

101 American Museum of Natural History, n.d.

102 Cui & Xu, 2019; Suter, 2020.

103 Cui & Xu, 2019.

104 American Museum of Natural History, n.d.; interview with Richard Lair, August 2014.

105 Suter, 2020.

106 Various researchers have studied the range areas of wild Asian elephants. Poole and Granli (2009) suggest a fluctuating average range of 34–800 km² for female Asian elephants and 200–235 km² for males, while a study by Alfred et al. (2012) in Borneo estimated range areas of 250–400 km² in non-fragmented forest and 600 km² in fragmented forest – pointing to the increased range size required in areas of human habitation. A further study by Fernando et al. (2008) estimated that wild elephants in India occupied a range area of 64–114 km².

107 Poole and Granli, 2009, p. 4; Sukumar, 2003, p. 161. Home ranges appear to fluctuate or differ based on location and environmental conditions.

108 Wemmer & Christen, 2008, p. 1.

109 Braverman, 2015, p. 10.

Chapter 4

110 Sukumar, 2003, p. 137.

111 Poole & Granli, 2009, p. 9.

112 Poole & Granli, 2009, pp. 9, 10.

113 Poole, 1989.

114 Sukumar, 2003, pp. 113–114.

115 Bansiddhi et al., 2018, pp. 16, 3.

116 Rittichainuwat et al., 2021 p. 59.

117 Taylor et al., 2020, p. 116.

118 Gruen, 2011, pp. 37-38.

119 Taylor et al., 2020, p. 122.

120 Franklin, 1999, p. 35.

121 Schliesinger, 2010, pp. 71-72.

122 Bartsch, 2000, p. 197.

123 Sukumar et al., 1997, p. 266.

124 Shiva, 1997, pp. 8, 5.

Chapter 5

125 Lair, 1997.

126 Cohn, 2006.

127 Holdgate et al., 2016, p. 10; Oregon Zoo, 2018, p. 1.

128 Bansiddhi et al., 2018, p. 7; Godfrey & Kongmuang, 2009, p. 14.

129 Sukumar, 2003, p. 177.

130 Schulte, 2006, p. 35.

131 Hammersley, 2014, p. 870.

132 Fowler, 2006, p. 77.

Chapter 6

133 Godfrey & Konmuang, 2009, p. 15.

134 Lair, 1997.

135 Homkrailis, 2002, p. 22.

136 Homkrailis, 2002, p. 92.

137 H-ELP Foundation, 2021.

138 Lenhhardt & Galloway, 2008, pp. 179–180.

139 Lorimer, 2010, p. 492.

140 Baker & Winkler, 2020, p. 5.

141 See also Lair, 1997; Kontogeorgopoulos, 2009; Suter, 2020; and Baker and Winkler, 2020.

142 See Roberts, 2017.

143 See Guha, 1997.

144 Lair, 1997.

145 Gómez-Pompa & Kaus, 1992, p. 271.

146 Gómez-Pompa & Kaus, 1992; Guha, 1997.

147 Suter, 2019, 2020.

148 Cuasay, 2000, pp. 1–2.

149 Rueangdej, 2009.

150 Rueangdej, 2009.

151 Homkrailis, 2002, p. 50.

152 Siriprapakorn, 2017.

153 Siriprapakorn, 2017.

154 Homkrailas, 2002, p. 50.

155 Schleisinger, 2015, p. 42.

156 Vetayasuporn, 2007, p. 134.

157 Cuasay, 2000, pp. 3–4.

158 Cuasay, 2000, p. 5.

159 See also Baker & Winkler, 2020, p. 9.

160 Cuasay, 2002, p. 13.

161 Homkrailis, 2002, p. 8.

162 Srichandrakumara, 1929, p. 61.

163 Cuasay, 2000, p. 2.

Chapter 8
164 See Pousajja (1993) for further details of the eucalyptus industry in Thailand.

Chapter 9
165 Lair, 1997.

166 Kurt et al., 2008, p. 336.

167 Suter, 2020, p. 2.

168 Bhattacharya & Slocombe, 2017, pp. 2–3.

169 Telfer & Sharpley, 2015, p. 124; Wearing & McGehee, 2013, pp. 117, 126.

170 Wearing & McGehee, 2013, p. 126.

171 Asian Captive Elephant Working Group, 2021.

172 Baker & Winkler, 2020, p. 13.

173 Lainé, 2020, p. 2.

Chapter 10

174 Kurt et al., 2008, p. 341.

Chapter 11

175 Schliesinger, 2010, p. 43.

Chapter 13

176 Suter, 2020, p. 3.

177 Roberts, 2021.

178 Roberts, 2021.

Bibliography

Abrell, E. (2017). Introduction: Interrogating captive freedom: The possibilities and limits of animal sanctuaries. *Animal Studies Journal 6*(2), 1–8.

Alfred, R., Ahmad, A. H., Payne, J., Williams, C., Ambu, L. N., How, P. M. & Goossens, B. (2012). Home range and ranging behaviour of Bornean elephant (*Elephas maximus borneesis*) females. *PLOS ONE 7*(2), e31400.

American Museum of Natural History. (no date). Elephants return to the forest. Available at www.amnh.org/explore/videos/research-and-collections/wild-at-heart-the-plight-of-elephants-in-thailand/elephants-return-to-the-forest.

Asian Captive Elephant Working Group. (2021). Available at https://www.mandai.com/content/dam/wrs/documents/conservation/ACEWG_Statement_March2017.pdf

Asian Elephant Specialist Group. (2017). *Asian Elephant Range States Meeting: Final Report*. Available at www.asesg.org/PDFfiles/2017/AsERSM%202017_Final%20Report.pdf.

Baker, L. & Winkler, R. (2020). Asian elephant rescue, rehabilitation and rewilding. *Animal Sentience 28*(1) 296.

Bansiddhi, P., Brown, J. L., Thitaram, C., Punyapornwithaya, V., Somgird, C., Edwards, K. L. & Nganvongpanit, K. (2018). Changing trends in elephant camp management in northern Thailand and implications for welfare. *PeerJ* 6: e5996, https://peerj.com/articles/5996/.

Bansiddhi, P., Brown, J. L., Thitaram, C., Punyapornwithaya, V. & Nganvongpanit, K. (2020a). Elephant tourism in Thailand: A review of animal welfare practices and needs. *Journal of Applied Animal Welfare Science 23*(2), 164–177.

Bansiddhi, P., Brown, J. L. & Thitaram, C. (2020b). Welfare assessment and activities of captive elephants in Thailand. *Animals 10*(6), 919.

Bartsch, H. (2000). The impact of trekking tourism in a changing society: A Karen village in northern Thailand. In J. Michaud (Ed.), *Turbulent times and enduring peoples: Mountain minorities in the South-east Asian Massif* (pp. 195–215). Richmond, Surrey: Curzon Press.

Barua, M. (2013). Circulating elephants: Unpacking the geographies of a cosmopolitan animal. *Transactions of the Institute of British Geographers 39*(4), 559–573.

Bekoff, M. (2000). Animal emotions: Exploring passionate natures. *BioScience 50*(10), 861–870.

Bekoff, M. (2008). *The emotional lives of animals: A leading scientist explores animal joy, sorrow, and empathy – and why they matter*. Novato, CA: New World Library.

Bhattacharya, J. & Slocombe, S. (2017). Animal agency: Wildlife management from a kincentric perspective. *Ecosphere 8*(10), e01978.

Braverman, I. (2015). *Wild life: The institution of nature*. Redwood City, CA: Stanford University Press.

Carter, B. & Charles, N. (2013). Animals, agency and resistance. *Journal for the Theory of Social Behaviour 43*(3), 322–340.

Cavalieri, P. (2003). *The animal question: Why nonhuman animals deserve human rights* (trans. C. Woollard). Oxford: Oxford University Press.

Chaipraditkul, N. (2011). Thai views of nature. Repository of Ethical World Views of Nature: Eubios Ethics Institute. Available at www.eubios.infc/yahoo_site_admin/assets/docs/ECCAPWG2Thailand.242151120.pdf.

Choudhury, D. K. L. (2008). Elephants and people in India. In C. Wemmer and C. A. Christen (Eds.), *Elephants and ethics: Towards a morality of coexistence* (pp. 149–164). Baltimore, MD: Johns Hopkins University Press.

Clifton, J. & Benson, A. (2006). Planning for sustainable ecotourism: The case for research ecotourism in developing country destinations. *Journal of Sustainable Tourism 14*(3), 238–254.

Clubb, R. & Mason, G. (2002). *A review of the welfare of zoo elephants in Europe*. Oxford: University of Oxford Animal Behaviour Research Group.

Clubb, R., Rowcliffe, M., Lee, P., Mar, K. U., Moss, C. & Mason, G. J. (2008). Compromised survivorship, fecundity and population persistence in zoo elephants. *Science 322*(5908), 1649.

Coghlan, A. & Gooch, M. (2011). Applying a transformative learning framework to volunteer tourism. *Journal of Sustainable Tourism 18*(6), 713–728.

Cohn, J. P. (2006). Do elephants belong in zoos? *BioScience 56*(9), 714–717.

Corman, L. (2017). Ideological monkey wrenching: Nonhuman animal politics beyond suffering. In D. Nibert (ed.), *Animal oppression and capitalism (Vol. 2)* (pp. 252–269). Santa Barbara, CA: Praeger.

Cropper, M., Griffiths, C. & Mani, M. (1999). Roads, population pressures, and deforestation in Thailand, 1976-1989. *Land Economics, 75*(1), 58–73.

Cuasay, P. (2000). Are Thai elephant people Thai? Marginal animals and a magical minority of South Isan. In G. Hainsworth (ed.), *Globalisation and the Asian economic crisis: Localized responses, coping strategies and governance reform in Southeast Asia.* Vancouver: CSEAR Publications, University of British Columbia.

Cui, Q. & Xu, H. (2019). Situating animal ethics in Thai elephant tourism. *Asia Pacific Viewpoint, 60*(3), 267–279.

Delang, C. O. (2005). The political ecology of deforestation in Thailand. *Geography 90*(3), 225–237.

Derrida, J. (2002). The animal that therefore I am (more to follow). *Critical Inquiry 28*(2), 369–418.

Despret, V. (2013). From secret agents to interagency. *History & Theory, 52*(4), 29–44.

Donaldson, S. & Kymlicka, W. (2013). Reply: Animal citizenship, liberal theory and the historical moment, *Dialogue, 52,* 769–786.

Donaldson, S. & Kymlicka, W. (2016). Comment: Between wild and domesticated: Rethinking categories and boundaries in response to animal agency. In B. Bovenkerk & J. Keulartz (Eds.), *Animal ethics in the age of humans: Blurring boundaries in human-animal relationships* (pp. 225–239). New York, NY: Springer.

Doyle, C. (2014). Captive elephants. In L. Gruen (ed.), *The ethics of captivity* (pp. 38–56). Oxford: Oxford University Press.

Duffy, R. (2002). *A trip too far: Ecotourism, politics, and exploitation.* Sterling, VA: Earthscan.

Duffy, R. (2014). Interactive elephants: nature, tourism and neoliberalism. *Annals of Tourism Research 44,* 88–101.

Emel, J., Wilbert, C. & Wolch, J. (2002). Animal geographies. *Society & Animals 10*(4), 407–412.

Fennell, D. A. (2012). *Tourism and animal ethics.* London: Routledge.

Fernando, P., Wikramanayake, E. D., Janaka, H. K., Jayasinghe, L. K. A., Gunawardena, M., Kotagama, S. W., Weerakoon, D. & Pastorini, J. (2008). Ranging behavior of the Asian elephant in Sri Lanka. *Mammalian Biology - Zeitschrift fur Saugetierkunde 73*(1), 2–13.

Fiske, J. (1991). Cultural studies and the culture of everyday life. In L. Grossberg, C. Nelson & P. Treichler (Eds.), *Cultural studies* (pp. 154–173). New York and London: Routledge.

Fowler, M. E. (2006). Physical restraint and handling. In M. E. Fowler & S. K. Mikota (Eds.), *Biology, medicine, and surgery of elephants* (pp. 75–90). Ames, IA: Blackwell Publishing.

Francione, G. L. (2004). Animals – property or persons? In C. R. Sunstein & M. Nussbaum (Eds.), *Animal rights: Current debates and new directions*. London: Oxford University Press.

Franklin, A. (1999). *Animals and modern cultures: A sociology of human-animal relations in modernity*. London, Thousand Oaks, CA, and New Delhi: Sage.

Garner, R. (1994). *Animals, politics, and morality*. Manchester: Manchester University Press.

Garner, R. (2010). A defense of a broad animal protectionism. In G. L. Francione & R. Garner, *The animal rights debate: Abolition or regulation?* (pp. 103–174). New York: Columbia University Press.

Godfrey, A. & Kongmuang, C. (2009). Distribution, demography and basic husbandry of the Asian elephant in the tourism industry in northern Thailand. *Gajah 30*, 13–18.

Goldenberg, S. Z. & Wittemyer, G. (2020). Elephant behavior towards the dead: A review and insights from field observations. *Primates 61*(1), 119–128.

Gómez-Pompa, A. & Kaus, A. (1992). Taming the wilderness myth. *BioScience 42*(4), 271–279.

Gray, A. (2003). *Research practice for cultural studies: Ethnographic methods and lived cultures*. London, Thousand Oaks, CA, and New Delhi: Sage.

Greenfield, S. & D. Verissimo (2019). To what extent is social marketing used in demand reduction campaigns for illegal wildlife products? Insights from elephant ivory and rhino horn. *Social Marketing Quarterly 25*(1), 40–54.

Gruen, L. (2011). *Ethics and animals: An introduction.* Cambridge, MA: Cambridge University Press.

Guha, R. (1997). The authoritarian biologist and the arrogance of anti-humanism. *The Ecologist 27*(1), 14–20.

Hammersley, L. A. (2014). Volunteer tourism: Building effective relationships of understanding. *Journal of Sustainable Tourism 22*(6), 855–873.

Haraway, D. J. (2003). *The companion species manifesto: Dogs, people, and significant otherness.* Chicago: Prickly Paradigm Press.

Haraway, D. J. (2008). *When species meet.* Minneapolis, MN: University of Minnesota Press.

Harnad, S. (2016). Cross-species mind-reading. *Animal Sentience 1*(4), https://doi.org/10.51291/2377-7478.1120.

Hemer, S. R. & Dundon, A. (Eds.) (2016). *Emotions, senses, spaces: Ethnographic engagements and intersections.* Adelaide: University of Adelaide Press.

Hermes, R., Hildebrandt, T. B. & Göritz, F. (2004). Reproductive problems directly attributable to long-term captivity–asymmetric reproductive aging. *Animal Reproduction Science, 82–83,* 49–60.

Heuschmann, G, (2007). *Tug of war: Classical versus 'modern' dressage: Why classical training works and how incorrect 'modern' riding negatively affects horses' health* (trans. R. Abelshauser). North Pomfret, VT: Trafalgar Square Books.

Hodgetts, T. & Lorimer, J. (2020). Animals' mobilities. *Progress in Human Geography 44*(1), 4–26.

Holdgate, M. R., Meehan, C. L., Hogan, J. N., Miller, L. J., Soltis, J., Andrews, J. & Shepherdson, D. J. (2016). Walking behavior of zoo elephants: Associations between GPS-measured daily walking distances and environmental factors, social factors, and welfare indicators. *PLoS ONE 11*(7), e0150331.

Homkrailis, P. (2002). *Ta Klang: The Elephant Valley of Mool River Basin.* Bangkok: Thunkamol Press Limited.

Horton, M. (2011). A little responsible tourism is a dangerous thing… *Progress in Sustainable Tourism, 1,* 94–101.

Human Elephant Learning Programs (H-ELP) Foundation. (2021). The H-ELP Elephant Training Technique. Available at https://h-elp.org/the-h-elp-elephant-training-technique.

Huspek, M. (1994). Critical ethnography and subjective experience. *Human Studies 17*, 45–63.

Jürgens, U. M. (2017). How human-animal relations are realized: From respective realities to merging minds. *Ethics and the Environment, 22*(2), 25–57.

Kim, C. J. (2015). *Dangerous crossings: Race, species, and nature in a multicultural age.* New York: Cambridge University Press.

Kirksey, E. & Helmreich, S. (2010). The emergence of multispecies ethnography. *Cultural Anthropology 25*(4), 545–576.

Kontogeorgopoulos, N. (2009a). The role of tourism in elephant welfare in northern Thailand. *Journal of Tourism 10*(2), 1–19.

Kontogeorgopoulos, N. (2009b). Wildlife tourism in semi-captive settings: A case study of elephant camps in northern Thailand. *Current Issues in Tourism 12*, 429–449.

Kurt, F., Mar, K. U. & Garaï, M. E. (2008). Giants in chains: History, biology, and preservation of Asian elephants in captivity. In C. Wemmer and C. A. Christen (eds), *Elephants and ethics: Towards a morality of coexistence* (pp. 327–345). Baltimore, MD: Johns Hopkins University Press.

Lainé, N. (2020). Anthropology and conservation: Commentary on Baker & Winkler on Elephant Rewilding. *Animal Sentience*, 310.

Lair, R. C. (1997). *Gone astray: The care and management of the Asian elephant in domesticity.* FAO-RAP 1997/16. Bangkok: Food and Agriculture Organization Regional Office for Asia and the Pacific. Available at www.fao.org/3/ac774e/ac774e00.htm

Lakanavichian, S. (2001). Impacts and effectiveness of logging bans in natural forests: Thailand. FAO RAP 2001/08. Bangkok: FAO RAP. Available at www.fao.org/3/X6967E/x6967e09.htm.

Laohachaiboon, S. (2010). Conservation for whom? Elephant conservation and elephant conservationists in Thailand. *Southeast Asian Studies, 48*(1), 74–95.

Laule, G., & Desmond, T. (1998). Positive reinforcement training as an enrichment strategy. In D. Shepherdson, J. Mellen, & M. Hutchins (Eds.), *Second nature: Environmental enrichment for captive animals* (pp. 302–312). Washington, DC: Smithsonian Institution Press.

Lea, J. P. (1993). Tourism development ethics in the Third World. *Annals of Tourism Research 20*(4), 701–715.

Leader-Williams, N. & H. Dublin. (2000). Charismatic megafauna as 'flagship species'. In A. Entwistle & N. Dunstone (Eds.), *Priorities for the conservation of mammalian diversity* (pp. 53–81). Cambridge: Cambridge University Press.

Lenhhardt, R. & Galloway, M. (2008). Carrots and sticks: people and elephants: Rank, domination, and training. In C. Wemmer and C. A. Christen (Eds.), *Elephants and ethics: Towards a morality of coexistence* (pp. 149–164). Baltimore, MD: Johns Hopkins University Press.

Locke, P. (2017). Elephants as persons, affective apprenticeship, and fieldwork with nonhuman informants in Nepal. *Hau: Journal of Ethnographic Theory 7*(1), 353–376.

Lohanan, R. (2002). The elephant situation in Thailand and a plea for co-operation. In I. Baker & M. Kashio (Eds.), *Giants on our hands: Proceedings of the International Workshop on the Domesticated Asian Elephant* (pp. 231–238). Bangkok: FAO Regional Office for Asia and the Pacific.

Long, M. (2019). Ecotourism reconsidered: Chinese and Western participation in the Thai elephant industry. Bowdoin College Honors Projects, 128. Available at https://digitalcommons.bowdoin. edu/honorsprojects/128.

Lorimer, J. (2007). Nonhuman charisma. *Environment and Planning D: Society and Space* 25, 911–932.

Lorimer, J. (2010). Elephants as companion species: The lively biogeographies of Asian elephant conservation in Sri Lanka. *Transactions of the Institute of British Geographers 35*(4), 491–506.

McIntosh, A. J. & Zahra, A. (2007). A cultural encounter through volunteer tourism: Towards the ideals of sustainable tourism? *Journal of Sustainable Tourism, 15*(5), 541-556.

Magda, S., Spohn, O. Angkawanish, T., Smith, D. A. & Pearl, D. L. (2015). Risk factors for saddle-related skin lesions on elephants used in the tourism industry in Thailand. *BMC Veterinary Research 11*, 117.

Maggio, J. (2007). 'Can the subaltern be heard?' Political theory, translation, representation, and Gayatri Chakravorty Spivak. *Alternatives: Global, Local, Political 32*(4), 419–443.

Mahoney, D. (2007). Constructing reflexive fieldwork relationships: Narrating my collaborative storytelling methodology. *Qualitative Inquiry 13*(4), 573–594.

Mason, G. & Rushen, J. (2008). *Stereotypic animal behaviour: Fundamentals and applications to welfare.* Oxfordshire and Cambridge, MA: CABI.

Matharu, H. (2015). Elephant gores handler to death and runs off into Thai jungle with tourists on its back. *Independent*, 27 August. Available at www.independent.co.uk/news/world/asia/elephant-gores-handler-to-death-and-runs-off-into-thai-jungle-with-tourists-on-its-back-10474003.html.

Moscarello, J. M. & Hartley, C. A. (2017). Agency and the calibration of motivated behavior. *Trends in Cognitive Sciences, 21*(10), 725–735.

Oregon Zoo. (2018). How Elephant Lands enhances elephant welfare – executive summary. Available at www.oregonzoo.org/sites/default/files/downloads/Elephant%20Lands%20Enhances%20Elephant%20Welfare%2CReport%20and%20Summary%20OC%20May2018.pdf.

Pearce, D. G. (1992). Alternative tourism: Concepts, classifications and questions. In V. L. Smith & W. R. Eadington (Eds.), *Tourism alternatives: Potentials and problems in the development of tourism* (pp. 15–30). Philadelphia, PA: University of Pennsylvania Press.

Phuangkum, P., Lair, R. & Angkawanith, T. (2005). *Elephant care manual for mahouts and camp managers.* Bangkok: Forestry Industry Organization, Ministry of Natural Resources and Environment.

Pintavongs, W., Chaeplaivej, P., Boonyasart, B., Kidyhoo, S., Pravai, W., Rattanakunuprakarn, J., Ounsiri, S., Lorsanyaluck, B., Sunyathitiseree, P., Jittapalapong, S., Wajjwalku, W. & Thongtip, N. (2014). Domestic elephant population structure and health status in Thailand. *Journal of Kasetsart Veterinarians 24*, 16–24.

Plotnik, J. & de Waal, F. B. M. (2014a). Asian elephants (*Elephas maximus*) reassure others in distress. *PeerJ* 2:e278.

Plotnik, J. & de Waal, F. B. M. (2014b). Extraordinary elephant perception. *PNAS, 111*(14), 5071–5071.

Plotnik, J. M., de Waal, F. B. M. & Reiss, D. (2006). Self-recognition in an Asian elephant. *Proceedings of the National Academy of Sciences 103*, 17053–17057.

Plumwood, V. (1993). *Feminism and the mastery of nature.* London and New York: Routledge.

Poole, J. (1989). Announcing intent: The aggressive state of musth in African elephants. *Animal Behaviour, 37*(1), 140–152.

Poole, J. H. & Granli, P. (2009). Mind and movement: meeting the interests of elephants. In D. L. Forthman, L. F. Kane & P. Waldau (Eds.), *An elephant in the room: The science and well-being of elephants in captivity*. Medford, MA: Tufts University Cummings School of Veterinary Medicine's Center for Animals and Public Policy.

Poole, J. H. & C. J. Moss. (2008). Elephant sociality and complexity. In C. Wemmer & C. A. Christen (Eds.), *Elephants and ethics: Towards a morality of coexistence* (pp. 69–98). Baltimore, MD: Johns Hopkins University Press.

Pousajja, R. (1993). Eucalyptus plantations in Thailand. FAO RAP 1996/44. Bangkok: FAO RAP. Available at www.fao.org/3/ac772e/ac772e0m.htm.

Pratt, M. L. (1986). Fieldwork in common places. In J. Clifford & G. E. Marcus (Eds.), *Writing culture: The poetics and politics of ethnography* (pp. 27–50). Berkeley and Los Angeles, CA: University of California Press.

Racine, T. P. (2016). The grounds for animal subjectivity and intersubjectivity: Commentary on Harnad in Other Minds. *Animal Sentience 1*(3), 093, https://doi.org/10.51291/2377-7478.1108.

Regan, T. (1986). The case for animal rights. In M. W. Fox & L. D. Mickley (Eds.), *Advances in animal welfare science 1986/87* (pp. 179–189). Washington, DC: The Humane Society of the United States.

Regan, T. (2001). *Defending animal rights*. Urbana and Chicago, IL: University of Illinois Press.

Regan, T. (2004). *The case for animal rights*. Berkeley, CA: University of California Press.

Rittichainuwat, B., Scott, N. & Laws, E. (2021). Drivers of elephant tourism in Thailand. In E. Laws, N. Scott, X. Font & J. Koldowksi (Eds.), *The elephant tourism business*. Oxfordshire: CABI International.

Roberts, J. (2017). Elephant tourism: The harms of received wisdom. The "Good Tourism" Blog. Available at https://goodtourismblog.com/2017/06/elephant-tourism-harms-received-wisdom/.

Roberts, J. (2021). Thailand's tourism elephants lose when pragmatism gives way to politics, ideology. The "Good Tourism" Blog. Available at https://goodtourismblog.com/2021/06/thailands-elephants-lose-when-pragmatism-gives-way-to-politics-ideology/.

Rueangdej, B. (2009). การอพยพย้ายถิ่นของชาวกูย [History of Guay people's migration] (trans. S. Akkaraphot). วารสารวิชาการมหาวิทยาลัยราชภัฏบุรีรัมย์ /Journal of Buri-am Rajabhat University 2, 18–27.

Sadashige, J. (2015). The Mother of Elephants: 'Lek' Chailert, Elephant Nature Park, and the gendering of elephant husbandry. *Gender Forum: Gender, Animals, Animality, 55*, 83–106.

Savvides, N. (2013). Living with dogs: Alternative animal practices in Bangkok, Thailand. *Animal Studies Journal, 2*(2), 28–50.

Schliesinger, J. (2010). *Elephants in Thailand Vol. 1: Mahouts and their cultures today.* Bangkok: Booksmango.

Schulte, B. A. (2006). Behavior and social life. In M. E. Fowler & S. K. Mikota (Eds.), *Biology, medicine, and surgery of elephants* (pp. 35–44). Ames, IA: Blackwell Publishing.

Seidensticker, J. (2008). Foreword. In C. Wemmer & C. A. Christen (Eds.), *Elephants and ethics: Towards a morality of coexistence* (pp. xi–xiii). Baltimore, MD: Johns Hopkins University Press.

Serpell, J. (2019). How happy is your pet? The problem of subjectivity in the assessment of companion animal welfare. *Animal Welfare 28*, 57–66.

Shiva, V. (1997). *Biopiracy: The plunder of nature and knowledge.* Boston, MA: South End Press.

Sin, H. L. & Minca, C. (2014). Touring responsibility: The trouble with 'going local' in community-based tourism in Thailand. *Geoforum, 51*, 96–106.

Singer, P. (2001). *Animal liberation.* New York: Ecco Press.

Singer, P. (2011). *Practical ethics*, 3rd edn. Cambridge, MA: Cambridge University Press.

Siriprapakorn, Y. (2017). ปะกำซาง: ความเชื่อในพลังศักดิ์สี ทิธขี องกลุมชาวไทยกูย ในจังหวัดสุ นิ ทร [Pakhamchang: Belief in Pakham holy power among Thai Guay people in Surin Province]. (trans. S. Akkaraphot) *Journal of Graduate Studies Review MCU Phrae 3*(2), 78–88.

Smith, M. & Duffy, R. (2003). *The ethics of tourism development.* London: Routledge.

Smith, R. J., Veríssimo, D., Isaac, N. J. B. & Jones, K. E. (2012). Identifying Cinderella species: Uncovering mammals with conservation flagship appeal, *Conservation Letters 5*(3), 205–212.

Smuts, B. B. (1985). *Sex and friendship in baboons.* New York: Aldine Publishing Company.

Smuts, B. B. (2001). Encounters with animal minds. *Journal of Consciousness Studies 8*(5–7), 293–309.

Sobocinska, A. (2014). Following the 'hippie sahibs': Colonial cultures of travel and the hippie trail. *Journal of Colonialism and Colonial History 15*(2).

Spivak, G. C. (1995). Can the subaltern speak? In B. Ashcroft, G. Griffiths & H. Tiffin (Eds.), *The post-colonial studies reader,* 2nd edn. Oxford and New York: Routledge.

Srichandrakumara, P. I. M. / Giles, F. H. (1929). Adversaria of elephant hunting (together with an account of all the rites, observances and acts of worship to be performed in connection therewith, as well as notes on vocabularies of spirit language, fake or taboo language and elephant command words). *Journal of the Siam Society 23*(2), pp. 61–96.

Steward, H. (2009). Animal agency. *Inquiry 52*(3), 217–231.

Stiles, D. (2004). The ivory trade and elephant conservation. *Environmental Conservation 4,* 309–321.

Sukumar, R. (2003). *The living elephants: Evolutionary ecology, behavior, and conservation.* Oxford: Oxford University Press.

Sukumar, R. (2006). A brief review of the status, distribution and biology of wild Asian elephants. *International Zoo Yearbook 40,* 1–8.

Sukumar, R., Krishnamurthy, V., Wemmer, C. & Rodden, M. (1997). Demography of captive Asian elephants (*Elephas maximus*) in southern India. *Zoo Biology 16,* 263–272.

Suter, I. (2019). In defence of elephant tourism: The role of captive elephants in the 21st century. *Gajah 50,* 38–40.

Suter I. (2020). Rewilding or reviewing: Conservation and the elephant-based tourism industry. *Animal Sentience 28*(3), 304.

Taylor, J. L. (1993). *Forest monks and the nation state: An anthropological study and historical study in northeastern Thailand.* Singapore: Institute of Southeast Asian Studies.

Taylor, M., Hurst, C. E., Stinson, M. J. & Grimwood, B. S. (2020). Becoming care-full: contextualizing moral development among captive elephant volunteer tourists to Thailand. *Journal of Ecotourism 19*(2), 113–131.

Telfer, D. J. & Sharpley, R. (2015). *Tourism and development in the developing world*, 2nd edn. London: Routledge.

Thitaram, C., Dejchaisri, S., Somgird, C., Angkawanish, T., Brown, J., Phumphuay, R., Chomdech, S. & Kangwanpong, D. (2015). Social group formation and genetic relatedness in reintroduced Asian elephants (*Elephas maximus*) in Thailand. *Applied Animal Behaviour Science, 172*, 52-57.

Tipprasert, P. (2002). Elephants and ecotourism in Thailand. In I. Baker & M. Kashio (Eds.), *Giants on Our Hands: Proceedings of the International Workshop on the Domesticated Asian Elephant*. Bangkok: FAO Regional Office for Asia and the Pacific.

van Dooren, T. (2019). *The wake of crows: Living and dying in shared worlds*. New York, NY: Columbia University Press.

Van Maanen, J. (2011). *Tales of the field: On writing ethnography*, 2nd edn. Chicago, IL: University of Chicago Press.

Van Patter, L. E. & Blattner, C. (2020). Advancing ethical principles for non-invasive, respectful research with nonhuman animal participants. *Society & Animals 28*(2), 171–190.

Varner, G. (2008). Personhood, memory and elephant management. In C. Wemmer & C. A. Christen (Eds.), *Elephants and ethics: Towards a morality of coexistence* (pp. 41–67). Baltimore, MD: Johns Hopkins University Press.

Veasey, J. (2006). Concepts in the care and welfare of captive elephants. *International Zoo Yearbook 40*, 63–79.

Verissimo, D., D. C. MacMillan & R. J. Smith (2011). Toward a systematic approach for identifying conservation flagships. *Conservation Letters 4*(1), 1–8.

Vetayasuporn, P. (2007). Development guideline for sustainable eco-tourism development of 'Suay' village in Surin Province. Unpublished PhD thesis. Silpakorn University, Thailand.

Walpole, M. J. & N. Leader-Williams (2002). Tourism and flagship species in conservation. *Biodiversity & Conservation 11*(3), 543–547.

Wannitikul, G. (2005). Deforestation in northeast Thailand, 1975-91: Results of a general statistical model. *Singapore Journal of Tropical Geography, 26*(1), 102-118.

Wearing, S. (2001). *Volunteer tourism: Experiences that make a difference*. New York: CABI International.

Wearing, S. & McGehee, N. G. (2013). *International volunteer tourism: Integrating travellers and communities*. New York: CABI International.

Webb, L. E., Veenhoven, R., Harfield, J. L. & Jensen, M. B. (2019). What is animal happiness? *Annals of the New York Academy of Sciences 1438*, 62–76.

Wemmer, C. & Christen, C. A. (2008). Never forgetting the importance of ethical treatment of elephants. In C. Wemmer & C. A. Christen (Eds.), *Elephants and ethics: Towards a morality of coexistence* (pp. 1–13). Baltimore, MD: Johns Hopkins University Press.

Whatmore, S. (2002). *Hybrid geographies: Natures cultures spaces*. London: Sage Publications.

Wolfe, C. (2003). *Animal rites: American culture, the discourse of species, and posthumanist theory*. Chicago, IL: University of Chicago Press.

Yasui, S. & Idani, G. (2022). Characteristics of social relationships in a group of captive Asian elephants (*Elephas maximus*) in the Elephant Village in Thailand. *Animal Behavior and Cognition, 9*(1), 89-105.

www.ingramcontent.com/pod-product-compliance
Lightning Source LLC
Chambersburg PA
CBHW031502270326
41930CB00006B/209